# The
# Middle
# Five

# Francis La Flesche

# The Middle Five

Indian Schoolboys of the Omaha Tribe

Foreword by David A. Baerreis

University of Nebraska Press
Lincoln and London

Copyright © 1963 by The Regents of the University of Wisconsin
Originally published in 1900


*First Bison Book printing: 1978*

Most recent printing indicated by the first digit below:

1    2    3    4    5    6    7    8    9    10

**Library of Congress Cataloging in Publication Data**

La Flesche, Francis, d. 1932.
  The Middle Five.

  Reprint of the ed. published by the University of Wisconsin Press, Madison.
  1. Omaha Indians—Children. 2. Omaha Indians—Education. 3. La
Flesche, Francis, d. 1932. 4. Omaha Indians—Biography. 5. Indians of
North America—Nebraska—Children. 6. Indians of North America—Ne-
braska—Education. I. Title.
[E99.04L165  1978]      970'.004'97      78-17409
ISBN 0–8032–2852–X
ISBN 0–8032–7901–9 pbk.

Bison Book edition published by arrangement with the University of
Wisconsin Press.

Manufactured in the United States of America

To The Universal Boy

# Foreword

For many years the American Indian has been alternately folk hero and villain, but constantly a thorn in the American conscience. Inequities based on inadequate compensation for land or other rights have been and still are being rectified. But the greatest problems, and these in large part still remain with us, have come about through the conflict of cultures rather than of people. In the face of expanding white settlement, the tribal mode of life in all of its ramifications could not persist. Intimate contact led to the disintegration of this tribal life and brought much personal disorganization and tragedy to the Indian. Education was early seen as a key to this situation, a means by which the Indian could become assimilated in a new culture or at least adjusted to a new mode of life. Examination of some of the earlier educational programs, all of varying degrees of effectiveness, is of considerable value in understanding the strengths and weaknesses of particular techniques and approaches and in gaining a better appreciation of the Indian situation. But while formal reports and evaluations of the educational systems can be found, it is exceedingly difficult to obtain any perspective on the schools from the Indians' point of view. Thus Francis La Flesche's informal account of his experience as an Omaha child in a mission school of the mid-nineteenth century is a unique document, interesting as a story and valuable in its implicit insights. It is also more than just an account by a native participant in the events described. Francis La Flesche was a scholar, an ethnologist who produced outstanding studies of the Omaha and Osage tribes, and his *Middle Five* reflects similar high standards of accuracy combined with sympathetic understanding.

The Omaha, one of five tribes speaking the Dhegiha group of the Siouan language (the others being the Kansa, Quapaw, Osage, and Ponca), had in prehistoric times moved into the eastern fringe of the Plains area. Their life in the early historic period involved further migration for they ranged as far north as the border country between Minnesota and South Dakota in the vicinity of Pipestone. They subsequently withdrew to northeastern Nebraska, an area which has become regarded as their traditional home and where the bulk of the Omaha reside today. Successive land sales gradually reduced the territory they claimed and in 1882 a law was passed which permitted the allocations of reservation lands in severalty. Although the Omaha farmed and lived in substantial villages of dome-shaped sod-covered houses like many other village tribes of the Plains, hunting activities were also an important part of their economy. Periodic hunts, particularly for bison, engaged the entire village both to provide a source of food and to acquire furs and hides that could be exchanged with traders for new goods that had gradually become necessities. The shrinkage of tribal lands, increase in white settlement, and decline of the great buffalo herds and other wild game provoked a crisis in Omaha life requiring profound modifications if the Omaha were to survive as a people. The generally accepted solution in the latter half of the nineteenth century, so far as governmental officials and friends of the Indian were concerned, was for them to adopt the white way of life and become self-sustaining farmers.

Missionary work among the Omaha was initiated in 1846 b ythe Board of Foreign Missions of the Presbyterian Church when agency headquarters for the Oto and Omaha tribes was at Bellevue, south of the city of Omaha in Sarpy County. In the following year plans for a boarding school to serve the two tribes were initiated and the first students (including some Pawnee children) were received in 1848. The school continued at this location until, as a result of the treaty of March 16, 1854, the Omaha ceded these lands and the tribe moved north in the following spring to their new location in what is now Burt, Cuming, and Thurston counties about 80 miles north of the city of Omaha. A new mission headquarters and school was constructed in 1857 at the agency headquarters in Thurston County on a terrace overlooking the Missouri River. The mission building, built of native stone, was three stories in height and dimensions were seventy-five by thirty-five feet. Its seventeen rooms were designed to accommodate approximately fifty boarding students as well as the mission staff and their families. The school continued in operation until 1869 when federal support, provided through educational funds set aside by the tribe according to treaty provisions, was removed for a period in favor of a system of day schools to be located in several villages. One of the day schools operated for a short period in the mission building, but the boarding school reopened in 1879. In its final stage, beginning in 1883, it was limited to girls.

The mission school would appear to have been operated in accordance with sound principles for the day. Thus in 1861, for example, it was reported that the school was divided into eleven classes, four being reading classes, three geography, one writing, one arithmetic (mental and written), and two primary classes. In this year the most advanced of the reading classes used McGuffey's *Fourth Eclectic Reader*, while in 1863 the *Fifth Eclectic Reader* was used as well as the texts by Monteith and McNally for the intermediate geography class. Lessons in vocal music were also given. An important aspect of the training program, however, was practical in character. Older boys participated in various kinds of farm work while the older girls were taught household work. In keeping with the mission sponsorship of the school, the students were treated as members of a Christian family and had their meals and worshipped with the members of the mission staff.

Is Francis La Flesche a typical product of the school? To understand him, we need to know something of his family. His father, Joseph La Flesche, was the son of a French trader and an Omaha woman. While he was raised among the Indians, Joseph later accompanied and assisted his father on trading expeditions. Exposed to both white and Indian cultures, he chose the latter and rose to the position of principal chief upon the death of Big Elk, who had adopted him as a son. Though Joseph La Flesche had chosen to become an Omaha, he saw that the ultimate future of the people would require adjustment to white culture and became the leader of a faction, the "young men's party," which favored such a program. Clearly this man of remarkable insight and qualities of leadership influenced his own children as much as they were influenced by the mission school to which he sent them or by their white teachers. One sister of Francis La Flesche, Susette (Mrs. T. H. Tibbles; perhaps better known as "Bright Eyes") was also an author, a noted lecturer, and a champion of Indian rights. Another, Dr. Susan Picotte, has been described as the first woman of her race to receive the degree of Doctor of Medicine. She graduated from the Philadelphia Woman's Medical College and served as a physician in the Omaha tribe.

Francis La Flesche in 1881 was appointed a clerk in the office of the Commissioner of Indian Affairs. While serving in the Office of Indian Affairs he attended the National University and received a degree from the School of Law in 1893. Like his father, he was much interested in seeing the Indian customs of his tribe recorded and early collaborated with Alice C. Fletcher in her studies and assisted another noted scholar of the Omaha, J. Owen Dorsey. This interest became a professional one when he transferred to the Bureau of American Ethnology in 1910 and continued work with that organization until his retirement on December 26, 1929. His scholarly career was a distinguished one and well merited the honorary degree of Doctor of Letters awarded by the University of Nebraska in 1926. La Flesche's close and distinguished family and the pioneer anthropologists with whom he collaborated stimulated him to achievements perhaps as much as his early educational experiences.

In *The Middle Five*, La Flesche does not tell us when he attended the mission school. His birth is recorded by Hartley B. Alexander, who provides us with most of the readily available information concerning him in his excellent obituary in the *American Anthropologist* (Volume 35, No. 2, 1933), as December 25, 1857. The date may not be given with unimpeachable accuracy since vital statistics on the frontier are largely reconstructions from memory. We know from the account that one of La Flesche's best friends was a boy who preceded his entry in the school, Brush. The *Report of the Commissioner of Indian Affairs* for 1857 (Washington, 1858) is the only printed report of the mission school which contains a list of the names of pupils. Among these we find Francis Vinton Brush (Matzhe-zin-zah), aged four, the youngest scholar at the school. The ages of the boys, at this period, were given as ranging between 4 and 17. Another clue given in the book is that the white names assigned to the students include such names as William T. Sherman, Andrew Johnson, Ulysses S. Grant, and Philip Sheridan, suggesting the war years or immediately thereafter. While these names need not be real ones, all appear as individuals to whom allotments were given in 1900, though the name of Francis Vinton Brush does not appear. Brush's death is described in the final portion of *The Middle Five*. But perhaps the most specific clue to the time at which the action of the tale takes place is the account of the treatment accorded the poor Winnebago child, which is closely coupled with a description of the mourning of an Omaha woman whose husband had been killed during the summer buffalo hunt. The Winnebago Indians came to the Omaha reservation in a condition of great destitution in 1864 and it was this same year that the Commissioner of Indian Affairs reports several Omaha killed while on their summer hunt. The mid-1860's (it will be recalled that the date must be prior to 1869 when the school was closed) would represent a reasonable guess as to the time sketched in the book.

Except for the addition of a few illustrations and the correction of a few typographical errors, the text to follow is a faithful rendering of the 1900 edition. A few bracketed editorial additions were made either by La Flesche himself or by his earlier editors. The original subtitle of the book, "Indian Boys at School," has been slightly expanded.

*David A. Baerreis*

*Department of Anthropology*
*The University of Wisconsin*

# Preface

As THE OBJECT of this book is to reveal the true nature and character of the Indian boy, I have chosen to write the story of my school-fellows rather than that of my other boy friends who knew only the aboriginal life. I have made this choice not because the influences of the school alter the qualities of the boys, but that they might appear under conditions and in an attire familiar to the reader. The paint, feathers, robes, and other articles that make up the dress of the Indian, are marks of savagery to the European, and he who wears them, however appropriate or significant they might be to himself, finds it difficult to lay claim to a share in common human nature. So while the school uniform did not change those who wore it, in this instance, it may help these little Indians to be judged, as are other boys, by what they say and do.

It is not my purpose to give a continued story with a hero in the following pages, but, in a series of sketches, to present the companions of my own young days to the children of the race that has become possessed of the land of my fathers.

This introduction is a genuine one, for all the boys who appear in these sketches have really lived and played a part in the incidents herein recorded. Each little actor, including the writer, made his entrance upon the stage of life in the "tee-pee" or in the dome-shaped earth lodge; for, in the years when we boys were born, only the aboriginal dwellings were in use among our people, the Omaha tribe of Indians. Like all the infants for countless generations in the line of our ancestry, we too had to pass through the cradle-board period while our bones "ripened," as the Indians say, and grew strong eonugh to bear the weight of our bodies. When at last our mothers gave us liberty to creep and to toddle about, we promptly used that freedom to get into all sorts of mischief as we explored the new and wonderful world in which we found ourselves.

Among my earliest recollections are the instructions wherein we were taught respect and courtesy toward our elders; to say "thank you" when receiving a gift, or when returning a borrowed article; to use the proper and conventional term of relationship when speaking to another; and never to address any one by his personal name; we were also forbidden to pass in front of persons sitting in the tent without first asking permission; and we were strictly enjoined never to stare at visitors, particularly at strangers. To us there seemed to be no end to the things we were obliged to do, and to the things we were to refrain from doing.

From the earliest years the Omaha child was trained in the grammatical use of his native tongue. No slip was allowed to pass uncorrected, and as a result there was no child-talk such as obtains among English-speaking children,—the only difference between the speech of old and young was in the pronunciation of words which the infant often failed to utter correctly, but this difficulty was soon overcome, and a boy of ten or twelve was apt to speak as good Omaha as a man of mature years.

Like the grown folk, we youngsters were fond of companionship and of talking. In making our gamesticks and in our play, we chattered incessantly of the things that occupied our minds, and we thought it a hardship when we were obliged to speak in low tones while older people were engaged in conversation. When we entered the Mission School, we experienced a greater hardship, for there we encountered a rule that prohibited the use of our own language, which rule was rigidly enforced with a hickory rod, so that the new-comer, however socially inclined, was obliged to go about like a little dummy until he had learned to express himself in English.

All the boys in our school were given English names, because their Indian names were difficult for the teachers to pronounce. Besides, the aboriginal names were considered by the missionaries as heathenish, and therefore should be obliterated. No less heathenish in their origin were the English substitutes, but the loss of their original meaning and significance through long usage had rendered them fit to continue as appellations for civilized folk. And so, in the place of Tae-noo'-ga-wa-zhe, came Philip Sheridan; in that of Wa-pah'-dae, Ulysses S. Grant; that of Koo'-we-he-ge-ra, Alexander, and so on. Our sponsors went even further back in history, and thus we had our David and

Jonathan, Gideon and Isaac, and, with the flood of these new names, came Noah. It made little difference to us that we had to learn the significance of one more word as applied to ourselves, when the task before us was to make our way through an entire strange language. So we learned to call each other by our English names, and continued to do so even after we left school and had grown to manhood.

The names thus acquired by the boys are used in these sketches in preference to their own, for the reason that Indian words are not only difficult to pronounce, but are apt to sound all alike to one not familiar with the language, and the boys who figure in these pages might lose their identity and fail to stand out clearly in the mind of the reader were he obliged to continually struggle with their Omaha names.

In the talk of the boys I have striven to give a reproduction of the peculiar English spoken by them, which was composite, gathered from the imperfect comprehension of their books, the provincialisms of the teachers, and the slang and bad grammar picked up from uneducated white persons employed at the school or at the Government Agency. Oddities of speech, profanity, localisms, and slang were unknown in the Omaha language, so when such expressions fell upon the ears of these lads they innocently learned and used them without the slightest suspicion that there could be bad as well as good English.

The misconception of Indian life and character so common among the white people has been largely due to an ignorance of the Indian's language, of his mode of thought, his beliefs, his ideals, and his native institutions. Every aspect of the Indian and his manner of life has always been strange to the white man, and this strangeness has been magnified by the mists of prejudice and the conflict of interests between the two races. While these in time may disappear, no native American can ever cease to regret that the utterances of his father have been constantly belittled when put into English, that their thoughts have frequently been travestied and their native dignity obscured. The average interpreter has generally picked up his knowledge of English in a random fashion, for very few have ever had the advantage of a thorough education, and all have had to deal with the difficulties that attend the translator. The beauty and picturesqueness, and euphonious playfulness, or the gravity of diction which I have heard among my own people, and other tribes as well, are all but impossible to be given literally in English.

The talk of the older people, when they speak in this book, is, as well as I can translate it, that of every day use.

Most of the country now known as the State of Nebraska (the Omaha name of the river Platt, descriptive of its shallowness, width, and low banks) had for many generations been held and claimed by our people as their own, but when they ceded the greater part of this territory to the United States government, they reserved only a certain tract for their own use and home. It is upon the eastern part of this reservation that the scene of these sketches is laid, and at the time when the Omahas were living near the Missouri River in three villages, some four or five miles apart. The one farthest south was known as Ton'-won-ga-hae's village; the people were called "wood eaters," because they cut and sold wood to the settlers who lived near them. The middle one was Ish'-ka-da-be's village, and the people designated as "those who dwell in earth lodges," they having adhered to the aboriginal form of dwelling when they built their village. The one to the north and nearest the Mission was E-sta'-ma-za's village, and the people were known as the "make-believe white-men," because they built their houses after the fashion of the white settlers. Furniture, such as beds, chairs, tables, bureaus, etc., were not used in any of these villages, except in a few instances, while in all of them the Indian costume, language, and social customs remained as yet unmodified.

In those days the Missouri was the only highway of commerce. Toiling slowly against the swift current, laden with supplies for the trading posts and for our Mission, came the puffing little steamboats from the "town of the Red-hair," as St. Louis was called by the Indians, in memory of the auburn locks of Governor Clark, — of Lewis and Clark fame. We children used to watch these noisy boats as they forced their way through the turbid water and made a landing by running the bow into the soft bank.

The white people speak of the country at this period as "a wilderness," as though it was an empty tract without human interest or history. To us Indians it was as clearly defined then as it is to-day; we knew the boundaries of tribal lands, those of our friends and those of our foes; we were familiar with every stream, the contour of every hill, and each peculiar feature of the landscape had its tradition. It was our home, the scene of our history, and we loved it as our country.

[*Francis La Flesche*]

[1900]

# Contents

# Illustrations

# The
# Middle
# Five

# 1

---

# The
# Mission

LEANING against the wall of a large stone building, with moccasined feet dangling from a high wooden bench on the front porch, sat a little boy crying. His buckskin suit, prettily fringed and embroidered with porcupine quills of the brightest colors, indicated the care bestowed upon him by fond parents. Boys and girls were at play around the house, making the place ring with their merry laughter as they chased each other among the trees, but the little boy sat all alone, sobbing as though his heart would break. A big boy came and sat by his side, put an arm around him, and in a kindly tone said, in Indian:

"What are you crying for? Don't cry, — I'll play with you and be your friend. I won't let the boys hurt you."

"I want my mother! I want to go home!" was all the homesick little chap could say, crying harder than ever.

"You will see your mother soon, we can go home every bathing-day (Saturday). It is only three days to wait, so don't cry. I have to go away, but I will be back soon. Play with this dog until I come"—putting into the hands of the little boy a wooden dog.

A bell rang, and from every direction came boys and girls crowding and pushing one another as they entered two of the large doors of the building. The big boy came running, and, grasping the little one by the hand, fairly dragged him along, saying: "Come, quick! We are going to eat."

They entered a large room filled with people. Parallel to the walls stood tables of great length, at one of which the two boys took seats. After considerable hard breathing and shuffling by the children, they suddenly became very still, every one bowed his head, then a man with gray hair and whiskers, who sat at the end of one of the tables, spoke in a low tone. He finished speaking, then followed a deafening clatter of a hundred tin plates and cups. Young women carrying great pans of steaming food moved rapidly from table to table. One of these girls came to the two boys, and put into the plate of the younger a potato. "Give him two, he's hungry," whispered the big boy to the girl.

Everything was strange to the little new-comer and he kept looking all around. The lamps that were fastened to the walls and posts, the large clock that stood ticking gloomily on a shelf, and the cupboard with its tin door perforated in a queer design were objects upon which his eyes rested with wonder.

The supper over, the boys and girls who sat on the inner side of the tables turned to face the centre of the room, and folded their arms. Then they all sang. When this was done, they dropped on their knees and the gray-haired man

4

began to talk again. The little boy watched him for a while, then laid his head on the hard bench,—the tones of the old man grew fainter and fainter until the boy lost all consciousness of them. Suddenly there burst upon him a noise like thunder. He arose to his feet with a start, and, bewildered, he looked around. Everything seemed to be in a whirl. He took fright, ran to the door that first caught his sight, and went with a thud down to a landing, but did not lose his balance; he took another step, then fell headlong into a dreadful dark place. He screamed at the top of his voice, frightened almost into a fit. A woman picked him up and carried him in her arms up a flight of stairs, speaking to him in a language that he could not understand.

This was my first experience at the boarding school established by the Presbyterian Board of Foreign Missions for the instruction of the children of the Omaha tribe of Indians.

The Mission school, the founding of which had marked an epoch in the tribe, was located among the wooded bluffs of the Missouri on the eastern part of the reservation. The principal building was of stone, plain and substantial, and plastered inside and out. It was three stories high and had an attic. This attic was perhaps the most interesting part of the structure, for we boys were quite sure it was tenanted by ghosts, and that the devil, who figured considerably in the instruction given us, had full sway in this apartment.

There was a large square hole close to the head of the stairs that led up to the attic. This hole had the greatest terror for us; there was a constant whistling within it, and out of it came sounds like distressing moans and sighs. I remember once, when Gray-beard had sent me up to the attic for something, that I never hurried so on any other errand as I did on that one. I found the article he desired, put it under my arm, and cautiously approached the head of the stair, keeping an eye on the dark hole, then suddenly I made a dash past it, and with amazing rapidity thundered downstairs. "Lad, you will break your neck!" exclaimed Gray-beard. I told him I liked to run downstairs!

Under the attic was the boys' dormitory. The beds were placed close together, and some were wide enough for three boys. The room was large, and in the middle of it stood a post. I have reason to remember this, for one night I got up in my sleep and ran with all my might against this post, making such a noise as to awaken Gray-beard and the superintendent, who came up in great haste with candles in their hands. I was laid up for days after this exploit, but I never ran in my sleep again.

Beneath our dormitory were the parlor and the bedroom of Gray-beard, our teacher and disciplinarian. This name was not inherited by him, nor was it one of his own choosing; the boys gave it to him because his beard was iron-gray, and the Indians adopted it from the boys. In his room at night he might have heard strange noises from the cherubs in the dormitory above, in fact he came up there quite often, rod in hand, as a reminder that such sounds made sleep impossible.

Under Gray-beard's rooms was the school-room where we struggled with arithmetic, geography, history, and

A B C, up to the Fifth Reader. This room corresponded in size to our dormitory, but it had no middle post.

The dining-hall, where on my arrival I had taken fright and stampeded head foremost into the cellar, was in the middle of the first story. It was very large and held, beside the three long tables, a big stove in the middle between two large posts. I remember these posts very well, I kept close company with one of them, on my return from a run-away expedition; and it was on this occasion that I had my first love adventure—but I must not anticipate.

The rooms on the two stories above the dining-hall were occupied, one as play-room for the girls, the others by the various employees.

On the same floor with the school-room and the dining-hall, at the north end of the building, was the chapel. Here we sat in rows on Sunday mornings, afternoons, and evenings, and on Thursday evenings, ranged on long, high, wooden benches without backs, our feet scarcely touching the floor, and listened (sometimes) to sermons which were remarkable for their length and sleep-enticing effects. I had many delightful dreams in this chapel, about Samson and his jaw-bone war club, the fight between David and Goliath, and of the adventures of Joseph the dreamer,— stories that were the delight of my boyhood. Brush, one of my dearest friends at the school, knowing my weakness, secured a seat back of mine on purpose to support me when I was in a slumberous mood. I shall never forget his goodness; he now sleeps in the cemetery just above the Mission.

The two large rooms over the chapel were occupied by our superintendent and minister. Above his apartments was the girls' dormitory, while over all stretched the haunted, ghostly attic.

There were other buildings grouped around: to the back stood the store-house and the smoke-house; out of the latter came our delicious hams and our sermons, for a part of this building was used as the minister's study. Then there was the great barn where we boys played hide-and-seek in the hay-mow; the corn-crib with its yellow wealth showing between the boards; and the dusty wheat-bins with padlocked doors. Below on the bottom were the Government saw and grist mills, where we often went to see the grinding of the Indians' grain and the large trees sawed into lumber for Agency use or for the Indians' houses. The carpenter and blacksmith shops were also down there, and a long wooden house for the occupancy of the Government employees. All of these buildings stood for the fulfilment of the solemn promises made by the "Great Father" at Washington to his "Red Children," and as a part of the price paid for thousands and thousands of acres of fine land.

Although there were high hills just back of the school, from which one could get excellent views of the surrounding country, we boys preferred to go up into the belfry on the top of the main building for our observations. We did not go often; two difficulties were in the way: the securing of permission from the superintendent, as but few boys could be trusted up there; and we must go through the haunted attic to get to the belfry. No boy during my school days ever went up there alone.

My friend Brush, being quite a favorite with the superintendent, often had permission to go, and took me with him. When we were once in the belfry, we felt safe from the

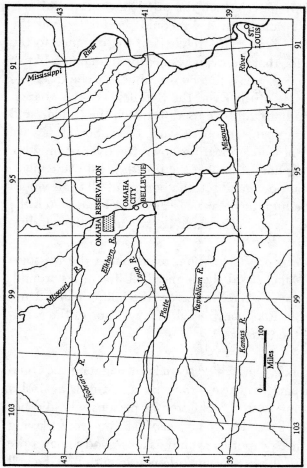

Map limits show country known to the Omaha Indians. The Mission School was located on the west bank of the Missouri River in the Omaha Reservation area shown. Drafted by the University of Wisconsin Cartographic Laboratory from Plate 21 of *The Omaha Tribe* by Alice C. Fletcher and Francis La Flesche, in the *27th Annual Report of the Bureau of American Ethnology.*

annoyances of the devil and the other horrible things in the attic. The superintendent, without the asking, let Brush have a big spy-glass, which the other boys were not permitted to use, and with it we could see far beyond the river and the valley that stretched in the distance to the opposite bluffs, that were always nearly hidden in a bluish haze. Bringing the glass to a closer range, we could see below, on our side of the river, the rich fields of the Mission and of the Indians; and we used to watch the Indians and the hired men of the school at work there. Sometimes we caught sight of a steamboat far down the river coming up, trailing a long line of smoke; then, with great excitement, we would run down and tell the boys, and all of us would hasten to the highest point near the school and watch the "mystic boat" as it slowly made its way along the winding stream.

To the south of the Mission, overlooking the Missouri and a small lake, stood the highest hill for miles around. This was known by the Indians as "the hill on which Um'-pa-ton-ga (Big Elk) was buried." He was one of the greatest chiefs of the Omahas.

Before schools of any kind were known among the Omahas, Indian parents warned their boys and girls against a free association with the children of persons who did not bear a good character. "Who was that you were playing with?" a father or mother would ask. "Nobody knows the child's family,—beware of him, do not go with him, he will throw upon you the habit of lying or stealing. Go with children whose parents are respected by the people." Such advice would be given by the reputable men and women

of the tribe to their children as to choosing their play-
fellows.

At the school we were all thrown together and left to
form our own associates. The sons of chiefs and of prominent men went with the sons of the common people, regard-
less of social standing and character. The only distinction
made was against cowardice; the boy who could not
fight found it difficult to maintain the respect of his mates,
and to get a place among the different "gangs" or groups of
associates the boys had established among themselves. I
learned this from my friend Brush, to whom I complained
one day of being abused by the boys when he was not near.
"You must look out for yourself now," he said. "If the boys
know you won't fight, they will tease you all the time. You
must fight."

So the next boy who rudely shoved me aside and knocked
my hat off received a painful surprise, for my right fist came
so hard against his cheekbone that he stood for a moment
as though stunned. Then he moved, and I moved, and the
boys standing near could hardly tell which was which until
we separated, pretty well bruised. After that the boys were
careful not to knock my hat off my head; if they did, they
took pains to let me know that it was not intentional.

I told Brush about this set-to, and he approved of it.
"That's right," he said; "fight any of them, even if you know
that you're going to get licked; then they won't tease you."

My father was the principal chief of the tribe and leader
of the village of the "make-believe white-men;" he had
plenty of horses, the standard of Indian wealth, yet that
did not entitle me to a place in any of the different "gangs"
in the school; I had to show that I was not afraid to stand

11

up and fight. Even good-natured Brush had to bristle up at times and engage in a lively tussle, else there would have been no peace for him. Now I was wanted by the smaller "gangs" and invited by them to their places of sport; but Brush held on to me and kept me out.

Among the boys there was the "gang" of the "Big Seven" which Brush had been trying to enter; but, for some reason which I did not then understand, they would not admit him. He did not care to go into any of the "gangs" of smaller boys, of which there were quite a number. I thought the "Big Seven" did not want him, because he was too small; but later I found out there was another reason for it.

As time passed, I learned more and more of the peculiar ways of the boys at the school, of the teachers, and of my books. It was not long before I felt quite at home and independent; but Brush and I were still without a "gang."

# 2

---

# Brush

"FRANK you're learning fast!" said Brush one afternoon as I was laboriously writing my lesson on a slate with his help. "I'm glad; I want you to catch up with me so we can be in the same classes."

I felt proud of his praise and worked all the harder. We had gone through the alphabet swimmingly, and once, when I said it without a break, he slapped me on the shoulder and exclaimed, "That's good!" When I was able to read short sentences, I felt quite sure that I should soon take my place among the advanced pupils.

In and out of school Brush helped me along; in our play and when our work brought us together, he always managed to teach me something of the English language, and I was a willing student because he taught me in a way that made the work a pleasure. Gray-beard, not knowing what a kind and patient assistant he had in Brush, thought he had in me an exceptionally bright scholar, for I made rapid headway in learning to speak English, won several promotions, and soon found myself in the Second Reader class.

Brush was a bright fellow and quite a student. He and I sat at the same desk in the school-room, side by side at the dining-table, and we were bed-fellows. From him I learned many things he had gleaned from the superintendent's library, for he was a great reader, and the superintendent, who liked the boy, favored him in various ways, loaned him books to read, and talked with him about them.

Of all the stories he used to tell me, and he knew a great many, I liked best to hear him recount the old stories out of the Bible. He was familiar with them all, and told them in a way that delighted me, for he fitted them to my notions. He made them very real. One day he read to me a story, but I could not understand it as well as when he told it in his own simple way, so I asked him not to read them to me any more. The time for the telling of stories was at night after Gray-beard had gone downstairs to his own rooms, having warned us against loud talking.

My friend always seemed happy, yet at times, particularly on Saturdays, I noticed he would appear sober, almost melancholy. He did not go home as the rest of us did, and I wondered at this very much. He had a way of disappearing about the time I was ready to start home, so I never had a chance to invite him to my house, as I had often intended to do. I tried a number of times to bring him to speak of himself, but he would throw me off that line of talk, and my curiosity went unsatisfied for a long time.

"Say, Brush, where do you live?" I asked one afternoon as we were in the belfry. "You don't go home Saturdays like the rest of us."

"There's a man on the top of the hill near Big Elk's grave," he said evasively as he looked through the spy-glass.

I could see the man with my naked eyes as he stood on the topmost point against the clear, blue sky.

"Take the spy-glass and look at him," continued Brush, as though to put off my question.

"Do you live on the other side of that hill?" I persisted.

"Frank, I live here, I don't live anywhere else. This is the only home I have," said the boy sadly. "Do your father and mother ask you who you play with at the Mission?"

"N-o, they never did, maybe they will sometime, I don't know."

"I think they will, that's why I'm going to tell you who I am, then they will know," said Brush, seriously. After a pause he went on, "My father and mother died when I was very small, but I remember my grandfather. He was a very old man. He used to go to your father's house; maybe you have seen him, but I guess you can't remember. He was one of the chiefs, Tae-son' was his name. Once we went to Omaha to buy a lot of things, and coming home we camped just this side of the town; there he died. He was the last relative I had. Now I have no mother, no father, no sister, nothing—no home." He uttered the last word slowly as though thinking. "That's why the Big Seven—that man's gone, you take the spy-glass and look for him."

"If you have no home, why don't you go home with me?" I asked, looking through the spy-glass. "I know my father and mother would like you the same as I do."

"If I go home with you, I know I'll have a good time, but I haven't any home to ask you to. All the boys in the Big Seven do that way."

"I don't care what the Big Seven do, I want you to go home with me."

Saturday came. At breakfast I was anxious to have prayers over, Brush was to go home with me, and we anticipated much pleasure for the day.

"Don't eat much," I whispered to him; "we're going to eat again when we get home. My mother will give us something good, she always does."

After breakfast Brush went to the barn and filled the stalls with hay for the horses, which was part of the work assigned him. Then he ran up to the superintendent to report, and as soon as he came down we were off.

On the hill we were joined by two white boys, children of one of the Government employees at the mill. "Hello! Going home?" asked one of them. "We're going to the village. They say they're going to have a horse race there to-day. We want to see it."

Instead of taking the well-beaten path to the village, we all turned off into one that led directly to my father's house, and that passed by the burial-place on the bluffs. The two white boys were ahead, and when they came to a freshly made mound surrounded by a neat fence they stopped, and peered between the palings. "Pemmican!" exclaimed one of them. When Brush and I came up, we too looked in and saw on the grave a wooden bowl of pemmican. It was tempting these white boys, for they had learned to like this peculiar food.

"Jack, give me a boost?" said one of them, and soon he was over the fence filling his pockets out of the bowl. Then he offered the remainder to the other boy.

Brush and I were amazed and horrified at this action. We went straight on, taking no notice of the offer made by the

16

boys to give us some of the stolen food. "I bet one of those boys will die before the year is gone," said Brush, turning and looking back at the irreverent little rascals, who were now tipping their heads backward and putting pinches of the meat into their mouths.

"I bet so too!" I added. "It was awful the way they did. Let's go on fast; I don't want to be with them." And we sped down the hill on a brisk run.

At the door of the house my mother met us and led us into her room. We both began to tell her about the dreadful things the white boys had done, and expressed the belief that before the year was out one or both of them would die.

We sat down on the floor, and mother placed between us a pretty wooden bowl filled with freshly made pemmican, smiling at our childish notion that food taken after the spirits had tasted it meant death within the year. As we were eating with relish the food placed before us, my mother said, "You do not understand why the bowl of pemmican was placed on the little grave, and I must tell you. The spirit of the person buried in that grave, or the spirit of any other person dead and buried, cannot eat food; but people love their dead relatives; they remember them and long for their presence at the family gathering: it is this desire that makes them go and put a share of the food on the grave of those who have become nothing, and not the belief that the dead can return and partake of food the same as the living."

We listened with respectful attention as my mother explained to us this custom which arose from the tender longing that prompted the mourner to place on the little mound the food that might have been the share of the loved one who lay under the sod; but I am afraid we failed to grasp

17

the meaning of her words, and clung to the commonplace idea entertained by less thoughtful persons.

In the afternoon there was a general movement throughout the village, men, singly and in groups, walked with stately tread toward the edge of the bluff back of my father's house. Women, too, no less dignified, made their way in the same direction, followed by their grown-up daughters dressed in their gayest attire, their ornaments glinting in the sun. Little boys and girls chased each other hither and thither as they drifted that way, and soon there was a great gathering of people, all bent upon enjoying the excitement of the race. Brush and I mingled with the boys, and took part in their lively games, as preparations were going on for the sport of the day.

My father was in his corral trying to lasso a young horse to put on the track, a spirited little animal with bald face and large white spots on his side. When, with some difficulty, he was caught and bridled, he stood pawing the ground, impatient to go, tossing up his head from time to time and moving his ears excitedly. My father led him up to where the people were gathered; other men had already brought their horses there. Boys about Brush's size, lithe of figure, stood by the racers ready to mount when it was time to start.

My father looked around, and finally his eyes rested upon Brush. "Boy, can you ride?" he asked.

"I can," was the prompt answer.

My breath was fairly taken away at this reply. I did not know that Brush could ride well enough to mount a running horse at a race.

"I want you to ride my horse in this race," said my father.

"All right," replied the lad, taking off his school uniform. In a moment he was ready, stripped naked, with only a breech cloth.

Taking the reins and grasping the horse by the mane, Brush attempted to spring on his back, but the animal all excited trotted round and round. Father seized him by the bit, Brush lifted his right foot, father caught it, and in a twinkling the boy was on the horse. The mount was superb; the fiery creature sprang forward at a brisk gallop, but was checked by a skilled hand.

"Give him a canter a short distance; he'll quiet down," said father. Brush did so and soon returned, the horse prancing about most gracefully.

The course was on the bottom and as smooth as a floor. The twelve horses which were to run were taken to the farther end, about a mile away, and with them went the two men who were to manage the race. When the horses reached the starting point, they were ranged in line, and their riders were told to gallop them slowly and evenly to a point marked on the course. The two men rode along to see that the line was kept fairly; when the marked place was reached, the men shouted, "Ah—hu!" then every boy put his horse on the run.

To us on the hill, the horses looked like small specks in the distance; but, by the sudden rising of a cloud of dust, we knew when the signal was given to run. For a time they were too far away for us to distinguish those in the lead; but, as the horses came nearer, we began to recognize them; two in the front were well ahead, neck and neck.

"It's the roan!" shouted a tall man.

"No, it's the bald face!" cried another.

"Hurrah! Brush is in the lead!" yelled the freckled-faced white boy, swinging his ragged hat in the air as he ran up to where I was standing. "Gee whiz! look at him! look at him! My! I wish I could ride like that! "

Brush leaned forward a little, loosened the reins a bit; the horse gathered fresh speed and gained a length. The boy on the roan leaned forward too, and, raising his right arm, brought down his whip on the flank, the animal bravely sprang forward, but his strength was exhausted, he could do no more. On came the bald face, and reached the goal nearly three lengths ahead.

The men shouted themselves hoarse, and the women, with long-drawn breaths, praised the plucky little rider. Brush trotted up to my father, and delivered the horse.

"Who are you, little brother?" asked father.

For a moment Brush looked embarrassed, then lifting his eyes to father's face answered, "I am Tae-son's grandson and Sas-su's friend."

"Your grandfather was my friend," said my father, looking kindly at the lad: "I am glad you like the company of my boy. You must always come with him on his visits home from the House of Teaching."

Brush was touched by this recognition, and the tears started to his eyes. Seeing this, I intercepted the white boys who were running toward him. When I thought Brush had had time to master his feelings, I took the two boys to him, and they put their arms around him exclaiming, "Brush, that was grand!"

As this was his first visit to my home Brush did not feel quite easy, and long before the usual hour for my returning to the Mission, he suggested our going back. When we entered the school yard, which was deserted, for the boys and girls had not yet returned, we noticed a woman at the front gate holding a horse by a lariat and close beside her stood a colt mounted by two boys. She called to us and said she wanted to see the superintendent. Brush went to find him, and soon returned with that official.

"Tell the White-chest," said the woman to Brush, "that I have brought my two boys to stay here. They wanted to come, so I have brought them. Their father is dead; they have been my only comfort; but they want to learn to write. I hope he will be kind to them."

"They are bright-looking boys," said the superintendent, shaking hands with the mother. "I will take good care of them."

The boys dismounted, and the woman prepared to go. She kissed each of the little fellows and wiped a tear from her eyes.

"Don't cry, mother," said the older boy; "we'll be all right. We will come home often to see you."

We watched the mother as she went down the hill, leading her horse and the colt, until she disappeared at a turn on the bottom.

"Well, Brush, here's a job for you and Frank," said the superintendent. "Take these boys to the dormitory and give them a good wash, then bring them to the store-room, and I will see if I can fit them each with a suit of clothes."

We did as we were told, and while the superintendent was busy fitting the boys, Brush and I went into a large room and selected a bedstead for them. We put it together alongside of our bed, and began to cord it.

"Brush, why do the Omahas call the missionaries 'White-chests'?" I asked, as I pressed the cord from the foot to the head of the bed to tighten it.

"It's because the men wear stiff white shirts, and they show on their chests, that's why," he answered, throwing the mattress on the bed.

Brush and I soon became much attached to Lester and Warren, as the new-comers were named, and we lost no time in helping them along in their English. By our assistance and persistent use of the language with them, the two boys made rapid progress, and it was not long before they were chattering in broken English, like the rest of us.

# 3

## Edwin

In one of the little houses of the village of the "make-believe white-men" there sat on the floor of the room, which served as parlor, kitchen, dining, and bedroom, a man and a woman. There was but one window to the room, and, the weather being warm, the door stood wide open to let in more light for the workers within. The man was cutting with great care a large piece of moistened rawhide into narrow strips to be braided for a long lariat, and from time to time he softly whistled a tune that was running through his head. Directly under the window sat the woman; around her were strewn little workbags, awls, bits of deerskin, and shreds of sinew. Patiently she worked, pushing the point of the sharp awl through the edges of the leggings she was making, and drawing the finely twisted sinew thread through the perforation.

"We are the only ones in the village who haven't sent any children to the House of Teaching," said the woman, without looking up from her sewing, continuing a conversation the two were having. "Ma-wa'-da-ne has sent his boy, the only one he has. The man is lame, you know, and needs help; yet he wanted the boy to go, because he thinks some good will come of it to the child in the future. Then look at your friend E-sta'-ma-za, a man of great knowledge and foresight, he has sent his only boy and three daughters. There must be some good in it; we ought to send one of our boys at least."

The man took up a round stone and whetted his knife; then, as he felt the edge with his thumb, he replied, "I don't want the little one to go. Why don't you send the two big boys; they're hardly ever home anyway, and they might as well be at the house of the White-chests as anywhere else. What would the house be without the little one? We'd be very lonely, at least I'd be."

"I am just as fond of him as you are, and would miss him just as much; but he is the brightest of them all," said the woman, rising and stirring something that was boiling and sputtering in a pot on the stove. "He could learn faster than either of the older boys," she continued. "Before many years have gone, our dealings will be mostly with the white people who are coming to mingle with us; and, to have relations with them of any kind, some of us must learn their language and familiarize ourselves with their customs. That is what these men who send their children to the White-chests are looking forward to, and they love their boys as much as we do ours."

There was silence for some moments. The man fastened the ends of the rawhide strips to a peg in the floor and began to braid them. At length he said, "Where is the boy; he hasn't been in all the morning. When do you want him to go?"

"He might as well go now, to-day, the sooner the better. Of course he's down by the creek with his little bow and arrows."

"Well, wife, I wish you would go and call him. I don't want these strips to dry on me while I am braiding them."

The woman went to the banks of the little stream that ran by the village, and called in a shrill voice, "Oo-ma'-a-be! Oo-ma'-a-be!"

"I'm coming!" shouted a bareheaded, black-eyed little boy, just as he shot a blue-joint grass arrow at a frog that had poked his head above the surface of the water to see what was going on in the outer world. Forgetting the call, the lad went stealthily on up the stream with another arrow strung, looking for other frogs that might be hunting for flies or mosquitoes, or enjoying the kisses of the warm sunshine in some pleasant nook.

"What can the boy be doing?" said the woman to herself, then she called again, this time emphasizing the first syllable of the name to indicate that she was losing patience, "Oo'-ma-a-be!"

With reluctant steps the boy made his way toward his mother, peering as he went into the tall grass to see if a grasshopper or any other creature might be exposing itself to the arrows of a sport-loving lad.

"Why did you not come when I first called you?" asked the woman as she took the child by the hand and led him with quickened steps toward the little house.

As the mother and son entered, the father looked up with a pleasant smile, and addressing the boy said, "Your mother went to call you because she wants us to go to the house of the White-chests, where you are to stay and learn to write. Now wash your hands and face, and make yourself look nice, so they will be pleased with you; then we will go."

The mother had the water ready, and began scrubbing the face and neck of the lad, while the candidate for scholarship was pressing his lips tightly together and squinting his eyes to exclude the soap that persisted in getting into them. Then followed the brushing of the hair, which was equally irksome to the boy, and he unconsciously leaned farther and farther away until he was pulled to again by the fond parent.

When both face and hair shone, the mother kissed her boy and announced to her husband that the child was ready. The father rose to go with him, but the boy held back.

"What is it?" asked the father; "are you not willing to go?"

"I am willing to go," answered Oo-ma′-a-be, "but I want to put on my embroidered moccasins and leggings and my little buffalo robe."

The husband and wife looked at each other smiling, and let the youngster have his own way, so he was decked out in his gorgeous costume. He folded himself up in his robe, which was beautifully ornamented with porcupine quills of exquisite colors, he twisted his body and neck to see if he looked well, then said he was ready to go.

In the school-room a class of big boys and girls were learning to read in concert:—

> "The boy stood on the burning deck,
>   Whence all but he had fled."

Again and again the teacher made them read the lines, but each time some one would either lag behind or read faster than the others. While this was going on I was busy with my spelling lesson, as my class came after the one now hard at work with the boy "on the burning deck."

There was a click; I raised my eyes and looked toward the door; it slowly opened, then a tall man and a boy silently entered. I recognized them at once; the man was a friend of my father and the lad one of my playmates on my weekly visits home. The class on the floor was dismissed with a lecture on reading, and Gray-beard turned to call, "Next class," when he discovered the man and boy sitting on a bench near the door.

"How do you do, Wa-hon'-e-ga?" said Gray-beard, approaching the Indian with outstretched hand.

"Ka-gae'-ha!" (Friend) responded the Indian, his face brightening. Then in a low tone he called me to him and said, "I have brought your grandfather here to stay with you. Be as good to each other as you have always been, and try to learn the language of the White-chests."

The boy was a distant relative, and, following the peculiar system of kinship among the Indians, there was no impropriety in my addressing him as my grandfather, although we preferred to call each other friend.

"What does Wa-hon'-e-ga want?" asked Gray-beard, putting his hand on my shoulder.

"My friend," replied the Indian, looking with a kindly smile into the face of the teacher, "my wife wishes her son, this boy, to learn to speak the language of the Big-knives [English], so I have come with him. We have brought him up with great care, and I think he will give you no trouble."

27

"Tell him," said Gray-beard, "I am very glad he has brought the boy, and we will do our best for him."

The Indian turned and with silent dignity left the room.

"Now, children," said Gray-beard, taking out the school register and looking at us, "we have a new boy here, and we must select a good name for him; what have you to suggest?"

We promptly called him Edwin M. Stanton, and he was registered by that name.

Brush and I were detailed to take Edwin to the storeroom and fit him with a new suit of clothes. When he was dressed, we tied up his fine Indian costume in a neat bundle to be returned to his father.

At the supper-table Edwin and I sat together. I showed him how to bow his head when the blessing was asked, and to turn his plate. He silently followed my whispered instructions, and was very quiet while supper was going on, but during the religious exercises which followed, when we dropped on our knees, he became very anxious to know why we did so. He shuffled a good deal in his position, and after a while stood up and looked around. I pulled him down, and he demanded out loud, "What are we hiding for? This is the way we do when we are hiding in the grass."

I gave him a good dig in the ribs. "That hurts!" he cried. I whispered to him to be quiet, but before long he was fidgeting again. Just as the superintendent lowered his voice at an earnest passage in his prayer Edwin spoke out again, in a louder tone than before, "I've got a dog; he can catch rabbits!"

Gray-beard lifted his head, and the superintendent paused in his fervent appeal and looked toward us; he rapped with his knuckles on the table, and said, in a severe tone, "Boys, you must be silent and listen when I pray."

I whispered to Edwin that he must keep still until we got out.

As we were going to bed that night Edwin said, "Ka-gae'-ha [Friend], let you and me sleep together; I don't want to sleep with any one else."

Lester too wanted to sleep with me; so it was arranged among us that Brush and Warren should have the double bed, and Edwin, Lester, and I were to have the wide bed for three.

After we had settled down, Edwin began talking, "When we finished eating," he said, "we turned around and the old man began to talk, then you all sang. I like to hear you sing; you've got a good voice. Then we went down on our knees, just as though we were hiding in the grass; what did we do that for? The old man talked a long time; was he telling a story? I know a great many of them; I know one about a dog. He was a man, but he was turned into a dog. I'll tell it to you."

I didn't say anything, so Edwin began:

"Far back in the earliest times there dwelt in a little village a man and his wife. They had only one child living, a son whom they loved to adoration. He was so handsome a youth that whenever he walked through the village all eyes were turned upon him with admiration. One day he asked his mother to make him a separate tent. When it was done he went into it, and there spent four days and nights in solitude, neither eating nor drinking. Then he came out and spoke to his father and mother and said, "I am going away to be gone a long time, perhaps never to return. I go

29

to meet the White-swan, the magician who sent my brothers to the abode of shadows, and, in conflict, with magic opposing his magic, I will destroy him or die as my brothers have died." The father and mother, remembering the fate of their other children, wept and pleaded with their son not to leave them, but he was determined to go.

The young man travelled many days, when one morning he beheld a maiden sitting on the brow of a hill. He went to her and asked why she sat there all alone. Without lifting her eyes, modesty forbidding her to return his gaze, the maiden replied, "I go to marry Hin-hpe'-ah-gre." The youth was seized with fear lest the young woman might be the White-swan transformed to beguile him; but being struck by her maidenly bearing, and becoming enamoured of her beauty, he turned aside from suspicion and permitted himself to be persuaded that the fair creature before him was in reality one of his own kind. And so he spoke and said, "I am he, Hin-hpe'-ah-gre, the man whom you seek to follow." In reply the maiden said, "It makes my heart throb with delight to meet and to see with my own eyes the man I am to marry. Sit down and rest your head in my lap, and when the weariness of travel has left you, I shall follow you wherever you may lead." Joy filling the heart of the youth, and no longer troubled with misgivings, he laid his head upon the lap of the maiden and soon fell fast asleep.

"Tha! Tha!" exclaimed the woman, using a word of magic, and four times, in quick succession, she pulled the ears of the young man. He awoke with a start and attempted to rise, but a transformation had taken place, instead of a man standing upright, he found himself to be a four-footed beast. His body had changed, but his reason

30

was still that of a man. He turned to see his companion, and lo! he beheld, not the beautiful maiden in whose lap he had fallen asleep, but one who looked down upon him with contempt, and whom he knew to be the White-swan. The thought that he had been outwitted came to the young man like a flash, and as swiftly his magic word returned to his mind. He tried to utter it, but he only yelped and gave a dismal howl like that of a dog. A cringing, mangy, lop-eared dog, he now followed the White-swan and—Are you asleep?"

I was almost asleep, so I did not answer him, then he became silent. When I awoke Edwin was gone; I called him but he did not answer. Brush and I went downstairs and called softly in the school-room, but the boy was not there, then we went to the large door of the hall and found it unbolted. We returned to the dormitory and went to bed, and I soon fell asleep again.

Toward morning I was awakened by strange sounds on the stairs leading up to our dormitory. I recognized the footsteps of a human being, but there were other footsteps that were like those of a four-footed beast. They approached my bed; they came near, and a voice said in Indian in a loud whisper, "Lie down, lie down!"

"Is it you, Oo-ma′-a-be?" I asked.

"Yes, I've been after my dog," he answered, getting into bed with his clothes on.

"Get up and undress; you can't sleep with your clothes on! What did you go after the dog for?"

"I wanted you to see him, and I thought we'd keep him here. He is a fine dog; he can swim too!"

"But were you not afraid? It was dark."

"I forgot all about being afraid, and I went right by that big grave too,—the one they say a ghost comes out of and chases people. I ran, though, all the way to my house. The dog was lying near the door; he was so glad to see me he almost knocked me down."

It was nearly morning, and we went right off to sleep. Suddenly we were aroused by a furious barking. Brush, Edwin, and I sprang out of bed, and rushed for the dog that with legs spread was defending the top of the stairs.

"Boys, what have you up there?" called Gray-beard from the foot.

"Edwin went after his dog last night," answered Brush. "He wants to keep it here."

"He does, eh! Will it bite?"

"No, it won't bite; you can come up."

# 4

## Little
## Bob

THE AFTERNOON SESSION was over; Gray-beard tapped his bell; we put away our books, folded our arms, and when there was silence the teacher spoke: "Frank will remain here until he finishes correctly the sum he is working on. He has neglected his arithmetic lesson during school hours, so he will have to do the work after school."

Such punishment had not happened to me before. It had frequently come to other scholars, and I had felt sorry for them; but now the disgrace had fallen on me, and I felt it keenly.

Gray-beard led the song about "The Little Brown Church in the Wild Wood," and the whole school sang; but just then I did not care for brown churches or churches of any other color, so my voice did not mingle with that of the other pupils. Then they sang "Lord dismiss us," but as I was not dismissed I did not join in the singing of that familiar hymn.

Brush, Edwin, and the rest of my companions lingered awhile in the school-room to keep me company; but as they had work to do they could not stay long, so I was left alone to struggle with a lot of ugly fractions. My thoughts ran in every direction, off to my home, to the boys at play, and anywhere but on my task. I made a desperate effort to bring myself around to the problem that held me a prisoner by keeping a steady gaze into the deep blue sky through the open window, and then slowly the solution of that detestable sum came to my mind, and I had it. I put it on my slate, compared it with the answer left me by Graybeard, found it correct, and my work was done.

I arose, put my books away, and stood near the teacher's desk wondering what to do next, when all of a sudden the door burst open and in rushed a little boy, crying. He was without his hat, his coat unbuttoned, and shoestrings untied. Following swiftly on the little chap came a large boy who, for some reason, was angered at the fleeing lad, and was now pursuing to punish him. The little boy ran around the stove, then toward me and got behind me. The big boy pushed on in his vengeful pursuit, and reached to grasp the object of his anger when I struck at him with my fist. The blow fell on his forehead, he stood for a moment stunned; then he sprang at me; we dealt each other blow after blow, and in our mad charges we knocked over benches and desks. How it happened I do not know, for in my excitement I could not tell where I struck him, or where he struck me, but suddenly my antagonist put his hands to his stomach, doubled over and could not breathe. I became frightened. At length, with a succession of hiccoughs, the boy recovered his breath, picked up his hat, and went out.

I straightened out the benches and desks that we had knocked over, and then sat down to cool off. When I had rested, I called to the round-headed little chap who stood trembling in the corner holding up his trousers, for in his attempts to escape he had lost the buttons to his pants, "What did you do to that boy; what did he want to hit you for?"

"I didn't do nothin'," he answered, hitching up his garments as he came toward me.

"What's your name?"

"Robert Brown."

"Where you live?"

"In your village, in that little house near Ou-ni-ja-bi's."

"That's Ne-ma-ha's house."

"Yes, that's my father."

And so it was the son of that man for whom I was all bruised up.

Ne-ma-ha was the poorest man in my father's village, and had no recognition among the prominent men of the tribe, although he had been the priest or hereditary keeper of the sacred tent of war. It was only by the performance of valorous deeds that men won honors in the tribe; but this man had no ambition to win such honors. As a hunter he was also a total failure, consequently his worldly possessions were not such as could give him distinction. Like his brother, who was struck by lightning, he deserted his sacred charge through craven superstitious fear, and, having lost his priestly position, he had become a useless member of the tribe.

"What's your Omaha name?" I asked, as I pinned his trousers to his suspenders with sharp sticks and nails.

"They call me Hae-th'na'-ta," he replied, wiping his face with the end of his coat sleeve.

The youngster belonged to the Elk band of the tribe, hence the boy's name, the English translation of which is, horns forked, meaning the forked-horned elk. How he came by his English name I do not know.

From this time on the lad was always near me, and gradually became my devoted follower. Although at first I did not care for him much, he finally won my friendship by his faithfulness and good nature. He always assisted me as far as his strength would permit in the work assigned me about the school; thus it was that Little Bob, as he was familiarly known, became a satellite to the group to which I belonged, and so safe from the attacks of the other boys.

Brush, Edwin, Warren, Lester, and I were now recognized by all the boys of the school as a "gang," and were spoken of as "the Middle Five." We had fallen into this close companionship without any formal arrangement, and we were regarded as the strongest group between the Big Seven and the other "gangs."

# 5

## Warren

BRUSH was a genius as a whittler. He had only one tool, and that was a rusty jack-knife with a single broken blade, and that blade was kept sharp almost to the keenness of a razor. He would take a shapeless piece of wood, cut here, cut there, scrape at one place, then at another, and go through a series of twists and turns of his strong, deft hands, and at last, with a triumphant smile, hold up to view a wooden horse, buffalo, or some other animal. He had just now finished a little plough which he had been carving for some time, and we, the Middle Five, sat in the shade of a tree noisily discussing the accuracy of the work.

"Brush, that's pretty good, it's just like the ploughs I've seen," I remarked as I passed the toy to Edwin.

"'Tain't good," said Edwin, after he had examined it a while. "I think the handles are too straight."

"This ought to be kind of crooked, come down like this,"

put in Lester, indicating with his finger the outline of the beam as it should have been, according to his notion.

Our heads were close together looking at the plough, when a sudden consciousness as of the presence of some-things disagreeable stole upon us. A sound like the snapping of a twig made us all look up, and there stood Jim, a big boy, one of the worst that ever entered our school, and who had been excluded from all the "gangs" on account of his vicious, meddlesome disposition. With a contemptuous grin, he passed his eyes from one boy to the other, as though to discern the character of each one. When this unpleasant stare fell upon Warren, he bristled up, gave back a defiant look, and kept it steadily upon the unwelcome visitor. Without relaxing the mirthless smile, so characteristic of him, Jim addressed the boy, "Warren, I just come from the spring, where a lot of boys was talking. I heard Gid say that he could lick you. I told him I'd come and tell you what he said. Then he says, 'I don't care, I ain't 'fraid of him!'"

"You go and tell Gid," said Warren, springing to his feet, "I can lick two like him, and I'll show him any time he wants me to."

The mischief-maker had read well the character of Warren, and had won from him the expected reply.

We resumed our examination of the plough thinking that our interview with the tale-bearer had ended. Jim thrust his hands into his pockets, and walked uneasily about; he came to where little Bob was sitting, and, pulling out a warty hand, he pointed his finger at the boy's face, making a hissing sound between his teeth. Jim never passed by a chance to tease a smaller boy. Bob put his hands to his face and began crying. We all rose to our feet; Edwin moved forward in a threatening attitude, and said, "Jim, you let that boy alone. What you want to tease him for?"

Jim turned away, looked up into a tree, threw a stone at a bird, and then slowly sauntered off.

We sat down again to resume our talk about Brush's little plough, but our minds seemed to turn in another direction.

"I don't want Warren to fight Gideon," said Edwin; "he's a bad fellow, that Gideon is. He don't fight fair."

"But he can't back out," spoke up Lester, "and I don't want him to. I don't want the rest of the boys to think he's 'fraid."

"Warren's got to fight Gid," exclaimed Brush. "If he only kept quiet and didn't say anything when Jim told him what Gid said, it would be all right and no fight; but now everybody knows what Warren said, and he can't back out without the boys thinking he's a coward. We will see that Gid fights fair, and, if he don't, we will thrash his whole 'gang.' Warren can use his arms and fists all right; but he can't wrestle very good. Frank, you'd better show him some of those new holds."

Warren and I took several rounds in which I showed him a number of new tricks I had learned from a good wrestler. There was quite an important one of which he was ignorant; I gave him some lessons in that; then we sat down to talk over the challenge again with the rest of the boys.

"I think Warren can throw Gid right easy," I said; "if he can remember that waist and chin trick, and the way to break it, he can down Gid every time."

"Remember that!" warned Lester, looking at his brother. "If Gid plays that waist and chin trick, you do just what Frank showed you to do to break it."

While we were talking, we heard the slapping of bare feet upon the hard ground, and soon a boy appeared before us, imitating the actions of a spirited horse. "Whoa'p! Whoa'p!" he called repeatedly, as with loud snorts the imaginary steed reared and plunged about; finally the excited animal came to a standstill. Looking at Warren, the boy said, "Gid told me to come and tell you, he will meet you down below the barn, at the east gate, right after school this afternoon. He told me to tell you again he can lick you good."

After some prancing about, the boy ran off, clapping his hips with his hands to imitate the sound of galloping hoofs.

Gideon had accepted Warren's challenge, and we had no misgivings as to the outcome, for we had every confidence in Warren's courage and strength. What concerned us most was Jim's meddling with us and the means by which we could prevent his further interference with our peace. He had made trouble with other "gangs" just in this way. We were still discussing this matter when the school-bell rang, and we went to the house together.

The boys who had already taken their seats looked up at us as we entered the school-room, then they turned their glances upon Gideon to see how he would behave. The two boys, Gideon and Warren, stared at each other defiantly; the rest saw there was no courage lacking in either, and they expected a lively battle between the two. Jim pretended to be studying; but we knew that he was closely watching the victims of his machinations to see how they would act. Jim never studied; he was always at the foot of his class, and boys younger than he were far in advance of him.

At last the monotonous recitations came to an end. We sang a song about "Pretty little zephyrs," then Gray-beard closed the school with the usual religious exercises.

The boys gathered in groups and walked down to the place designated for the combat. We followed slowly, as we wanted time to give all the instructions necessary to Warren. A large ring had been formed by the boys, and Gid was already in the centre with his coat off and his sleeves rolled up. Jim glanced at us as though impatient for our coming. As we neared the ring, some one said, in a voice loud enough for us to hear, "They're not coming very fast. I guess they're 'fraid!"

Brush stepped hastily forward and asked, "Who said we're afraid? Whoever said it, let him come out here and I'll show him whether we're afraid or not!"

No one answered. There were few boys in the school who would without fear accept a challenge from Brush.

A place was cleared for us, and Warren, after handing me his coat, entered the ring. The two boys approached each other and stopped within a few feet.

"Did you tell Jim you could lick me?" asked Warren, looking his opponent square in the eye.

"Yes. And I can do it too," was the bold reply.

"You can't do it!" exclaimed Warren, striking Gideon in the chest.

Then followed an exciting scene. Gideon rushed at Warren, and aimed blow after blow at his face, but our boy skilfully parried each attack. Round and round within the ring the two boys carried on their strife, neither one prevailing. For a while no serious blows were dealt, finally, in an unguarded moment Warren received a hard thrust in the left side which made him gasp; whereat Gid's gang shouted in chorus, "Choo-ie!" (An exultant exclamation in Omaha.) After this success Gideon grew reckless and struck wildly, and Warren was a little too anxious to put in a good hit before the proper moment. Gid made another effort at his antagonist's ribs, but the blow fell short; then Warren made a lunge at Gid's face; he dodged, but not quickly enough to save his ear from a bad scraping from Warren's knuckles. "Choo-ie!" cried Lester and the rest of us at this success; but Gid's next movement threw us into dismay, he had suddenly seized Warren around the waist while his arms were uplifted. Gid put his chin against Warren's chest and began pulling in his back. Warren tried to twist Gid's neck; but there was no use in that, Warren was slowly giving way. If he should fall the battle would be won by Gideon.

"Put your arms under his and push!" I said to Warren in an undertone. I couldn't help doing it.

Isaac, a blustering little chap and one of Gid's "gang" overheard me; stepping forward and pointing his finger at me, he angrily exclaimed, "Frank, you know that ain't fair, we don't do that way."

"You do worse than that," I retorted. "The whole four of you jumped on me in the school-room; that wasn't fair, but I licked you! Wait till Warren and Gid get through, then I'll see you!"

Warren had heard my words, and acted on them at once, and so released himself from Gideon's dangerous grasp. Then they went to sparring again. In making a thrust Warren stumbled on a round stone and fell on one knee, before he could rise Gid put in a blow that cut Warren's under lip. "Choo-ie!" exclaimed the friends of Gid. It seemed for a moment as though the victory would be against us. The struggle now became desperate. Gid was blowing hard, but there was still considerable reserve of strength in Warren. Gid repeatedly tried to grasp his antagonist's waist, but was every time cleverly brought about again to fists.

Warren's shirt front was bloody and his short hair stood up, giving him a frightful aspect. Gid's thrusts and parries now grew visibly weaker, but he showed no signs of yielding. He lowered his fists to give an under cut, thus leaving his face unguarded, quick as a flash Warren's right arm shot out, and with a sickening thud his fist landed square on Gid's nose. The blood spurted; the boy was stunned, and, before he could recover, he received another blow on the eye.

The fight was ended, and Gid's friends dragged him away more dead than alive.

Warren came to us smiling as widely as his swollen lip would permit.

"You did first rate, old boy!" said Brush, slapping Warren's back.

"He'll never want to fight you again," added Lester.

I helped Warren to put on his coat, then I looked around to see where Edwin was. I saw him standing before Jim, who was watching us with his wicked grin. They both spoke, but I could not hear them for the noise of the talk around me. Suddenly Edwin's long arm darted out, his fist came square on Jim's cheek with a resounding whack. Jim's face became livid, and the spot upon which the blow fell twitched convulsively. When the natural color returned to

43

his face, Jim deliberately pulled off his coat; he was going to fight Edwin. It was an uneven match; Jim stood a head taller and was heavier than Edwin.

"What's the matter?" asked Brush, as he came up; "what are you going to do?"

"We're going to fight," replied Edwin; "I hit him because he made that trouble."

"Jim," said Brush, stepping forward and rolling up his sleeves, "I don't think it would be unfair for two of us to fight you. You are bigger than any of us, so I am going to help Edwin to thrash you. You've been making mischief for others, now it's going to come to you."

The boys gathered around the three to see another fight, but were disappointed. Jim made no further demonstration, but stood looking at the two boys; at last he muttered something to himself, and, picking up his coat, pushed his way out of the crowd.

All the boys pointed their fingers at Jim, and shouted, "Ah, coward!" Jim turned his head and looked at them sulkily, but went on, and no one cared to follow him.

# 6

---

# Lester

THE HANDS of the little clock on Gray-beard's desk indicated the hour of two. The midsummer's sun hurled its rays with unrelenting force to the earth, and the wind, as though consenting to the attack, withheld its refreshing breezes. All the windows of our school-room were thrown wide open, and the hum of busy insects and the occasional cry of a bird were the only sounds that relieved the monotonous stillness outside.

A class, with Warren at the head, was on the floor. The girl at the foot was reading in a tone that made it difficult to resist the drowsiness that attacked every one in the room. She came to a hard word, and, according to our custom, she spelled it. Gray-beard, who was sitting with eyes shut, pronounced it for her through a suppressed yawn. A few more words brought her to the end of the paragraph.

A long pause followed; Warren stood with book uplifted, but was gazing intently on something outside. The teacher, recovering from an overbalancing nod, opened his eyes slowly, and lazily called, "Warren!" The boy did not stir. Brush and I looked up from our desk, and shuffled our feet to attract his attention. "Warren!" again called Gray-beard, in a louder tone. Still there was no response.

Brush tore a fly-leaf out of his book, rolled it hastily into a ball, and threw it at Warren's head, but missed it.

Gray-beard turned in his chair, his eyes rested upon the boy, who was still looking fixedly out of the window. Then he rose, stepped softly up to Warren, seized him by the shoulders and shook him violently, saying, "Are you asleep?"

"Swarming!" rang out the last word of the sentence which Warren was making a desperate effort to utter.

Gray-beard, following the eyes of the lad, looked out of the window, "Quick, boys, to the dining-room, take anything you can make a noise with!" he exclaimed, as he sprang to the door, threw it open with a bang and disappeared.

We leaped over desks, and tumbled over each other as we rushed with impetuous haste to the dining-room. Brush caught up an enormous tin pan, Edwin a milk pail, and I the school triangle; the rest of the boys took tin pans and plates, or whatever they could lay their hands on, and we all ran out into the yard. Warren was already following the humming black cloud, ringing the school-bell with all his might. We caught up with him, and began beating on the tin pans with our knuckles, keeping up a constant yelling like a lot of savages. The noise we made was enough to drive the bees and ourselves insane. It was bedlam let loose. On we went through the barnyard, up the hill, and into the woods, closely following the flying black mass. Three boys carrying small mirrors kept throwing flashes of light into the swarm.

The bees made a straight line for a tall oak, hovered over the end of a high branch, and then settled on it. We gathered around the tree, and continued our unearthly noise until Gray-beard, with a box and a saw on his shoulder, and a coil of rope on his arm, came up puffing and all in a perspiration.

"Have they settled?" he asked, shading his eyes and looking up into the tree.

"Yes, there they are," answered Brush, pointing to the writhing black mass on the branch.

"Who can climb?" said Gray-beard, looking around among the boys. No one answered. After a while Edwin spoke up, "Lester climb tree like wild-cat."

Lester turned and looked daggers at him. Brush and I nudged each other and giggled. Edwin was playing a joke on Lester.

"Come," said Gray-beard, "there's no time to be lost." And he proceeded to tie the end of the rope around the waist of Lester, who had not recovered from his astonishment and was given no time to put in a disclaimer to the title of climber.

Gray-beard lifted the lad up as high as he could, then the boy began to clim. He went up slowly but surely, dragging the rope after him. Edwin shouted words of encouragement. "That's good, go ahead!" he would exclaim as the climber made now and again six inches or so.

"Wait till I get down, I show you!" Lester called back. Then Edwin turned to us and grinned.

The limb upon which the bees had settled was at last reached; the boy pulled up the hand-saw that was tied to the other end of the rope. He looked down at us with mischief in his face, then straddled the branch with his face toward the trunk of the tree and began to saw. Gray-beard, seeing this, called up in great excitement, "Stop! stop! Lester, stop! Turn the other way." The boy, having had his fun, turned, and, moving as near to the bees as he dared, began sawing slowly until the branch hung down, then he severed it. It did not fall because before he began to saw he had tied one end of the rope near to the bees, and had fastened the other part near to the place where he was sitting, so that he was able gradually to lower the bees to the ground.

We did not know that anything had happened to Lester until he came down, then we saw that he was stung on the eyebrow and his face was swollen. Brush moistened a bit of earth and smeared it around the injured part to prevent further swelling, but it did no good.

Gray-beard put the box over the bees and began pounding the top, "Look under there, Frank, and see if they are going up," he said; "if the queen goes, they will all go."

I crouched to the ground and looked into the box; there was great activity and noise. "I think they are going up," I said.

Suddenly the pounding on the box ceased; I heard an outcry and a groan; I looked up, and there was Gray-beard rolling on the ground. He was badly stung in the face. Brush went to his assistance and painted his wounds with mud. I went to the box and pounded as Gray-beard had done.

"Look under, Warren, and see what they are doing," I said.

Warren put his head to the ground and looked, "I guess that old king went up; they're all gone," he said; "I can't see them."

Having recaptured our bees, we securely fastened the box so that the wind could not blow it over; we gathered up our pans, milk pails, and bells and formed a homeward procession. Brush headed it, leading Gray-beard, whose eyes were now both closed and bandaged with his white handkerchief, and in this way we reached Mission building.

The ladies and the school girls were waiting on the porch for our return, and as we approached the gate a number called out, "How many of you are stung?"

"Two!" cried the boys; "teacher and Lester."

When we were passing the girls on the porch to go to our quarters, pretty little black-eyed Rosalie, my sweetheart, came up to me and asked, "Frank, was you stung?"

"No; but the bees wouldn't go in the box for anybody but me," I answered proudly.

"But I wish you was stung like Lester," she said; "his girl is telling the rest of them all about it, and they think he's right smart because he got stung."

Some of the big girls, overhearing this confidence, put their aprons up to their faces to hide their laughter. The teachers never knew that there were lovers among the pupils and that little romances were going on right under their eyes.

Gray-beard could not see us to bed that night, so the superintendent took his place.

"Good-night, boys, keep quiet and go to sleep," he said

as he went downstairs after he had heard us say our prayer.

"Warren, you've earned ten cents to-day," said Brush; "I think Lester earned something too. I don't know how much it's going to be, but I'll go and see the superintendent about it to-morrow."

"Say, Brush, I think that bee that stung Lester was a drone; that's why his face is all swelled up," I said.

"Oh! go 'long!" he answered. "Whoever heard of a drone having a sting. They have no sting, and they can't sting. It's only the working bees that have a sting."

"But those drones are big fellows, two times as big as the working bees. The superintendent showed me one when he was moving a swarm to a new box in the bee house."

"They haven't any sting, though. There are three kinds of bees: there's the queen, then there's the drone, and there's the working bees. When the drones get too many, and eat too much, the working bees, they get mad and they sting them to death."

"I think that work bee thought Lester was drone," remarked Edwin.

"Wait till I get well," threatened Lester; "I'll show you drone!"

"What is the queen?" asked Warren. "And what does it do?"

"Why a queen is a female king," explained Brush, who was authority on a great many things. "She doesn't do anything but sit on a big throne and tell people what to do. If they don't mind her, she makes her soldiers cut their heads off. It's the same with bees: they have a queen,—I

50

don't think she sits on a throne, but she tells the rest of the bees what to do; and if they don't mind her, she gets up and goes; then all the rest have to follow her, because they won't know what to do unless she tells them. That's what that old queen did today."

"Why don't the 'Mericans have a king?" asked Edwin. "They got a President, but I don't think he's big like a king."

"They had one," said Brush; "but they didn't like him, because he put a terrible big tax on tea. The 'Mericans are awfully fond of tea, and when they saw they'd have to pay the trader and the king, too, for their tea, they got mad; and one night, when everybody was asleep, they painted up like wild Indians, and they got into a boat and paddled out to the tea ship and climbed in. They hollered and yelled like everything, and scared everybody; then they spilted the tea into the ocean."

"What did the old king do?" asked Lester.

"Well, he was hopping mad, and he lifted his great big sceptre, and he went up to the man that brought the news, and knocked him over. Then he walked up and down talking loud, and when he got tired he went to his throne and sat down hard."

"What is a sceptre?" I asked, interrupting the story.

"Why, it's something like a war club; when the king tells people to do things, he shakes it at them, so they will get scared and mind what he says."

"I wouldn't mind him," said Warren; "I'd make a big sceptre for myself and shake it at him."

"Well," continued Brush, "the old king sat still for a long time; then he said to his soldiers, you go and fight those

51

'Mericans. And they did fight, and had the Rev'lution. That war lasted eight years, and the king's soldiers got licked. Then the 'Mericans made General George Washington their President because he couldn't tell a lie."

The next morning Brush went to the superintendent's study, and soon came out calling for Warren and Lester. Edwin and I waited under the walnut-tree in front of the school. When the three came to us, they showed us a bright silver dime and an equally bright quarter of a dollar. According to our notions, Warren and his brother were rich, the former having earned the reward offered for the discovery and report of the swarming of the bees, and the latter earning the quarter by climbing the tree on which the swarm had settled.

Brush announced to us that Lester and Warren had been detailed to go after the mail. The post-office was in the trader's store three miles away from the school, and boys were always very glad to be sent on this errand.

In the afternoon, when school was out, Brush went up to the superintendent's room to borrow the spy-glass, while Edwin and I went in search of Lester and Warren, who had slipped away from us. We could not find them, so we returned to the school-room, where we met Brush, and we all went up to the belfry.

The Indians were at work in their fields, and we each took the glass in turn to see if we could recognize our friends. Suddenly Edwin said, "Something's going to happen; look at those girls."

Two girls were going through the yard arm in arm, now and again glancing over their shoulders toward the boys' play-ground. They reached the farthest corner of the yard,

52

then turned and looked along the dividing fence. Two boys sauntered towards them on the other side, following a narrow path.

"There's Lester and Warren," said Brush; "they're up to something, keep your eyes upon them."

We did. The four met at the corner, sat down and appeared to be talking to each other. When they had been there for some time, the boys handed through the palings to each of the girls a brown parcel.

"I see now why those boys wanted to go after the mail this morning," said Brush.

The girls arose and walked toward the house, opening their parcels, and we saw through the spy-glass that they were eating candy. The boys slowly returned, one following the other along the narrow path. Edwin thrust his fingers into his mouth and whistled, imitating the cry of the robin, which was the signal we five had adopted. The boys stopped suddenly as the sound reached them, and looked all around. Seeing no one, they went on. Again Edwin whistled; then I touched the bell very lightly with the clapper. The boys looked up to the belfry; but we kept out of sight.

At breakfast the next morning the two girls appeared at the table with their hair neatly done up in bright-colored ribbons. Edwin leaned over toward Lester and said in a whisper, "Your girl's got a right pretty ribbon!"

"Yours hasn't got any!" retorted Lester.

# 7

## The Splinter,
## the Thorn,
## and the Rib

Oн! oн! oн! Aunt, that hurts. Oh!" "Keep still, now, keep
still! You have a big stick in your toe, and I must take it
out. If you keep pulling like that, I might run the point of
this awl into your foot."

I lay flat on my back on the ground with my sore foot in
the lap of this good woman whom I called Aunt, while she
probed the wound to withdraw a splinter. After considerable wincing on my part, the cause of my agony was removed and held to view. The splinter was long and very
large; the relief was great, and already I felt as though I
could walk without limping. The kind woman took from
her work-bag a bit of root, chewed it, and put it on my sore
toe; then she bandaged the foot with a piece of white cloth
which also came from the handy bag.

My Aunt laid the splinter on a piece of wood and cut it
into fine bits, just as I had seen men cut tobacco for smok-

ing. "Now," said she, as she scattered the bits in every direction, "that thing cannot do any more harm. But what is this?" she asked, holding the old bandage up between the tips of her thumb and index finger of her right hand, and in her left the bit of pork that had been tied on my toe.

"Why, Aunt," I replied, "that thing in your right hand is the old bandage, and that in your left is the pig-fat that was put on my toe."

"Why did they put pig-fat on your poor sore toe; who put it on? Bah! It's nasty!" she exclaimed, as she threw it away as far as she could.

"The white woman who takes care of the children at the school put it on to draw the splinter out."

"To draw the splinter out!" she repeated in a tone of contempt. Then she tossed up her fine head, gave shouts of laughter, and said between the paroxysms; "Oh! this is funny! This is funny! Your White-chests might as well hitch a bit of pig-fat to their wagon and expect it to draw a load up the hill! And how long has this pig-fat been tied on your foot?"

"About four days."

"Without bathing the foot and renewing the bandages?"

"Yes."

"If this white woman takes as much care of the other children as she has of you,—I'm sorry for them. No children of mine should be placed under her care,—if I had any."

My Aunt gathered her awl, knife, and other little things into her work-bag; I looked all about to see if any boys were watching, then I put my arms around her dear neck and kissed her.

"Are you going to see my mother today?" When she answered yes, I said, "Tell her to come and see me,—very soon."

"I will; but don't keep her running over here all the time," and she started to go. She had not gone very far when she turned and shouted to me, "Wash your foot to-morrow morning and turn the bandage over. You will be well in a day or two."

A boy passing by cried out, "Bell has rung!" and I limped into the school-room to attend the afternoon session.

When school was out, Lester suggested that we go on the hill to sit and talk. Turning to me, he asked if I could walk as far as that; I assured him that I could, so I hobbled along with the boys up the hill. We found a beautiful grassy spot, and three of us—Lester, Warren, and I—lay down and looked up into the deep blue sky. Brush sat near by, carving a horse's head out of a piece of oak. Clouds lazily floated far above.

"Say, Lester," I called, "you take that one that looks like a buffalo; Warren, you take that one that is shaped like a bear; and I will take this one that's like a man smoking a pipe. Now, let's rub them out!"

So, fixing our eyes upon the clouds, we began rubbing the palms of our hands together.

"Mine is getting smaller, right away, now!" cried Warren.

"Mine too!" echoed Lester.

Brush gave us a look of disgust, and said, "Boys, I think you are the biggest fools I ever saw,—rubbing out clouds, the idea!"

But we rubbed away, and paid no attention to the contemptuous glances our friend gave us. My hands began to come down lower and lower; and then I felt myself rising from the ground, higher and higher I went, just like a big bird, and suddenly landed on a heavy black cloud. I looked down; there were the boys still rubbing away, and Brush still carving. I could see the winding river far below and the birds flitting about. I wondered what it all meant. I felt the cloud moving away with me; the boys were growing smaller and smaller, and I noticed that I was passing over the Indian village. Where is the cloud going with me, and will it ever stop? I heard a sound that seemed familiar to me,—is it a bell? Could there be bells in the cloud? I asked myself.

"Wake up, you fools! Supper-bell has rung! Rubbing out clouds, were you!" said Brush, in derisive tones.

Warren sat up, blinking his eyes, and asked, "Where are we?"

That night, when the boys had settled down in their beds and Gray-beard had gone downstairs, Edwin asked, "Boys, where've you been this afternoon? You came to supper late; Gray-beard looked hard at you."

"We've been up the hill," I answered; "I told the boys to hurry along and leave me; but they wouldn't."

"Who was that Indian woman talking to you before dinner-time?"

"That was my aunt; she saw me when she was going by, and she made me sit down and she looked at my foot. She took a great big splinter out of my toe. My! it hurt."

"You're going to get well now. Why didn't you put that splinter into some buffalo hair, then 't would've turned into a baby."

"Nonsense!" said Brush, "who ever heard of such a thing."

"There's a story like that," replied Edwin.

"Tell that story! tell that story!" cried the boys in chorus.

"But you don't listen; you go to sleep, or you ask fool questions and stop me."

"We won't stop you; we're going to lie awake."

"All right. I'll tell you that story. Say 'ong!' pretty soon, then I'll know you're awake."

We all snuggled down, then in chorus cried, "Ong!" and Edwin began:

"'Way long time ago, four brothers lived on earth. Good hunters, they shoot straight, kill deer, buffalo, elk, and all kinds of animals. They got plenty of meat and skins. One night, the youngest man came home very lame; his foot was all swelled up; he had to use his bow for a cane, and he was groaning, groaning all the time. He lay down and was real sick, one, two, three days. The other men, they went hunting. When they were gone, the youngest man got up, took his knife, cut open his toe, and took out a big thorn, a great big—"

Whack! whack! whack! Quick as a flash the boys put their feet against the foot-board and pulled the bedclothes taut so that the rest of the blows fell harmless upon us. We had been surprised by Gray-beard. Edwin, in his earnestness, and in his belief that a foreign language can be better understood when spoken loudly, had been shouting his story in a voice that reached Gray-beard and woke him up. After warning us against loud talking, the old man went downstairs as stealthily as he had come.

"Well, boys," said Brush, "that came like a cyclone, didn't it?"

We all agreed that it did.

"Frank, did he hurt your foot?" asked Warren.

"No, the boys kept the quilt up, so he couldn't hit me."

"What did I say last?" asked Edwin.

"You said," I reminded him, "that he cut open his toe and took out a big thorn."

"Oh, yes," he continued; "he took out a big thorn, a great big thorn. He wanted to show it to his brothers, so he pulled out some buffalo hair from his robe and put the thorn inside and laid it away, way back in the middle of the tent. Then he went after some water to wash his foot. When he was coming back, he heard something crying like everything; not like raccoon, not like any kind of bird or animal, something different. He stood still and listened; it sounded like coming from inside the tent! So he went slow, easy, and looked in the tent; there was something moving and crying loud. Then the young man went inside the tent, and he saw a baby, a little girl baby, and no thorn. He knew that thorn had turned into a girl baby, crying like everything. The young man was very glad; he danced on his one well foot; he took up the girl baby in his big arms and moved like a tree when the wind blows, and he sang soft, and the girl baby shut her eyes and went to sleep, e-a-s-y,—just like you!"

"No! We ain't asleep. Go on."

"Well, those big brothers came home, and they were all very glad. They took the girl baby all round. Then the oldest brother, he said, 'She is going to be our sister. I wish she would grow right up and run round the tent.' Then he lifted her four times, and the girl baby grew quick, and ran round the tent, talking. Then another brother, he said, 'I wish my sister would grow up and get big enough to go after water.' Then he lifted the little girl four times, and she got big enough to go after water. Then the next one, he said, 'I wish my sister would grow big enough to make moccasins and cook and make lots of things.' Then he lifted her four times, and the girl grew right up and knew how to make lots of things. Then the youngest man, he said, 'I wish my sister grown up woman now.' Then he lifted her four times, and she was a big woman right away. So in one night that thorn girl baby grew up, and she was the first woman."

"Why!" said Brush, "that's just like the Bible story of Adam and Eve. You remember it says, that Adam was the first man God made, and He put him in a big garden full of flowers and trees. He told him he could eat everything there except the berries of only one tree, and He showed him that tree. God made Adam go to sleep, and then He cut open his side and took out one rib, and out of that bone He made a woman, and He named her Eve."

"Did He whittle that rib bone just like you whittle a piece of wood and make men, and horses, and dogs, and other things?" asked Lester.

"Yes, I think He did. Then in that garden there were elephants, and lions, and tigers, and camels, and lots of other animals; but they didn't eat each other up. God gave Adam the camels to ride, so he wouldn't get tired. Camels ride easy, easier than a horse. You know a horse goes trot! trot! trot! and makes your stomach ache; but a camel goes just as e-a-s-y, like rocking, like that boat, you know, when we went on the river and the wind blew, and the boat went up and down. Why, you know, the difference is just like this: you ride in a big wagon and it shakes you like everything; you ride in the superintendent's carriage, and it rides just as easy as anything."

"How do you know?" broke in Warren. "You never rode a camel, and you never rode in the superintendent's carriage."

"Yes, I have too. I've ridden in the superintendent's carriage that time I went to interpret for him down to the big village. I rode with him in his carriage."

"You boys said you wouldn't stop my story," protested Edwin, yawning.

"Say, Brush," I asked, "when that bone was whittled, and it became Eve, what did she do?"

"Well, one morning she went down to the creek to swim, and, just as she was going to step into the water by a big willow-tree, she saw a snake in the tree with a man's head on, and the snake—"

"It wasn't a snake," interrupted Warren; "it was the serpent, the Sunday-school teacher said so."

"Well, it's the same thing,—the snake and the serpent is the same thing."

"No, they're not. The serpent is the kind that's poisonous, like the rattle-snake; and the snake is like those that don't poison, like the garter-snake and the bull-snake."

"Brush, go on with your story," I broke in impatiently. "Don't mind Warren; he doesn't know anything!"

"No, he doesn't. Well, the serpent was Satan, and Sa—"

"How can Satan be a serpent and a snake?" asked Lester.

"First you said it was a snake; then you said it was a serpent; now you say it was Satan!"

"You boys are bothering my story all the time. I'm going to stop."

"Go on, Brush," I urged; "don't mind those boys; what do they know? They're all way back in the Second Reader, and you are in the Fifth, and I am in the Third."

"All right, I'll go on; I don't care what they say. Well, the Devil spoke to Eve and said—"

"Your snake has turned into a Devil now," sneered Edwin. "Boys, why don't you let me go on with my story; Brush doesn't know how to tell a story."

"Yes, I do too. Boys, you don't know anything; you don't know that the Devil and Satan and the serpent and the snake are the same thing; they're all the same. If you would listen when the teacher talks to you in the school-room, and when the minister speaks to us in the chapel, you would learn something. All you got to do is to listen, but you don't. When you are forced to sit still, you go to sleep; and when you are awake you tickle those that are asleep with straws, or stick pins in them. How are you going to learn anything when you do like that? You must listen; that's what I'm doing. I want to know all about these things so I can be a preacher when I get big. I'm going to wear a long black coat, and a vest that buttons up to the throat, and I'm going to wear a white collar, and a pair of boots that squeaks and reaches to my knees, and—"

"Edwin, go on with your story, I want to hear that," called Warren.

"He's asleep," said I.

"Only last Sunday," resumed Brush, "the minister told

us that the Devil went about like a roaring lion seeking whom he may de— de— What's the rest of that word, Frank?"

"Vour."

"Yes, 'vour, devour. The Devil went about like a roaring lion seeking whom he may devour."

"Bully for you, Brush!" exclaimed Lester. "That's good; you didn't cough big though, like the preacher does."

"Don't make fun of the old man, boys, he is here to help us; he wants to do us good."

"Yes," answered Warren; "I guess he wanted to do you good last week, when he switched your back for you!"

"I think I deserved it."

"No, you didn't. You didn't do anything; you only threw Phil Sheridan down and made his nose bleed."

"I shouldn't have done it. I saw a good chance and I did it, and the old man was looking at me. Now, boys, what did the preacher mean when he said the Devil went around like a roaring lion?"

"I s'pose," said Edwin, "he means the Devil is like some of our big medicine men who can turn themselves into deer and elk, and any kind of animal, and the Devil can change himself into a hungry, howling lion and—"

"And into a Satan," suggested Lester.

"And into a serpent," added Warren.

"Into a snake," I chimed in.

"And put a man's head on!" ejaculated Edwin.

"And talk to women when they go swimming!" said Lester, with a laugh.

"There's no use talking to you boys. I'm going to sleep," and Brush turned over.

One by one, sleep overcame these boys. Brush made a peculiar noise as he breathed, and Lester puffed away like a steamboat.

A whippoorwill sang in one of the cottonwood-trees near the corner of the house. Fainter and fainter grew the sound, and so the day passed into yesterday, and the morrow began to dawn.

# 8

## Fraudulent Holidays

"THIRD READER," called Gray-beard, and some ten or twelve boys and girls marched to the place of recitation, and put their toes on a straight crack in the floor. The reading lesson was some verses on "Summer," prettily illustrated with a picture of a boy and a dog, the lad racing over a meadow, and the dog frisking at his side.

"Now, Robert, begin!" said Gray-beard to little Bob, who in some unaccountable way had reached the head of the class.

The boy put his index finger on the first word, and slid it along as he read, in a low, sing-song tone, "Come, come, come, the Summer now is here."

"Read that over again," said Gray-beard. "Read it loud, as though you were out of doors at play."

Bob read again, but in the same manner, and had hardly gone through half the line when the sharp crack of Gray-beard's ruler on the desk made us all jump.

"That's not the way to read it!" he exclaimed with some impatience; and he repeated the lines to show how they should be given. "Now, begin again."

Bob began, but in the same lifeless tone, never taking his finger from the words.

"Next!" interrupted Gray-beard. "The same verse; read as though you were wide awake and calling to your playmates, not as if you were going to sleep."

The boy addressed straightened himself up and shouted out:

"Come, come, come, the Summer now is here!" going through the verse without a break, then he glanced proudly toward the girls, only to see them giggling behind their books.

"Silence!" cried Gray-beard, striking his desk. "That was well done!"

The door slowly opened, and the farmer entered, hat in hand, and addressed Gray-beard, "I want to transfer a sow with a litter of pigs from one pen to another, and I've come to ask if you could let me have the help of some of the boys?"

When permission had been granted, a number of willing hands went up, and as many faces turned with eager expectancy to the farmer, who looked around, and then said, "Brush, Frank, Lester, and Warren will do."

We followed the farmer to the pen, and at once jumped in, each one seizing a little pig; but, before we could turn, the sow made such an onslaught upon us that we dropped the pigs and scrambled over the fence; but Lester, who was last, left a piece of his trousers in the jaws of the angry beast. After this exciting experience, at which the farmer could hardly stop laughing, we held a consultation with him, and agreed upon a plan which we immediately proceeded to carry out.

We threatened the sow with our hats; she retreated into a corner with her young; then Brush slyly went up, and, reaching his hand through the fence, caught one of the little pigs by the legs and held it fast; it squealed lustily, and the infuriated mother made savage attacks upon the fence. Then Lester, Warren, the farmer, and I sprang into the pen, caught the frightened little pigs, and ran with them to the new pen. Brush released his prisoner, and the cry of the transported little ones brought the mother to the pen where she was secured.

While the farmer was fastening the gate, we boys walked around the hog-yard; Warren, who was ahead, discovered a weak place in the fence, and beckoned excitedly for us to hasten.

There were times when the pupils became very tired of their books, and longed to take a run over the prairies or through the woods. When this longing came upon them, they sought for ways and means by which to have the school closed, and secure a holiday. I remember once, it was in the fall, the members of the Big Seven loosened the joints of the long stove-pipe during recess. When school opened in the afternoon, and their class was called, they marched to the place of recitation, keeping step and jarring the room so that the sections of the pipe fell rattling to the floor, filling the room with smoke, and covering floor and desks with soot. As it would take some time for the pipe to cool and be put up again, and the room cleaned, the school was dismissed, giving us a half holiday.

Now, in the weakness of the hog fence, there was a chance for an afternoon out of school, and Warren saw it.

He told us his plan, and the rest of us fell in with the scheme. After dinner we took some corn and scattered it outside of the fence at the weak place; then we went to the school-room, where Gray-beard, when he came to ring the bell to summon the scholars, found us hard at work on our arithmetic lessons.

The geography class was up, and Brush was describing the rivers of South America, when the door was thrown open by the superintendent, who exclaimed, "Hurry, boys! The pigs are out and going to the Indians' cornfield!"

We did not wait to be ordered a second time; but, snatching our hats from the pegs in the hall, we ran down the hill with wild shouts and cries. All the afternoon we chased pigs, and had a glorious time, while the girls had to stay in school and be banged at by Gray-beard.

It was almost supper-time when we finally drove the pigs into the yard and repaired the weak places in the fence. Flushed with our exciting chase we entered the dining-room when the bell rang, and took our places at the table for the evening meal; then the superintendent, looking at us with a kindly smile, thanked us for the good service we had rendered that afternoon!

The few hours' release from the tasks of the school-room had brought about a general good feeling among the boys; so, when we had partaken of the simple fare, we gathered on our play-ground and joined in a number of lively games in the long twilight. So interested and excited had we become in our play that we took no notice of the fading light and the lateness of the hour until the first bell for bed sounded.

Our school was an industrial one, and in the assignment

to the larger boys and girls of various duties in and about the building, I was given the care of the hydraulic ram that pumped the water from the spring to the house. In the morning I started it, and in the evening shut it off. The ram was located in a wooded ravine a quarter of a mile from the school, and I usually stopped it while it was yet light, for, like many a foolish boy, I was afraid to go away from the house alone in the dark. Now in the excitement of play I had forgotten all about the ram until I heard the bell calling us to prepare for bed, nor had I realized till then that it was dark, and that the sky in the west was black with storm clouds through which the lightning zigzagged, and that there was an incessant rumble of thunder. The myriad of fireflies that filled the air with flashes of red light only made the darkness seem yet darker.

Stricken all at once with fear, I called loudly for Brush and the rest of the boys, but none of them responded. I was afraid to go to the ram alone in the dark, but if I should let it pump all night the water would overflow the kitchen, and that would mean a disgraceful punishment for me. I went from boy to boy, trying to secure a companion; but not one of them dared to go with me, they were all afraid of ghosts. Marbles could not tempt them, nor could a much coveted gun-lock, which for the first time I was willing to part with, induce any boy to go. The time for the last call for bed was fast approaching, and I dared not wait longer trying to secure an escort, so I started on a run, frightened nearly out of my wits at everything I saw, but on I went as if racing for life.

I reached the place and stood over the square pit in which the ram was placed, and was about to go down the ladder into it, when I saw something move rapidly at the bottom. I nearly fell over backwards as I jumped away. I ran toward the house, but the thought of the overflow in the kitchen, and the punishment that was sure to follow, came back to my mind. For a moment I struggled between a known and an unknown fate, and decided to meet the latter. With set teeth and clenched fists I jumped into the pit, backed into the nearest corner, yelled at the top of my voice, while I struck right and left with my fists and kicked out with my feet. Let it be ghost or beast, I was determined to fight it and die game. I kept on striking, kicking, and yelling, but nothing put itself in my way. I dropped to the ground, panting, but kept an eye on the white thing which had also moved into a corner. I made a feint at charging upon it and it fled to another corner; then I put my head close to the ground to discover the shape of my enemy, when, to my joy, I discerned the outline of a rabbit. With a long-drawn breath of relief I stood upright, turned off the ram, made a rush upon the rabbit and caught it. Hastily rolling it up in my jacket, I climbed the ladder, ran up the hill as though a dozen ghosts were after me, and reached my bed just in time to say "Amen" to the evening prayer.

When Gray-beard had gone down, I whispered to Lester and Edwin, "I've caught a white rabbit!"

"Let's scare the boys," said Lester.

So we dropped the little creature on the floor, and it ran around the room as hard as it could go, while one of us cried out in a loud whisper "Ghost!" Then every boy in the room pulled the bedclothes over his head, and did not dare to uncover again.

We kept the rabbit for a pet, and made a box for it. We

liked to watch it eat, and it did not suffer for want of food so long as we had it. One of the "gangs" among the small boys came to us one day while we were feeding our pet, and offered us some clay marbles for it. We looked upon their offer with contempt, for we all knew how to make clay marbles ourselves, and had all we wanted.

"I'll tell you what we'll do though," said Brush to the would-be purchasers. "If you will give each one of us seventeen cakes, you can take the rabbit."

The boys retired and held a private consultation, then came back, and the leader said, "We'll take the rabbit."

These boys must have coveted the rabbit very much, for there was not a boy in the school who did not love cake, and the one slice of brown ginger-cake we were each given for Sunday noon lunch was the only delicacy we tasted. This cake became a currency among the boys, and all contracts for cakes were faithfully kept. I know of only one instance where a boy failed to keep his bargain, and he was so persecuted by the other scholars that he was obliged to pay his debt in order to live in peace.

Brush thought he had put the price of the rabbit so high that it would not be accepted; but as we could not back out of our agreement, we were obliged to part with our ghost rabbit for eighty-five cakes.

As the number of the "gang" purchasing the rabbit was the same as ours, for seventeen Sundays these five boys went without their cakes, while each one of us enjoyed a double share.

# 9

---

# William T.
# Sherman

HE STOOD on the third board of the fence from the ground, and leaned with his elbows on the top one, now and again kicking with his moccasined foot a loose panel. How long he had been standing there rattling that loose board no one knew, but in time one of the boys noticed him, and suddenly he became an object of the greatest interest among the boys of all sizes at the school. Boys who were playing down by the river, up by the spring, and over by the saw mill came running to see the stranger; and how the word reached them was as much of a mystery as the appearance of the little figure on the fence.

Every one was eager to pelt him with a question, and get as close to him as possible. He answered the questions in monosyllables; but he showed objection to any near approach, by freeing his bare arms from his little buffalo robe and pointing a wooden pop-gun at the eye of the boy who was inclined to be too familiar. We kept at him until we found out that his name was Thin'-je-zhin-ga, which, translated into the language of the Missionaries, signified Little Tail.*

He had come over from the village to see the school, and was as much interested in us as we were in him. All at once something attracted his attention; his black eyes sparkled, out came one arm from under his robe, and he pointed with a very dirty little finger and said, "Give me one of those!"

The coveted object was a brass button on the jacket of one of the small students. When Little Tail was asked what he wanted to do with it, he said, "Tie it to my scalp-lock." This sounded very funny to us, and we all laughed. The little chap retreated into his robe, covered his head, and looked out at us with one eye.

The bell rang for dinner; and there followed a general scramble to appear promptly at the table, and no thought was given to the queer little visitor. Being the last boy to enter the house, I turned to look back at him, and there he stood perched upon the fence, staring after us as though he wondered why he was so suddenly deserted.

When we came out from dinner, he was still on the fence, but he was busy. He had an ear of roasted corn and was shelling the kernels; when he had nearly a handful he tipped his head back, poured the grains into his mouth, and ate them with relish. After he had stripped half of the cob, he seemed to be satisfied, and the remainder disappeared

* He belonged to a band in the Omaha tribe known as Mon'-thin-ka-ga-hae, people of the underground world; in other words, animals that burrowed and lived in the earth; such had small tails, and the name Little Tail referred to this peculiarity.

in the recesses of his robe. As he finished his corn dinner, one of the school-boys said to him, "Little Tail, how would you like to stay and live with us here?"

"I would like it," he promptly replied.

"Will you stay?"

"Yes."

It was soon reported to the superintendent that a new pupil had come. When the afternoon session opened and the pupils were seated, Little Tail was given a seat at one of the desks, but to our delight he slid down and sat on the floor. The teacher rapped the top of his desk with a ruler and cried, "Silence!" and order was restored.

"What is the name of the new boy?" he asked.

"Thin'-je-zhin-ga," answered one of the boys.

Gray-beard tried to repeat the name, but only set the whole school laughing. While this was going on, Little Tail reached down to his belt and drew out a roll of milkweed fibre. It was his ammunition. He tore off enough to make a bullet, chewed it, and, bringing the breach of the pop-gun to his mouth, inserted the ball, twisting the gun with his hands while he pressed the wad in with his teeth, making many motions with his head. By pounding the butt of the rammer on the floor, he drove the ball to the firing point; then raising the gun he began forcing the ball with vigorous thrusts, aiming it at a mischievous boy who sat opposite making faces at him. Bang! went the weapon; the bullet, instead of hitting the object aimed at, struck Gray-beard in the face, and made him throw his head back. We covered our faces to suppress the giggles that bubbled up at this mishap. The wounded man looked sharply at the young artillerist, who, seeing the mischief he had done, very slyly thrust his gun into his robe, and, keeping an eye on his victim, sat perfectly still.

The teacher looked serious, then we became scared. After a moment his face relaxed, and he said in a pleasant tone, "We must have the name of the new boy on the Register, but we cannot have any name that is unpronounceable. We shall have to give him an English name. Will you suggest one?"

A number of hands went up and as many historic names were offered and rejected. Finally it was determined to call him William T. Sherman and that name was entered upon the Register.

After school a few boys were detailed to wash and dress the new arrival; so, with arms full of clothing, towels, and other bathing appliances, the lad was taken up to the boys' dormitory. The first thing to be done was to cut his long hair. A towel was put around his neck, and soon the shears were singing a tune about his ears. He seemed to enjoy it, and laughed at the jokes made by the boys; but when by some chance he caught sight of his scalp-lock lying on the floor like a little black snake, he put his fists into his eyes and fell to sobbing as though his heart would break.

"Pshaw!" said little Isaac, rubbing his closely cropped head, "mine was longer than yours when it was cut off, but I didn't cry!"

"Mine too!" exclaimed Abraham, picking up the braided lock and putting it where his had been; at which the rest of the boys laughed.

When the bath was over, William T. Sherman was dressed. He was delighted with his brand-new clothes, particularly with the long row of brass buttons that adorned the front of the jacket. When it came to the shoes, his grief for the lost scalp-lock was clean forgotten, and he strutted about to show the boys that his shining black shoes sang to his satisfaction.

William T. Sherman was quick to learn, and by the time winter was over he was speaking the peculiar English used by the boys of the school; he said, "fool bird," for quail; "first time," for long ago, and other Indian expressions turned into English. He was fond of arithmetic, and spent much time ciphering on his slate; he would write down the figure 1, 2, or 3, add to it a string of aughts, and then try to read them off. Grammar he abhorred, and in the spelling class, he held a permanent place at the foot. In outdoor sports he excelled; he could beat any boy of his size in leaping and running, and we had yet to learn other things in which he was expert.

One day, during the great June rise, all the boys were at the river watching the huge drift logs floating down the muddy Missouri.

"Say, boys!" exclaimed Ulysses S. Grant, thrusting his hands deep into his pockets; "I bet one hundred dollars that river is strong. I wouldn't like to swim in it; I'm sure the eddies would pull me under."

Gideon, who was always boasting of what his father could do, shouted, "My father could swim clear acrost and back again; he ain't 'fraid of eddies. He—"

"What's that?" cried a number of boys, startled by a heavy splash in the water. We all watched, and two brown feet came to the surface, wiggled, and disappeared. After a moment a round black head slowly arose. "Ha! Ha! I'm not 'fraid eddy!" shouted William T. Sherman, for it was he. A few vigorous strokes brought him to shore again.

76

"Take off your shirts and pants, boys, let's swim," he said.

We did so, and timidly splashed about the shallow edges of the water. A large tree was drifting down near the middle of the river. William ran up along the bank for quite a distance, and then plunged into the water. It was a beautiful sight to watch him as he threw his arms up and down, moving swiftly toward the tree; he reached it, dived under it, and came up on the other side; then he scrambled on the trunk and shouted for us to come, but none of us dared to go. After a moment he stood up on the tree, flourished an imaginary whip, and cried, "Git up, there!" with a succession of swear words,—genuine swear words. He was imitating the Agency teamster, and did not know what he was saying. He had heard the servant of the Government urge on his horses by such terms, and he was merely repeating them. Those of us who had been at the Mission a long time, and had all the Shorter Catechism in our little heads, and were orthodox by compulsion, if not by conviction, were horrified to hear those dreadful words uttered by a pupil of our school; for we knew some severe punishment awaited the little sinner should there be a traitor among us to make it known to Gray-beard.

Before we had fairly recovered from our shock at hearing this swearing, we were startled by a cry, "Job is drowning!" Not one of us moved, we were so frightened; but, quick as a flash, William T. Sherman sprang from his imaginary wagon, swam swiftly to the boy, caught him by the hair as he was going down for the last time, and brought him to the surface. "Kick! Kick!" he shouted; "make your arms go! Don't stop!" And after a hard struggle the two boys landed.

Job had swallowed considerable water, and become very sick. We didn't know what to do for him; but after we had rubbed and pommelled him, and held him by the heels head downward, he felt better; then we took him to the Mission and put him to bed.

On our way back Sherman spoke very little, but those of us who had been frightened into helplessness had much to say as to what we did or might have done to save Job.

At supper Gray-beard as usual counted the boys, and found one missing, "Where's Job?" he asked.

"He's got the th'tomick ache," said Daniel, his mouth full and his spoon raised half way with a new supply.

School went on the next morning as though nothing had happened. The teachers had not heard of the drowning and the rescue; but the girls had learned all about it and threw admiring glances at Sherman: to them he had become a hero, and each of the different gangs among the boys now wanted this hero as a member.

The recitations for the afternoon session were over, and the bell was tapped as a signal to put away our books and slates, and struck again to call us to order. When all arms were folded, there followed an ominous silence. Gray-beard slowly looked around the school-room, as though to read every face turned up to him, then he spoke:

"I have been told that some of the boys in this school are in the habit of swearing; that is one of the things you are forbidden to do. It is wicked to swear, and any boy that I find has been doing so I shall punish very severely. I want you to remember this. After the closing exercises William T. Sherman will come to my room; I have something to say to him."

All eyes on the boys' side turned toward William as we chanted the Lord's prayer; then Gray-beard made his usual supplication, during which the big girls twisted their necks to look at their hero.

The exit from the school-room was quite orderly, but as soon as the groups of boys passed into the hall, they set up a shouting and singing, and made off to their different resorts for play. We, the Middle Five, were the last to go; and, as had been hastily arranged between us, I went to Gray-beard and asked some trivial question in order to give time for Brush to go and advise Sherman as to what answers to make if he was asked as to his being guilty of swearing.

"When he asks you if you been swearing, say, 'No, sir, I don't know what swear is,'" said Brush to Sherman.

"All right."

"Then tell him you been saying what you heard Agency man say to horses; but you don't know what those words mean, maybe they're swear words, you don't know."

Gray-beard went up to his room, followed by William T. Sherman, who for the first time entered that apartment. Boys who committed serious offences were disciplined in that place. I was taken there for fighting Andrew Johnson; Brush took his punishment there when he nearly cut Jonathan's ear off with a wooden sword. Most of us had had peculiar experiences in that room.

William T. Sherman had come to us direct from a tent; our bare school-room and play-room were all that he had seen of the furnishings of a civilized dwelling, so when he was suddenly ushered into Gray-beard's room he was quite dazzled by the bright draperies, pictures, and the polished furniture. He stood with hands in his pockets, mouth and

eyes wide-open staring at the things, although twice re-
quested by his host to sit down.

William timidly took the chair assigned him. It rocked
backwards, and up went his feet; he clutched wildly at the
arms, and the chair rocked forward; he got his footing, then
sat perfectly still, fearing the chair would fall over with him.

Gray-beard took a seat facing the boy, and began to
question him, "I was told that you had been swearing; is
it true?"

Bewilderment at new sights, and the fright of the rocking-chair had put Brush's promptings out of Sherman's
head, and in his confusion he answered, "Yes, sir—ma'am."

"It is wicked to swear, and you must be taught to know
that it is. Now say what I say," and Gray-beard repeated the
third commandment, until Sherman could say it without
assistance, and then bade him to keep on until told to stop.

Poor William sat in the treacherous rocking-chair repeating this commandment, while Gray-beard wrote at his
desk. William might as well have sat there imitating the
cry of some animal or bird, for his mind was not dwelling
upon the words he was uttering, but following his eyes as
they moved from one strange object to another,—the pictures, the gilt frames, the sea shells, the clock on the mantel-
piece, then something hanging near the window absorbed
his attention, and his tongue and lips ceased to move as
he drew with his finger on his knee the figure 1, adding to
it a number of aughts. Gray-beard noted the pause, and
said, "Go on, William, don't stop." After some little prompt-
ing, the boy resumed, but his finger kept moving, making
the figure 1 and a string of aughts after it.

When Gray-beard and William T. Sherman left the

80

school-room, Brush and I and the rest of the Five went toward the spring and sat under the large elm. Brush lay down on the grass and read a book he had borrowed from the superintendent, while the rest of us talked.

"I'd like to see that boy who told on William T. Sherman; I'd give him a licking," said Warren.

"I'd kick him hard," added Edwin.

"I bet it's that tell-tale Edson; he ought to be thumped!" I suggested.

While we were talking, William came and sat down with us. Every now and then a quivering sigh would escape him, although he tried not to show that he had been crying. Little Bob, believing as we did that William had been whipped, and, desiring to express sympathy, said, "Say, did it hurt?" William did not answer; nobody ever answered Bob.

"What did Gray-beard do to you?" I asked, turning to William.

"He made me sit down and say a commandment one hundred times."

"Which one was it? Say it to us."

"I don't want to say it; I said it enough." After a pause he asked, "What is swear?"

"When you call God names, that's swear," said Warren.

"I don't do that. I know God, it's the same Omahas call Wa-kon-da; but I don't know what means lord."

"It's a man just like big chief," explained Lester; "he has plenty of horses and lots of money. When he tells anybody to do anything, he got to do it; that's a lord."

"Is Gray-beard lord?"

"No, Gray-beard isn't lord."

"Say, boys, a one and six aughts is one million, ain't it?"

"Yes," we answered in chorus.

"Gray-beard is lord. He's got one million dollars. I saw it on a book hanging by his window; it had a name, I can't say it, then Bank and Cap'tal, and then a one and six aughts, —that's a million. He's got one million dollars!"

Brush threw his book down, raised himself on his elbow and looked at us with a smile; then he said, "I know that book William T. Sherman saw, it's the book Gray-beard counts the days by, and it's got on it what they call advertisement. That bank wants people to know it has one million dollars capital to go by; I learned that in my arithmetic. Gray-beard isn't a lord; he's a missionary,—the same kind that goes to Africa and Greenland's icy mountains."

# 10

## A Runaway

VACATION had come, and the Indians were about to start on their annual summer buffalo hunt. Some of the scholars were to accompany their parents, and others, after a brief home visit, were to return to the school and continue their studies while the tribe was away.

In the three villages there was great hurry and bustle in every family. Pack saddles were brought out of the caches where they had lain through the winter. The task of mending them fell to the older people of the household, while the younger folk busied themselves in retrimming their more ornate trappings. Goods not necessary for the journey were stored away, and the dwellings were made ready for the long absence.

At last there remained but one day before the time set for the departure of the tribe. In the afternoon I bade my parents goodby, and reluctantly returned to the school. Quite a number of the boys and girls had already come back, among them Lester and Warren. Brush had not left the school, so on my arrival I received from the three boys the usual greetings we accorded each other when one returned after an absence. We four paced the long front porch, arm in arm, for a while, and then went and sat down in the shade of a tree.

"Where is Edwin?" asked Brush; "isn't he coming back?"

"No," I replied; "his mother wanted him to; but his father didn't want him to leave him behind, so he's going on the hunt."

"He'll have lots of fun," said Warren; "I wish I could go!"

The next morning, immediately after breakfast, Brush borrowed the superintendent's spy-glass, and we went to a high point whence we could watch the movements of the people in the village nearest the school. We took turns in looking through the glass. Already the head of the great caravan had gone behind the first hill, but my family had not yet started. We looked toward Edwin's house, and saw that the people were just moving. It was a wonderful sight to us, the long procession on the winding trail, like a great serpent of varied and brilliant colors. At last I saw my father mount a horse and move forward, the rest of the family followed him, and I watched them until they finally disappeared beyond the green hills. It was nearly noon when the end of the line went out of sight.

While the movements were going on in the village, we could hear the neighing of horses, the barking of dogs, and the hum of voices, but now there was a stillness in the deserted village which brought upon us a sense of loneliness that was hard to overcome. We slowly returned to the Mission and ate our noonday meal without speaking. There seemed to be a general depression among the remaining pupils at the school. A silence pervaded all the surroundings which made each boy wish to retire from the other and to be alone.

At breakfast, the next morning, there was the same sense of stillness; even the superintendent and the teachers at their table seemed to be homesick, and they passed the dishes to each other in silence. The reading of the Scriptures and the prayer of the superintendent was in a tone that added to the gloominess which had taken possession of our simple little souls.

As we were slowly marching out of the dining-room, when the worship was over, the superintendent stopped Brush and said to him:

"I want you to go after the mail this morning; go on horse-back so as to get back soon. I have some work for you to do this afternoon. Take Dolly, and use the large saddle; the other one needs mending."

"Let's go down to the spring," said Lester to Warren and me.

So while Brush went to the barn to saddle up, we three went to the spring and sat under an elm that stood near by.

"Say, boys, I'm going to the hunt!" said Lester, startling us with the sudden announcement; "I heard that two families down at the Wood-eaters' village can't get away for two days yet, and I'm going down there so I can go with them. The Omahas always wait on the Wa-tae (Elkhorn River), for those that are last."

"If you're going, I'm going too," spoke up Warren; "I don't want to stay here."

"If you two go, I'm going!" I exclaimed.

"All right, let's all go then," said Lester, rising. "We must hurry up; some one might see us!"

We followed a narrow path that led through a ravine just beyond the spring. We were in the greatest excitement; every little sound aroused within us the fear of detection, and we frequently sought for a hiding place, while we carefully avoided all well-beaten paths. Silently we plodded our way through the bushes until we came to a hill where there were no trees, then we ran as fast as our legs could carry us for another wooded place.

We stopped a moment when passing to take a look at the village. Silence prevailed. Not a living thing was astir. Three whirlwinds chased each other along the winding paths between the houses, making funnel-shaped dust clouds as they sped on.

"The ghosts have entered the village," said Lester, in our own language, and in a melancholy tone; "they always do that as soon as the living leave their houses!"

Entering the ravine for which we were making, we continued our journey. The nettle weeds caused us much suffering, for we were barefooted, and wore short trousers. We came to an opening; before us lay the road to the Agency; we looked cautiously around, then started to cross it to go into another ravine that headed toward the big village, when the snorting of a horse was heard with startling distinctness.

"Quick! quick! get down!" exclaimed Lester in a loud whisper, as he dropped into the gully of the old abandoned wagon-road.

Warren and I followed hastily, pulling the tall grass over us. We heard the footsteps of the horse come nearer and nearer to our hiding place. It stopped and reached its head down, and began to nibble the grass under which I lay concealed. I looked up through a slight opening, and, behold! there on the horse sat Brush with one leg thrown over the pommel of the saddle, busily reading a book. I could see the boy's eyes and his lips moving as he read, and at times it seemed as though his eyes were looking right into mine. I was in great suspense while the horse stood there, but at length Brush picked up the reins and urged Dolly on. As soon as he disappeared at the bend of the road, we rose and darted across and ran down to the ravine.

We entered the big village of sod houses through which we had to pass. Here, too, we felt the sense of desolation that pervaded even the hills around. Somewhere from the midst of these peculiar dwellings came the doleful howl of a stray dog, the only sound that broke the stillness of the place. What sensations my companions experienced upon hearing the melancholy wail of that deserted beast I do not know; but, like the rapid advance of a fire over the prairie, a thrill that made the very roots of my hair creep vibrated through my body. Involuntarily we paused to listen; the long-drawn moan came to a close, and the ghostly echoes carried on the sound as though to mock the lost creature.

"Let's run!" exclaimed Lester, in a frightened tone; "let's get away from here!"

And so we sped on until, all out of breath, we were far beyond the limits of the village.

The shadows of the hills and the trees were beginning to grow long as we reached the foot of the bluffs where lay the village of the Wood-eaters. We followed a narrow but well-beaten path, wending our way among the tall trees. Suddenly a dog, with tail rigid and erect, and hair bristling, came barking at us with savage fury.

" 'Shta-du-ba!" 'Shta-du-ba!" called Lester, as he came near. "It is I, don't you know me?"

The dog, on hearing his name from a familiar voice, relaxed his aggressive appearance and assumed one of joyous welcome. He jumped upon us, licked our hands, wagged his whole body as well as his tail, and preceded us with leaps and barks of delight.

We came to a clear space, and there before us against the deep shadows of the woods stood a solitary sod house, the smoke lazily ascending to the sky from the top of the dome-shaped roof, making a picture of simple contentment. In the projecting doorway stood a man looking intently in our direction. The serious expression of his face changed to one of pleasure and amusement as he descried the three school-boys. When we were near enough for him to fully recognize us, his smile burst into a mirthful laugh in which we could not help joining, though to us our business was full of seriousness.

"Woo-hoo!" he mildly exclaimed, "what important thing is it that has brought you here at this time, when all are about going away? Your mother left yesterday," he said, addressing my companions, then turning to me remarked, "Your father must have gone to-day."

"We ran away from school because we want to go on the hunt," explained Lester. "I know my mother has gone; but my uncle has not left yet, so we are going to him."

"He is still here, we all go to-morrow morning early; but

Francis La Flesche, about 1905
*Courtesy Smithsonian Institution, Bureau of American Ethnology*

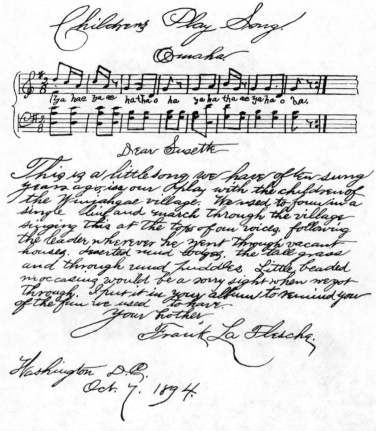

Letter from Francis La Flesche to his sister Susette. This handwritten version of the song differs slightly in the third measure from that printed on page 144. The letter from La Flesche to his sister was originally printed in a small book written by Fannie Reed Giffen and illustrated by Susette La Flesche Tibbles, *Oo-Mah-Ha Ta-Wa-Tha (Omaha City)*, published in 1898.

The Presbyterian Indian Mission School about 80 miles north of the
city of Omaha, setting of *The Middle Five*
*Courtesy Smithsonian Institution, Bureau of American Ethnology*

you should have stayed at the House of Teaching; you would get more good there than by going on the hunt. You know the way to Me-chah'-pe's house, just follow that path."

We trudged along to Me-chah'-pe's house. The family had gathered about an outside fire, and were eating their supper in the dusk. Upon our coming into the light of the fire we were recognized; the mother and grown daughter greeted us with exclamations of surprise and sympathy; while the father and the two sons glanced at each other with expressions of amusement. A place was assigned us in the circle, and soon we were busily engaged with the simple fare placed before us by the good and hospitable mother.

"Why do parents when they go away leave their children at the House of Teaching, I wonder?" commented the woman, as she apportioned the food for us. "Some people show no signs of affection for their sons and daughters until they sicken and die; then they tear their hair and rend the air with their loud wails. It is well enough while the parents are at home that they should place the young ones in the care of the White-chests; but, when going on a long journey like this, they should take the children with them."

By the side of every Indian house stands a raised platform made of poles, elevated upon posts, some seven or eight feet high, planted firmly in the ground. This platform is used for drying corn and squash, at the time of harvesting; but, through the summer when the people are at home, the young men and boys take possession of it, for sleeping in the open air. As weariness began to be felt, one by one, the family arose, and, without formality, each sought his place of rest. We school-boys and the sons of Me-chah'-pe repaired to the platform, climbing the "stairs" made of a single log, with notches cut in it for steps.

This was the first night I had ever spent out of doors. The novel experience, and the excitements of the day, filled my mind with strange speculations, and I lay awake long after my companions had gone to sleep. Now and then, I heard the chatter of birds and the whirring of their wings, as they flew by far above me, and I wondered if they could see in the darkness. The roar of the river filled the still air, and the crash of a tree uprooted by the current sent its echoes far and wide; then the sounds about me grew to faint murmurings, until I was conscious of them no more.

When I awoke, the dawn was coming, and the stars were beginning to turn pale. There was a gentle stir in the tent near by; a tall man came out, and his shadowy form passed from view into the slowly rising mist. A woman moved noiselessly to the fire-place, and, bending over, began to gather the embers together, blowing them to life with her breath. The gray streak along the horizon slowly turned to a rosy hue; here and there the birds began drowsily to peep and twitter, then, when the sun shot its rays through the heavens, a thousand voices burst into rapturous song.

My companions awoke, and one by one we climbed down the rude ladder to the ground.

When we gathered for breakfast, the mother, as she helped the food, asked, "Where is Na-zhe'-de-ah?" (Lester.)

Warren and I looked at each other; neither of us could explain his absence.

90

"Call him," said the good woman, addressing her son; "we must hurry, the sun is up!"

No response came to the young man's call. It was evident that Lester had slipped away before any one was awake.

Breakfast over, Me-chah'-pe and his sons saddled and packed the horses, while the wife and daughter gathered the various utensils. Warren and I tried to make ourselves useful by holding up the packs with our shoulders, as they were being placed on the horses.

Me-chah'-pe looked at Warren, then at me, as he shouldered his rifle, and said, "I am sorry that I have not enough horses for all of us to ride. You see those I have are heavily burdened; so we will have to do as our fathers did, take one step forward, then another, and keep stepping forward until we get to the place where we are going. Are we ready? Here we go!"

And we did go,—horses, dogs, and all. Soon we were joined by the man of the lonely sod house and his family, and together we made quite a cavalcade as we went up hill and down hill, and up hill and down hill again. By and by, we reached a long ridge, called by the Indians "the tortuous ridge," which zigzagged in a westerly direction, and along it lay the hunting trail.

The sun grew hot; Warren and I were drenched with perspiration as we plodded on. Every now and then Me-chah'-pe gave us an encouraging word, when we showed signs of lagging. We were determined to keep on, for were we not going to a buffalo hunt! The heat increased. The dogs did not now chase each other and run after birds as when we started out, but let loose their tongues and panted, keeping close to the shadows of the horses. On we all trudged, while the one baby slept on its mother's back, its little head rocking from side to side with the motion of her steps.

As we reached an elevated point on the ridge, Me-chah'-pe shaded his face with his hand and scanned the horizon. Far ahead of us his experienced eye caught sight of an object, like a mere speck. He pointed it out to us, saying, "There's somebody coming."

Warren and I looked at each other in alarm, and then kept our eyes on the speck, which grew larger and larger as the distance between it and us lessened.

"The horse looks like one of your father's," said Me-chah'-pe to me. "I think it is some one looking for you!"

My heart sank when I recognized the horse as father's, and the rider as my uncle, and, for the first time in my life, I was not glad to meet him.

Warren and I were captured, and there was no escape. We tried to be brave when Me-chah'-pe shook hands with us, as his party moved westward; but we were far from happy when, ignominiously mounted on father's horse, one behind the other, we followed my uncle, who walked so rapidly that the animal had to trot now and then to keep up. The road over which we had so laboriously travelled on our outward way was soon retraced, and the sun still high when my uncle, who had wandered all night in search of us, turned us over to Gray-beard.

It was thought best to punish us; so Warren was taken to the top of the house and locked up in the attic, where he was to reflect upon the wrong he had committed in running away. But I am quite sure he thought more about the devil and the ghosts in that horrid place than of anything else.

As for me, I was marched to the dinning-room, placed with my back to one of the posts, and my arms brought around it and tied; then I was left alone in this uncomfortable position,—to repent.

The afternoon was close and hot; the windows and doors were open, but the place was very quiet. Now and then I heard the cry of a bird, or the laughter of the happy wren. The time seemed very long as I stood there, with my arms thrown back around the post and my hands tied so that I could not defend myself against the flies that attacked my bare feet. A rooster came to the back door and entered the dining-room. He shied on discovering me; but, as I did not move, he began picking in the cracks of the floor. He spied my toe, looked at it curiously, turning his head from side to side, then stretched his neck and gave it a dab. I was in no mood to be amused by his actions, so I sent him flopping and squawking under the table. Recovering from his surprise, he ran around, sprang on the table, then on the sill of the open window, tossed up his head, flapped his wings, gave a lusty crow, and hopped out.

Immediately I saw eight little fingers hook themselves on the outer edge of the window-sill, and a head with black hair held back by a rubber comb rise higher and higher until two bright eyes gazed right into mine. The head disappeared, and shortly after a little figure cautiously approached the door, looked all around, and then came up to me. It was Rosalie. Her bright smiling face threw a sunbeam into my gloomy little heart. Without saying a word she wiped the perspiration from my face with the corner of her apron; then she went away softly in the direction of the kitchen. Soon she returned with a tin cup having in it bits of ice. She took a lump and put it in my mouth, then stood looking in my face. After a while, she said, "I like you, don't I?"

"'M h'm!" I assented with my mouth closed, nodding my head.

"When we get big, we're going to be married, ain't we?"

"'M h'm!" again I answered.

"We won't send our children to this horrid old place, will we?"

"'M 'm! 'M 'm!" I replied with emphasis, shaking my head and stamping the floor.

The little sweet-heart, seeing that the flies troubled my ankles, went out and came back with a linden branch and brushed away the pests. I slid to the floor and sat down with my legs stretched out. Rosalie dropped down too, and sat whisking away the flies.

Gradually things took on queer shapes, and the sounds seemed to come from afar; there was a moment of confusion and then,—I found myself on a wide prairie. Heavy clouds were swiftly approaching; the thunder rolled long and loud, and the lightning darted hither and thither. Off in the distance I saw a forest. I pushed toward it with all my strength so as to take shelter before the storm should come upon me; but as I labored on there crept over me a consciousness of a weight upon my back which, hitherto, I had not noticed. It retarded my progress, and from time to time I was obliged to stop and give a little spring to shift the burden higher up. A cry of terror came from the thing I was carrying; then I knew it was little Rosalie. I tried to speak words of encouragement to her, but my strength was fast failing. Great drops of rain fell, and the wind drove the dust into my face, blinding me. I tottered on with my load, but the timber was still far away. A vivid flash, a deafening crash, and I fell to the ground with a cry. I tried to rise, but my legs and arms were as though dead.

With a start I opened my eyes. The room was darkened; there was a great commotion; all through the house, windows were being rapidly closed and the doors swung to with a bang. A terrific storm had arisen, and the building was in danger of destruction. Rosalie lay asleep with her head resting on my knees.

# 11

## A New
## Study

It was a hot September afternoon; our gingham handker-
chiefs, which matched our shirts, were wet with mopping
our faces. We all felt cross; Gray-beard was cross, and
everything we did went wrong.

Warren, who had been sent to the spring for a pail of
cold water, leaned over his desk to Brush, and whispered
loud enough for the boys around us to hear, "A big black
carriage came up to the gate just now, and the Agent and
three other big fat men got out. The super'tendent shook
hands with them, and they went to his room."

While Gray-beard was shaking a boy to make him read
correctly, the news of the black carriage and the fat men
went from boy to boy. The girls were dying to know what
word it was the boys were passing around; but the aisle
that separated them from us was too wide to whisper
across. Warren's girl made signs to him which he at first
did not understand; when he caught her meaning, he tore

a fly-leaf out of his book, wrote on it, rolled it into a ball and threw it to the girl, who deftly caught it; these two were adepts at such transmission of messages. The girl unfolded the paper, read it, and passed it on; then the girls felt better and resumed their work.

The class in mental arithmetic took the floor. Not one of the boys knew his lesson. As the recitation went on Gray-beard's face darkened and his forehead wrinkled; he came to a timid youngster with a hard question. I knew there was going to be trouble for the little chap; so, to save him pain and distress, I thought of a plan by which to distract Gray-beard's attention. I reached under my desk and took hold of a thread which I carefully drew until my thumb and finger touched the stiff paper to which it was attached, then, as the boy stammered out the wrong answer and Gray-beard made an impatient movement toward him, I gave the thread a gentle pull, "Biz-z-z-z-z!" it went.

"Who's making that noise?" asked Gray-beard, turning toward our end of the school-room.

I loosened the pressure, and the noise ceased. When Gray-beard returned to the boy, I again pulled the thread, "Biz-z-z-z-z!" Something was wrong this time; the buzzing did not cease, it became louder and angrier.

"Who's doing that?" exclaimed Gray-beard.

Every boy and girl looked up to him as though to say, "I did not do it." The buzzing went on; I alone kept my eyes on my book, and so aroused suspicion. I did not dare to put my hand under the desk again to stop the buzzing, for I had lost the thread. Gray-beard came towards me and asked, "What have you there?" I did not answer.

"Stand up and let me see!" he exclaimed. Before I could give him any warning, he put his hand in the desk and felt about; he sprang back with a cry, "Ah! I'm bitten! Is it a snake?"

"No, it isn't," I answered; and, peering carefully into the desk, I drew out the buzzing thing and showed it to him; it was only a wasp fastened by its slender waist to a sheet of paper.

Although he felt relieved of his fright, the pain of the sting was arousing his anger, and I saw that there was trouble coming to me; but at that moment the door opened and in walked the superintendent and the four fat men. Gray-beard went forward and was introduced to them. There was a scramble by three of the large boys to get chairs from the dining-room for the visitors. When the gentlemen had made a quiet survey of our faces, they sat down and questioned Gray-beard about the branches taught at the school, and the progress made by the pupils. In the meantime I had released my prisoner; it went buzzing around the room, and then manœuvered over the bald head of one of the visitors, who beat the air with his hands to ward it off.

"Frank, catch that wasp," said Gray-beard.

I caught the troublesome creature in my hat and turned it out of doors.

When the questioning of the visitors was over, Gray-beard turned to us and said, "Now, children, pay strict attention; these gentlemen want to see what you have learned. I will put some questions to you."

We became so silent that we could hear a pin drop. The visitors smiled upon us pleasantly, as though to encourage us.

"Who discovered America?" asked Gray-beard. Dozens of hands went up. "Abraham, you may answer."

An expression of amusement spread over the faces of the scholars as the great awkward boy stood up. Gray-beard must have been bewildered by the sting of the wasp and the sudden appearance of visitors, else he would not have made such a blunder; for he knew very well what every boy and girl of the school could do; however there was no help for it now; Abraham Lincoln, standing with his hands in his pockets, had the floor; he put his weight on one foot and then on the other, the very picture of embarrassment; he cleared his throat, looked helplessly at me, and then at Brush,—"Come," said Gray-beard, "we are waiting."

"George Washington!" answered Abraham.

A titter ran around among the pupils. Gray-beard's face turned red, then white, as he said, "Abraham, take your seat. Brush, can you tell us who discovered America?"

"Columbus," promptly answered the boy. Then a series of questions were asked, which the children answered voluntarily, and did credit to their teacher. The visitors nodded approvingly to each other. When the examination was over, the Agent arose and, addressing the school, said:

"You have acquitted yourselves well in this sudden and unexpected test; I will now ask you to spell for me. Here is a book," said he, turning the leaves of a pretty gilt edged volume, "which I will give to the scholar who can spell best."

Taking a spelling book, he gave out the words himself. We all stood up, and those who misspelled a word sat down. One by one the pupils dropped to their seats, until only Brush, a big girl, and I remained on the floor; finally I went down, and the girl and Brush went on; they were now in the midst of the hard words. At last Brush failed; the girl also misspelled the word; but as the prize book could not be divided, it was given to her.

"Are the children taught music?" asked one of the strangers.

"No," replied the superintendent; "but they can sing nearly all of the Sunday-school hymns."

"They should be taught music as well as reading and spelling," remarked one of the gentlemen, then, addressing the children, he asked:

"Have your people music, and do they sing?"

"They do," answered one of the large boys.

"I wish you would sing an Indian song for me," continued the man. "I never heard one."

There was some hesitancy, but suddenly a loud clear voice close to me broke into a Victory song; before a bar was sung another voice took up the song from the beginning, as is the custom among the Indians, then the whole school fell in, and we made the room ring. We understood the song, and knew the emotion of which it was the expression. We felt, as we sang, the patriotic thrill of a victorious people who had vanquished their enemies; but the men shook their heads, and one of them said, "That's savage, that's savage! They must be taught music."

So it came about that every afternoon after this visit we spent an hour on a singing lesson. We learned quite a number of songs, but we sang them by ear, as it was difficult for us to understand the written music. We liked some of the songs we learned very much, and enjoyed singing them almost as well as our own native melodies. Although there were boys with richer voices, Brush was fond of hearing me sing a certain song we had been taught; we always had to give it when visitors came to the Mission. I can remember only the chorus:

> "Laura, Laura, still we love thee,
> Though we see thy form no more,
> And we know thou 'lt come to meet us,
> When we reach that mystic shore."

One day the teacher said that we must learn to sing in parts; hitherto we had been singing in unison as the Indians do; so he assigned the different parts to those scholars whom he thought could carry them. He met with no difficulty in selecting the soprano, contralto, and the tenor; but he could not find any boy who was willing to try the bass. He had given me the tenor, but as he could not find a bass, he said I must take that part as I was less timid about singing. I protested, but there was no escape for me. We learned fairly well to sing in parts a few pieces, but one day the teacher gave us a new song in which, at certain places in the chorus, the bass was unsupported. Our first attempt to render this song resulted in a failure, on account of my embarrassment. The teacher threatened and coaxed before I consented to make another trial. We sang very well together until we came to the chorus; when the leader indicated to me to remain silent, while the others drawled out the first two bars and came to a rest; then he motioned quickly to me, and I croaked, "Daisy Lee!" very much like a bull-frog. A smile rippled over the school, but the leader went on waving his arms and nodding to the others, who again drawled out, "My dar-ling Dai-sy Lee-e-e-e." This time I knew when to come in; so as soon as they reached

101

the rest, from the very depths of my chest I again croaked, "Daisy Lee!" This time the whole school went into convulsions; the teacher himself could not control his laughter; it was fun for everybody but me. For weeks afterwards whenever the boys saw me, they would mischievously shout in a bass voice, "Daisy Lee!"

This was not my only singing experience at the school. One afternoon the superintendent, Gray-beard, and all the rest of the men at the Mission were called away on some urgent business, and were not expected to be home for supper. At the table one of the ladies presided and asked the blessing over the evening meal. It being warm, the windows were thrown wide open while we ate. When supper was over, the children shifted their positions and waited as usual for the announcement of the hymn. The lady made the selection, but there was no one to lead; a hasty consultation was held at the first table, then she came over to me with her hymn-book, "Frank, you must lead the singing," she said; "none of us can do it."

I could not understand why I should be selected to lead singing; but I took the book and looked over the hymn that was chosen. I knew it by heart, and could sing it; but I was embarrassed by the prominent position given me; however, my pride would not permit me to make an excuse, so I struck an attitude, and thinking it the proper thing to do, I imitated the music teacher as well as I could, and searched for the pitch by making a sound like the whinnying of a horse. I was half-conscious that I had provoked some amusement at the teachers' table by this performance, but I boldly struck out, in a clear, loud voice. All joined in, and with an effort sang the first line. The second line began with two or three very high notes, difficult to reach even when the tune was sung at the proper pitch; I struck at them bravely, and just managed to reach them, only one voice, that of a girl, was with me; no one else had ventured. We two went on and finished the line; at the beginning of the next we were joined by a third voice; but it sang a very different tune. I turned to see who it was, and there, with his paws on the window-sill, was Edwin's dog howling with all his might!

# 12

## Ponka
## Boys

"Woo-hoo! Noo'-zhin-ga pa'-hon ba ma kae don'-ba i ga!"
(Oh! boys, get up and look at the snow!) exclaimed a new
student, ignorant of the rule against speaking Indian.

We scrambled out of bed and rushed to the windows.
Sure enough, there was snow on the ground, and the trees
that the frost had stripped of their verdant beauty now
stood resplendent in a mantle of white.

Summer had gone. The myriads of little creatures that
only a short time ago enlivened the hills and valleys had
withdrawn into the recesses of the earth, or other places of
safety, each according to its own peculiar habit.

Winter had come. And the school-boy, defying its chill-
ing blasts, dances about in the crisp snow, or on the ice,
shouting to his playmates. Delighting in the exercise of
every muscle, he races to the hill-top, blows his hot breath
on his tingling finger-tips, mounts his little sled, then dashes
down the hill with merry shouts of laughter, though the
snow whirls and flies about his ears and beaming face.

Again and again he takes this wild descent until he hears the calling of the school-bell; then, with reluctant feet, he enters the class-room, to study the divisions of the earth either by natural boundaries, or by the artificial ones made by aggressive man, to learn about weights and measures, or to memorize the great events that have changed the conditions of nations and of peoples.

Every one was up and dressed that morning when Graybeard came to the dormitory; and, after repeating our prayer, we hurried down the two flights of stairs, making a noise like thunder. We ran into the yard, where we wrestled for a while, then rubbed our faces and hands with snow.

One of the teachers asked why the boys did so. "All boys do that," answered Brush. "The old folks tell them to do it, because then their faces and hands won't get frozen."

When breakfast was over that morning, and the students had shifted their positions so as to face the centre of the dining-room, and had folded their arms, the superintendent, marking with his forefinger the chapter he had selected to read at the morning worship, looked up and spoke, "We want the boys to learn the use of tools, and to make things for themselves, so we have provided the boards out of which every boy in this school can make a sled for himself. The carpenter will give to any boy who asks, the materials and show him how to use the tools to make his sled. Of course this must be done before the school hour."

We looked at each other and smiled. The reading of the Scripture and the prayer seemed to us to be unusually long, but at last they came to an end. Then every boy hurried and scurried to the carpenter's shop. Soon dozens of hammers were going crack, crack, and the saws zip, zip.

"Be careful, boys! Look out for nails, or you will ruin

your saws," said the carpenter, and he smiled good-naturedly as he went on marking the boards for the next applicant.

Suddenly, in the midst of all the din some one exclaimed, "Hong!" which is Indian for Ouch! and a big boy danced about, shaking his hand violently in the air, then he brought it down and pressed it between his knees, twisting his body into all sorts of shapes, howling the while. The hammering and sawing ceased, and a dozen voices asked, "What's the matter?" Peter, who was always clumsy in his movements, instead of hitting the nail he was driving, had struck his thumb and smashed it. The traditional "Indian stoicism" was not in him, so he kept up his howling until the carpenter had put on a tobacco poultice and bandaged the injured thumb.

After a lively coasting on our new sleds one afternoon, we were gathered in the school-room, and every one was busy preparing lessons. The arithmetic class was before the blackboard, answering questions put by the teacher.

"Ulysses Grant," said Gray-beard, "suppose the boards, nails, and work upon your sled cost you fifty-five cents, and you sold it to Edwin Stanton for sixty-three cents, what would be your profit?' '

Ulysses moved uneasily, then began counting rapidly with his fingers.

"Stop counting your fingers. Do the sum with your head," said Gray-beard.

Just at this moment something like a shadow appeared at one of the windows, and all faces, except Gray-beard's, turned in that direction. We soon made out that the shadow was the face of an Indian boy with his buffalo robe drawn

106

over his head and spread against the glass to exclude the glare of the sun, so as to give him a better view within the room. His black eyes peered at us, and at every object within sight. The figure withdrew; then we heard a voice speaking in our own language, "Come quick! Come and look at them!"

Soon the windows were darkened by dozens of the queerest-looking heads we had ever seen. Over each face hung two long braids. As the boys pressed their noses against the glass, and wrinkled their brows in trying to see, they made the strangest and most comical of pictures. They pushed and climbed over each other in their eagerness to observe what was going on inside. We could not help laughing at their appearance.

Edwin nudged me and whispered, "They're Ponka boys; they wear their scalp-locks in front, and they always have two."

"Don't they look funny?" shouted a Ponka boy at the middle window. "See, see that one!" and he pointed at Warren; "he looks just like a little owl; his hair stands straight up, and he has such big eyes."

Study became impossible, and the class in arithmetic made horrible blunders. Gray-beard was disgusted; in vain he rapped the desk with his ruler; and his patience found a limit when Andrew Johnson said that Ulysses' profit would be eleven cents, if he sold his sled for sixty-three cents. He gave the boy a vigorous shaking. This act of discipline delighted the little savages at the window; they shouted with laughter and the ends of their little braids fluttered with the breath of every peal. They interspersed their merriment with comments on our appearance, our clothing, and the absence of scalp-locks on our heads.

107

"What are they saying?" asked Gray-beard, looking toward the windows.

"They're calling us names," answered Warren, who felt sore at being compared to an owl.

Gray-beard went to the door; as he opened it, the intruders ran swiftly to the fence, and sat astride of the top board.

"Get away from here!" said Gray-beard, in a loud voice. "Go home!"

"How do do! Goo-by!" shouted back some of the little rascals with boisterous jeers.

"Class in history," called Gray-beard as he closed the door; and a number of us stood in line at the usual place.

"Philip Sheridan, can you tell me something of George Washington?"

All eyes turned toward the youngster who answered to the name of George Washington, and who, neglecting his lessons, was now busy drawing on his slate a caricature of a boy against whom he had a grudge. Hearing his name, and thinking he had been caught in his mischief, he looked up with a startled expression, and rose to make a denial, when Sheridan, fixing his eyes upon him, slowly answered, "He chopped his father's choke-cherry-tree."

The little savages returned to the windows, and began chattering noisily. Suddenly a number of them stood in line, imitating the history class, while one of the big boys took a place before them, mimicking the actions of Gray-beard and the tones of his voice, by giving the peculiar rhythm of English to his own Indian words.

"Ah'-bru-zhe-dae!" he asked; "do you ever wash your face?" And the make-believe class went into fits of laughter.

108

"Ten sleeps ago," angrily retorted the boy addressed, "you stole some honey, and the smirches of it are still on *your* face!"

The boys were convulsed at this reply, and so were the boys in the school-room; but the mock teacher took a different view of the matter, and sprang at his impudent pupil, boxing his ears, whereat the two fell on each other in a lively tussle. We stretched our necks to see the struggle, and Gray-beard also watched the scene.

All at once a Ponka boy shouted, "I've found something! Come, come!" and the crowd moved away, leaving the two to finish their wrestling.

Before long we heard a great clatter in the hall-way, and then the Ponka boys were seen marching out of the yard with our sleds. We heard them coasting down the hill, and this made us very restless, so that we could not pay any attention to our lessons. By and by the shouting on the hill-side ceased, and Warren leaned over to Brush and whispered, "They're going off with our sleds!"

Brush raised his right hand; Gray-beard saw him, and asked what he wanted.

"Those Indian boys are going away with our sleds, and we want to go after them."

Permission being given, in a twinkling there were twenty or thirty school-boys charging up the hill, all mad as hornets. We overtook the Ponkas midway between the school and the village. The little savages turned and came to meet us.

"What do you want?" said the big boy who had played teacher.

"We want our sleds," said Brush.

"Come and get them!" was the defiant answer of the Ponka boys.

"That we will do!" answered Brush.

We all moved forward, and then followed a scene hard to describe. A terrific battle took place between us and the robbers; it was hand to hand, and shin to shin, for hands and feet were the only weapons used.

The Ponkas made a determined resistance. I cannot very well relate what happened around me; for I was engaged in a lively bout with an impish-looking little chap for whom I had taken a sudden and unreasonable spite. It was hard to get at him, for he was quick as a wild-cat in his movements, and he gave me a number of vicious blows before I could touch him. I noticed that he was more afraid of my brogans than of my fists; taking advantage of this, I pretended to lift my foot for a fierce kick; he hopped backwards, and, in so doing, bent his body toward me. Quick as a flash, I grasped his two braids, pulled his head down, and brought my right knee up against it with tremendous force, and he went sprawling in the snow.

"Frank, Frank, come here, quick!" It was Brush calling. I turned, and there he lay under two of the Ponkas, who were dealing him heavy blows. In a second I had dragged one of them off, and Brush had his footing again. Some one shouted, "They're running! they're running!" and the boys we were fighting broke loose. Then all of us school-boys chased the Ponkas, and drove them into their camp.

We were a bruised lot when we came back to the school; but we had our sleds.

# 13

## The Secret
## of the
## Big Seven

THE SMALL BOYS had been marched to bed at eight o'clock.
We, the Middle Five, who, for the first time, were permitted
to stay up until ten,—a privilege hitherto enjoyed only by
the Big Seven,—sat around the fire listening to Indian tales
told by Edwin in his animated way. There was no light in
the room save that which came through the open door of
the stove, in front of which the story-teller had taken his
place. The flickering fire cast a ruddy light upon the fine
features of the boy, and the shadows on the wall danced to
the caprice of the restless flames. We laughed heartily at
the mishaps of Ish-te'-ne-ke, a comical character that fig-
ures in the folk-tales of the Omahas, as they were vividly
portrayed in language and gesture.

Outside the wind was moaning and sighing through the
trees around the house, at times rattling the windows vig-
orously, as though threatening to rush in upon us; and
from the neighborhood of the graveyard came the mourn-
ful sounds of the hooting owl.

In the back part of the school-room, where it was dark, sat the Big Seven, carrying on an earnest conversation in low tones, as though to exclude us from their confidence.

The leader of this "gang" was a youth of peculiar appearance and manner. He was tall and muscular, with prominent nose and cheek-bones. Although he took an active part in the amusements and sports of the school, often inaugurating them himself, we never knew him to change the expression of his face, either in pain, anger, or mirth. We Five often had talks about the peculiarities of this singular youth. Brush said that "Aleck" (the boys addressed him by this name, for he was called after the Macedonian conqueror) was turned outside in, that all his laugh, anger, and sorrow were inside and couldn't be seen. Edwin declared that the boy had ceased laughing since the killing of his father by the Sioux, and that he was reserving his laugh for the time when he should take revenge.

The mysterious consultation in the back part of the school-room came to an end, and one by one the Big Seven approached the stove and mingled with us. Aleck, who was the last, did not sit down in the space left for him, but drew up a desk and perched on one end of it, resting his feet on the bench where he should have sat. He leaned over, supporting his body with his elbow on his knee, and shaded his eyes with his hand. We could feel that for some purpose he was looking into the faces of the Middle Five.

As the Seven took their places among us, Edwin brought his story to a close, and we fell into silence. After a few moments Aleck cleared his throat, and, without change of attitude, said in the Omaha language, fearlessly breaking one of the rules of the school:

"Boys, to you of the Five I speak. There is not a 'gang' in the school that has not its secrets. You of the Five have yours, no doubt; we of the Seven, who now sit with you, have ours. We respect yours, and we have every confidence that you respect ours. Ordinarily we do not interfere with each other's affairs; but now that you have the same privilege that we have had, and we are thrown together, we of the Seven think that your 'gang' should unite with ours in a secret that up to this time has been ours alone, and share in its pleasures. Are you willing to join in it?"

"Yes," answered Brush, knowing as the rest of us did, what this secret was; "we are willing."

"You of the Seven, are you satisfied with the answer?"

There was silence. "Then," continued the leader of the Seven, "I must have the answer of each one of the Five."

Brush again signified his assent, and the rest of us followed. Having arrived at a mutual understanding which awakened in each one a fraternal feeling, there ensued among all the boys a lively chattering. When the fervor of the friendly demonstration abated, Aleck, in his deep voice, said, "Wa'-tha-dae shu-ge'ha!" (The Word of Command approaches.)

Immediately there was silence, and each one held his breath expectantly, for we recognized the ritual words of "the Leader" in the game, "Obeying the Command," words which had been sacred to generations of boys who had preceded us.

"Those are the very words," whispered Edwin to me; "now listen, hear where the Command will come from, and where it will go."

"The Word of Command approaches," continued Aleck,

113

with unmoved face; "from the head of the Ne-shu'-de [the Missouri] it comes, wrapped in a black cloud, the mantle of thunder, like the mighty whirlwind it comes; the great trees of the pine-clad mountains bend to its fury; its voice echoes through the valleys, and the animals, big and little, tremble with fear. On it comes, sweeping over the wide plains; the angry lightnings dart from the cloud; it approaches the village of the Ponkas, at the mouth of the Niobrara, passes it and continues its course down the Ne-shu'-de; now it has come to the pictured rocks; it reaches the bluffs of the Cut-lake; but on it comes, swifter and swifter it comes; it is now at the old Omaha village, at the graves of the little ones; it comes—it is here!"

There was a pause, and we all waited in suspense. Just then the wind rattled the windows and the owl up in the graveyard hooted.

"George!" called the leader, in a solemn tone.

"Present!" promptly responded George in English, as though answering Gray-beard's roll-call. A ripple of suppressed laughter spread among the boys. Aleck, I doubt not, was giggling inside.

"Edwin!" continued the leader, in the same tone.

"Ah-ho!" said Edwin, giving the response and imitating the voice of a grown-up and serious warrior.

"The Word of Command is before you two," continued Aleck, "the Leader"; "and it is, that soon after Gray-beard has gone to bed you are to go to the village and enter the house of Hae'-sha-ra-gae, where you will see a woman making pemmican. You will say to her, 'Woman! we are the commanded and the bearers of the Word of Command. Of you we demand a bag of pemmican. Give willingly, and you shall go beyond the four hills of life without stumbling; there shall be no weariness in the pathway of life to hinder your feet, and your grandchildren shall be many and their succession endless!' Fail not in your mission. Your way out of the house shall be through one of the windows in our dormitory, and by a rope."

"It is bed-time, boys, come right up," called Gray-beard, from the head of the stairs. "See that the large doors are bolted."

When we were in bed, Gray-beard went softly downstairs, and we heard him open his door, close it, then lock it. Some of the youngsters were still awake, and, when they heard the closing of Gray-beard's door, began to talk. It seemed as though they would never stop and go to sleep, so that we could carry out the Word of Command. After a while Aleck thought of a plan, and started a game often played by small boys at night; he said, loud enough for the little boys to hear, "Tha'-ka!" Brush and the rest of us repeated the word, one after the other, and each of the wakeful little fellows, according to the rules of the game, was obliged in his turn to utter the word, and then there was silence, for no one can speak after he has said the word. Soon heavy breathing among the little ones gave sign that they had entered the land of dreams.

It was near the middle of the night when one by one the members of the Big Seven and the Middle Five noiselessly arose. George tiptoed to a corner and brought out a large coil of rope. We went with it to the window directly over that of Gray-beard's bed-room. I do not know why we selected that window, the only dangerous one in the dormitory, but there seemed be a fatality about it. Very softly the window was raised; George slipped the noose at the end of the rope around his body, then climbed through the window. Slowly we let him down the three stories to the ground. Then we hauled the rope up again, and let Edwin down in the same manner. We closed the window, leaving space enough for the rope, which remained dangling.

On entering the village, the two boys were met by a pack of noisy curs that snapped and snarled at their heels. As the dogs became bolder in their attacks, the lads struck right and left with the heavy sticks they carried; one dog limped away yelping, and another lay thumping his tail on the ground, stunned.

The door of the house designated by the leader of the Big Seven squeaked loudly on its rusty hinges as the boys swung it open without the ceremony of knocking. A woman at work in one corner of the room looked up at them, smiled good-naturedly, and said in a sympathetic tone:

"Such a dark night as this! On what errand do they come, and little White-chests, too?"

Four men were sitting on the floor around a flickering candle playing a game; they too looked up at the sound of the door.

"Oho!" said the man of the house, who was one of the players, "for a long time you have not entered my dwelling on a visit; I fear you will make it rain! Walk around the stove and break the charm."

"Don't mind him," said the woman, kindly; "tell me what you want. Won't you sit down?"

The two boys stood hesitating, then George began in a sepulchral voice, "Woman, we are the commanded, the bearers of the Word of Command. We come to demand of you a bag of pemmican. Give plenty—"

"Willingly," corrected Edwin, in a whisper.

"Willingly, and you shall go beyond the four hills of life without—without—"

"Stumbling," prompted Edwin.

"Stumbling; there shall be no weariness in the pathway of life—" and so on to the end of the ritual.

The woman clapped her hands, and shouted with laughter, as she exclaimed, "If your cloud and lightning and thunder do all you say they will do, they have more power than I supposed they had! Sit down and wait a while, and I will have some pemmican ready for you."

"Did those old White-chests teach you all that?" asked the husband. "If they did, they have been stealing the rituals of some of our priests, and—"

"Oh, let them alone!" said the wife; "they came to see me."

"They came in without knocking on the door; that's bad luck!" the husband continued in his banter; "before entering a house they should knock, as the White-chests do."

"Be careful, and don't spill it!" said the wife, as she handed a bag to George, who thanked her.

"There they come!" said one of the Seven in a loud whisper, as he felt a tug on the rope that was tied to his arm.

We hastened out of bed, being careful not to make any noise. George and Edwin sent the bag of pemmican first, then they were each pulled up and safely landed.

We had built a fire in a vacant room adjoining our dormitory; into this warm room we repaired with our bag, and sat in a circle on the floor, Indian fashion. On a little table stood the one candle allowed us, shedding a feeble light. Two of the boys had stolen down to the dining-room for plates. Alexander, before whom the bag was placed, divided the pemmican equally, while we listened to George and Edwin's account of their adventure. The plates were passed around; I put out my hand to help myself from my plate, when a member of the Big Seven stopped me. "Wait," said he; "there is something more to be done."

Aleck looked up; we all became silent; then he took a tiny bit of the pemmican, and held it toward the sky for a moment as a thank offering to Wakonda, then placed it with great solemnity on the floor in the centre of the circle. This done, we fell to eating, telling stories as we feasted, and had one of the most enjoyable nights of our lives.

From time to time through the winter we had these nocturnal banquets, taking turns in going to the village for our supplies; but misfortune overtook us before the season was fairly over.

One dark night we had our meeting as usual, and the Word of Command came to Lester and to Joel of the Big Seven. When the small boys had gone to sleep, we brought out our rope and let Joel down through the window. Then we put the noose around Lester and proceeded to lower him.

It chanced that Gray-beard had lain awake from toothache, and was at that very moment looking through his window, the curtain of which he had neglected to pull down when he retired, and he saw, slowly descending outside, two dark objects; they grew longer and longer, then they suddenly ceased to move. For an instant he felt a slight shock of fright; but quickly recovering, he gradually made out the form of two feet and two legs without a body. He sprang out of bed, threw open the window, and in a severe tone demanded, "What's this! Who are you; what are you doing?"

118

Lester struggled frantically to climb the rope; we tried to help him, but a large knot caught the edge of the window-sill, and we could not lift it over, nor could we let Lester down, for one of the Seven had entangled his legs in the coil, and before he had extricated himself, it was too late to save our companion.

"Who are you?" again called Gray-beard, grasping the boy by the trousers.

"It's me, Lester," replied the lad.

Seeing that the game was up, we gently let Lester farther down, and he entered Gray-beard's room through the window.

In the mean time one of the boys had run softly downstairs to open the hall door for Joel, who had not been discovered.

Gray-beard woke us up in the morning at the usual hour, but of the disturbance during the night he said nothing. At breakfast the subject was not mentioned, although we listened with anxious expectation.

To the twelve boys who were engaged in the escapade of the night, it seemed as though the preliminary exercises of the morning school session would never end, so desirous were we to have the punishment, whatever it might be, come quickly and we be rid of suspense. The last name on the roll was called; Gray-beard slowly closed the Register, put it in his desk, and during an impressive silence turned his eyes upon us to scan our faces.

"Lester!" said he, at last, "you will step up to my desk, if you please."

If there was a serious matter on hand, Gray-beard always said, "If you please."

Notwithstanding the very polite invitation extended to

him, Lester reluctantly walked to the desk. Every eye but two, those of Alexander, was fixed upon Gray-beard and Lester. Aleck had taken out his writing-book and was carefully copying the example given at the head of the page, "Honesty is the best policy." He took particular pains with the capital H, finishing the last part with concentric circles.

"What were you doing last night," asked Gray-beard of Lester, "when I caught you outside of my window?"

"I was going down to the ground."

"Were you running away?"

"No, sir."

"Where were you going?"

"I was going to the village."

"What were you going to the village for?"

No answer.

"Who was letting you down; some one must have held the rope in the dormitory, who was it?"

No reply.

"If you don't answer my questions, I shall have to whip you; who else was going with you?"

Lester looked appealingly to Brush, then to Alexander. Aleck was writing the sentence in his book; but, when he heard Gray-beard's threat to whip Lester, he arose without finishing the last word. All eyes turned upon him, and there was a stir among the pupils.

"What is it, Alexander," asked Gray-beard, "what do you know about this strange performance?"

"Lester is not to blame, sir; I made him go out of the window, and I held the rope to let him down."

"And I helped him to do it," came from a voice in another part of the room; it was Brush, who had silently risen; "we

120

compelled the two—we compelled Lester to go out of the window."

"You said there were two boys who were going out of the window, who was the other?" asked Gray-beard, determined to find out all the participants in the mischief.

Those of us who knew, looked toward Joel; an expression of fear stole over his face and he anxiously awaited Brush's answer.

"I did not say that, sir," he replied; "Lester was going down alone."

Joel gave a sigh of relief.

"What made you force the boy to go out of the window; where were you sending him?"

"We were sending him to the village."

"What were you sending him to the village for?"

"I refuse to answer," was the bold reply.

Gray-beard, seeing that there would be no use in questioning Brush, turned to Alexander and asked, "What were you sending Lester to the village for?"

"I was sending him to go there and return."

"Alexander, I want no foolishness; tell me what you were sending Lester to the village for?"

"I refuse to answer."

"This abusing of smaller boys by the large ones, and making them do things that are improper, must be stopped; it has gone far enough. Lester, you may take your seat. Frank, take this knife and get me two good hickory switches. Do you know a hickory-tree?"

"Yes, sir," I answered, as I took the knife. I knew every kind of tree growing around the school, and I had a suspicion that Gray-beard did not know the difference between a hickory sapling and some others. I cut two formidable-looking switches of linden, closely resembling hickory. I had time to fully doctor only one of the switches, by driving the knife-blade deep into the wood every two or three inches. When I entered the school-room, Gray-beard took a glance at the switches, then said:

"Alexander and Brush will step to my desk and take off their coats."

The two boys stood in their shirt sleeves; I kept watch of Gray-beard's eyes, and saw that he was going to take Brush first; so when he was ready I handed him the fully doctored switch.

"Is that hickory?" he asked, trying it on the air; "I suspect it isn't."

I made no reply.

"Stand in the middle of the floor," said Gray-beard to Brush.

He did so. Gray-beard brought down the stick heavily on Brush's shoulders, an inch of the sapling broke; then he struck faster and faster, and at each stroke a piece flew off. Brush stood with clenched fists, determined not to show any flinching; but we could see that he felt keenly the blows. He went to his desk, and buried his face in arms.

"I am afraid this isn't hickory," said Gray-beard, throwing on the floor the stump of the switch. "I know this one is," and he dealt blow after blow on the broad shoulders of Alexander, who gave no sign of pain. The boy stood unmoved, every muscle relaxed, even his hands were open, showing no emotion whatever. The stick was worn out, and Gray-beard threw the stump on the floor.

Aleck put on his coat, then, with head uplifted and unfaltering steps, went to his desk, took his pen, and completed the unfinished word of the motto.

# 14

---

# A Rebuke

It was saturday, a day of delight for the boys and girls of the Mission school, for to them it was a day of rest from the toil of study, and a visit home was permitted. On this morning the allotted chores were performed with redoubled energy; for the sooner the tasks were done, the earlier would be the start for home, the sooner the pleasures laid out for the day would begin.

The boys who had finished their work and had reported to the superintendent were already on their way to the village, shouting and singing as they went. Edwin watered the horses, and I started the hydraulic ram; then, having received our formal leave to go, we chased each other up the hill toward the village, and wrestled until we came to the place where the path branched; he took one way and I the other, but we continued to chaff back and forth until we were out of hearing.

After greeting my father and mother, the first thing I did

was to run over to the barn and see the horses. When I had rubbed the noses of Kushas and Hintu and the rest, and had pitched down from the loft a lot of hay for them, I stepped over to Ka-he'-num-ba's house and looked in at the door, which stood wide open. His wife was sitting near the stove, quietly working on a pair of moccasins.

"Where is Ga-im'-ba-zhe?" I shouted.

"Oh! how you startled me!" she said. "Your uncle has gone to the stable with other boys; he left word for you to go there when you came."

Hardly had she finished speaking before I was off like the wind. On the ground by a fire sat Ga-im'-ba-zhe and the boys, all busy making game-sticks, the Indian name of which we Mission boys translated into English as "bone slides." These were made out of willow saplings. After cutting the stick the proper length, the bark was removed, and a narrow strip of it wound around the peeled stick, which was then held over the blaze of the fire until the exposed part was scorched. When the binding was removed, the game-stick presented a mottled appearance, something like a snake.

The brown bodies of these partly nude little savages glistened against the sun as they worked, while the breezes played with their black totemic locks. They were not aware of my approach until I pitched a corncob into their midst, when they all threw up their heads to see who was coming.

"Ho! Little White-chest!" exclaimed Ga-im'-ba-zhe. "Have you come home?"

"Yes, I have come home," I replied; "but I don't want you to call me White-chest."

"Sit down," said one of the little brownies. "When we

124

have done, we will give you some, then you can play with us."

When the sticks were finished, I was given five or six of them. The tallest boy led the game. He grasped the small end of the game-stick with his right hand, bracing the top with a finger, then he took two or three quick side-long steps and threw the stick against the ground with all the force he could command; it bounded up and shot through the air like an arrow. The next boy threw one of his sticks in the same manner, and from the same place. All the others played, each in his turn. Then one of the boys shouted, "Your turn, little White-chest. Throw hard!"

I was familiar with the game, and by practice had acquired some skill in throwing the sticks. I selected one that seemed to have the proper weight and feeling, took the usual position, and crouching almost to the earth, I threw my stick with all the force that I could muster. We watched its flight until it touched the ground and slid along, far beyond any stick that had been thrown.

"Woo-hoo!" exclaimed the boys, "he has beaten us all; he's won all our sticks!"

"Kill him! kill him! He's nothing but a thieving Winnebago!" This cry came from the west end of the village, not far from where we were playing. Startled by the angry words, we paused in our sport, and looked in that direction. A crowd began to gather and move along the path that led out of the village.

"What are they doing? Let's go and see," cried Ga-im'-ba-zhe.

We all rushed forward on a keen run, and reached the crowd; there we saw a lad, a little larger than we were, struggling to get away from a swarm of boys and young men who were throwing stones and sticks at him. He was a pitiful object, and why they should abuse him so was more than we could understand. His legs and feet were bare; he carried on his arm something that resembled a worn-out blanket, and in his hand he held tightly a piece of bread. He belonged to the Winnebago tribe, against whom at that time there was much prejudice among the Omahas. Mud was thrown at him; he was pushed and jostled by the crowd, and some persons kicked him. Slowly the boy retreated, at times stopping to look with pleading eyes at his merciless persecutors. When he started to run, some one threw a stick of wood before him; he struck his foot against it and fell; then the crowd laughed.

"They are doing wrong!" exclaimed Ga-im'-ba-zhe. "They ought not to do that!"

"I think so, too," I added; "but what can we do?"

Just then I felt a tug at my sleeve. I turned to see who it was, and there stood the boy that did errands for my father. "Your father wants you to come home," he said.

I was a little troubled at this, for the boy spoke in a frightened tone. At that moment a man came up and cried in a loud voice:

"You are commanded to cease molesting the boy!"

Recognizing the speaker as a messenger coming from the chief, the rabble dispersed in groups, like angry wolves.

My mind was uneasy as I went toward home, and I felt guilty, though I could not understand why. As I entered the house I was ushered into my father's presence. He was talking earnestly to a number of men who sat on the floor smoking a pipe which they passed from hand to hand. Among them I recognized Ka-he'-num-ba (the father of

Ga-im′-ba-zhe), Te-o′-ke-ha, Du′-ba-mo-ne, Wa-hon′-i-ge (Edwin's father), and other prominent men of the village. My father seemed to take no notice of my entrance, but kept on talking. When he had finished speaking, his eyes rested on me, and after a moment's pause, he said, "Son, step to the middle of the floor." I did so. Then in a low tone he began:

"I speak not boastfully; all who are here have known me from boyhood, and will know what I am about to say to you is true. Even before I grew to be your size I was left to face the difficulties of life. I have felt the pangs of hunger and the chills of winter, but, by ceaseless struggles, I overcame poverty and gathered about me, as I grew to manhood, many of the things that make life bearable; yet I did not cease to struggle. I have won honors and position among our people, and the respect of the tribes having friendly relations with us. Success has attended me; but, remembering my early struggles, I suppressed vanity, and gave help to the poor. When journeying with my people, if I saw any of them weary and footsore, I gave them horses, and sent them away singing for joy. The stranger who entered my door never left it hungry. No one can accuse me of having tormented with abuse the poverty-stricken man. Early I sought the society of those who knew the teaching of the chiefs. From them I learned that kindness and hospitality win the love of a people. I culled from their teachings their noblest thoughts, and treasured them, and they have been my guide. You came into existence, and have reached the age when you should seek for knowledge. That you might profit by the teachings of your own people and that of the white race, and that you might avoid the misery which accompanies ignorance, I placed you in the House of

Teaching of the White-chests, who are said to be wise and to have in their books the utterances of great and learned men. I had treasured the hope that you would seek to know the good deeds done by men of your own race, and by men of the white race, that you would follow their example and take pleasure in doing the things that are noble and helpful to those around you. Am I to be disappointed?"

As his talk progressed, he grew eloquent, and louder and louder became his tones. My eyes were riveted upon him. In every feature of his handsome face there was reflected a mind, a will, a determination that nothing could break. He arose to his feet and continued, pointing his finger at me:

"Only to-day there crept to the door of my house a poor boy driven thither by hunger; he was given food by my command. Having satisfied for the time being his craving, he went away happy. Hardly had he left the village, when a rabble gathered about him and persecuted him. They threw mud at him, pointed at him their fingers in derision, and laughed rudely at his poverty, and you, a son of E-sta'-ma-za, joined the tormentors and smiled at the poor boy's tears."

I winced at this accusation. He could accuse me of almost anything; but of this I was not guilty. A hesitating small voice at the door said, "He did not join them!" It was the little boy that came after me who spoke. I was grateful for this defence, but, as though he had not heard it, my father continued.

"By your presence you aided and encouraged those wicked boys. He who is present at a wrong-doing, and lifts not a hand to prevent it, is as guilty as the wrong-doers. The persecution of the poor, the sneer at their poverty is a wrong for which no punishment is too severe. I have finished. Go, and think of my words."

Those at the door made way for me; I passed out and entered my mother's room. She looked up at me with a kindly smile; but I flung myself down on her bed, buried my face in the pillows, sobbing. My mother did not speak, but went on with her work. When I had regained my composure, she bade me come and sit beside her. I did so. She put an arm around me, and said in a caressing tone, "What is it that makes my little boy cry?" I told her. She sat in silence for a while, and then spoke:

"Your father is right; you must be guided by his words. You had a chance to do good; you let it slip away from you. That poor boy came and sat at the door, the humblest place in your house; he did not beg, but the eyes he turned upon your father and on me told a tale of suffering. At your father's bidding, I placed food with my own hands before the boy; when he had finished eating he arose without a word and, taking with him what was left of the food, he went out, giving me a look that bespoke his gratitude. My boy must learn to be good and kind. When you see a boy barefooted and lame, take off your moccasins and give them to him. When you see a boy hungry, bring him to your home and give him food."

The mild words and the gentle touch of her hand were like ointment to my wounds. When she had finished speaking, I put my arms around her neck and kissed her.

On my way back to the Mission I saw a lad standing at the fork of the paths. It was little Bob. "Come, hurry!" he said; "I've been waiting for you." Together we returned to the school.

After supper I went out and lay on the grass, looking up

into the blue sky, thinking. Twilight came, then darkness. A bell rang, and all the boys went upstairs to bed. I followed. We knelt by our beds; Gray-beard rapped on the banister with his pen-knife; when there was silence, he said slowly, and in a low tone, "Our Father who art in heaven, Hallowed be Thy name." We repeated with him this prayer that was taught over a thousand years ago. The tardy ones with labored breathing cut almost every word; but I repeated them carefully, and, although I had said them a hundred times before, now, for the first time since I had been in the school, I began to wonder what they meant.

Lester, Edwin, and I got into bed; my place was in the middle.

"Frank, what makes you so quiet?" asked Lester, nudging me with his elbow.

Before I could answer Edwin began tugging at the sheet, saying, "Lester, you've too much sheet over there!"

They both pulled the bedcovers and kicked at each other good-naturedly for a while, and then quieted down. I received some of the kicks too, but did not join in the fun. There was silence for a time and then Edwin said, "Say, boys, I've been feeling bad this afternoon. When I got home from the river, my father scolded me like everything. He said something about my being with some boys who teased a poor Winnebago boy, and he talked to me a long time. He never give me chance to say I didn't see a Winnebago boy today; I was all the morning down to the river swimming. I couldn't understand it, and I don't now. Say, Frank, does your father scold you sometimes?"

"Edwin, tell us a story," I said.

"Do!" exclaimed the other boys. "Tell us a story."

# 15

## Joe

IT WAS RECESS. The laughter and shouts of the boys, as they chased each other and wrestled, mingled with the song of the wren and other birds that inhabited the woods surrounding the school. Not less merry or boisterous were the laughter and calls of the girls, although their territory for play was limited and fenced in, to keep them from too free a communication with the rougher sex. Study and work were forgotten, and every boy and girl romped in the sunshine, and the atmosphere around seemed to be alive with happiness.

Suddenly the boys began to gather curiously around two objects upon the ground. The girls, seeing this unusual stir, came running to their fence, climbed up as far as they dared, and asked the nearest boys what it was that attracted so large a crowd.

It was a pitiful scene,—there, sitting on the green grass, was a crippled old woman of about seventy or eighty years, speaking in the kindest and gentlest of tones, with inflections of the voice hard to describe, but which brought to one's mind the twittering of a mother bird to its young, and passing her crooked fingers and wrinkled hands over the brown back of a miserable, naked, little boy who was digging his chubby fists in his eyes to squeeze away the tears that flowed incessantly.

"Don't cry! my little grandson," she was saying; "don't cry! These White-chests are kind; they will clothe and feed you. I can no longer take care of you, so I must give you to them. See these boys, what nice caps and coats and pants they have! You will have these things, too, and you will have plenty to eat. The White-chests will be good to you; I will come and see you very often. Don't cry!"

But the boy cried all the harder, twisting his fists into his eyes, and the old woman continued her caressing twittering.

The bell rang, and there was a rush for the school-room. When the hard breathing, coughing, and shuffling into position at the desks had ceased, the door was gently pushed open, and the old woman entered, tenderly urging the unwilling little brown body forward into the room, still weeping. Addressing Gray-beard, who was watching the scene with a queer smile on his lips, the old woman said:

"I have brought my little boy to give him to the White-chests to raise and to educate. On account of my age and feebleness, I am no longer able to care for him. I give him to you, and I beg that he be kindly treated. That is all I ask."

Without waiting for an answer, the poor creature, with tears streaming down her furrowed checks, limped out of

132

the room, making a cheerless clatter with her heavy stick as she moved away. The little boy, recovering from his bewilderment, turned to see if his grandmother was still near by, and, finding that she had gone, gave a piteous wail, and fell to the floor, sobbing violently.

Who was this wretched little boy? He was his mother's son, that's all. He had no father, that is, none to caress and fondle him as other boys had. A man had presented the name of the boy to the Agent to be entered on the annuity rolls, only to that selfish extent recognizing the lad as his son.

The mother died while the child still needed her tender care, and the little one was left all alone in this great world that plays with the fortunes of men and nations. The place of death was in a dreary little tent, the rags of which flapped and fluttered in the force of the merciless winds, as though in sympathy with the melancholy situation. No loving husband or father was there to prepare the body for its last resting-place, and to give the helpless babe the nourishment for which it cried. Not even a relative was there; the dead woman had none among the people; she belonged to another tribe.

As the mother lay an unburied corpse, and her child wailing, a figure bent with age was plodding by. It was an old woman; slowly she put her heavy stick forward, then took a step, as though measuring every movement. When she came near the tent, she stopped, for the distressing wail had pierced her ears. She raised her trembling hand to her brow, looked up to the tent, then to the surroundings. The wailing went on, and the decrepit old woman hastened toward the tent as fast as she was able to go, and entered. For a moment she stood still, contemplating the scene before her, then from the fountains of her tender heart arose tears, impelled not by the sympathy that naturally springs from the love of friend or kindred, but by that nobler and higher feeling which lifts one toward God,—the sympathy for human kind.

Thus it was that this kind-hearted old woman took the homeless little child to her tent and cared for him. The two were inseparable until the grandmother, as she was called by the boy, felt that she was fast approaching the time when she would be summoned to join her fathers in the spirit-land; so, to provide for the child's future, she had brought him to the school.

The naming of a new pupil was usually an occasion for much merriment, but this time there was no enthusiasm. The school seemed to be in sympathy with the grandmother who went away weeping. Instead of raising their hands, as was their wont, to suggest names, they sought to hide their feeling by poring over their books.

"Come," said Gray-beard, "we must have a name for this youngster. Be quick and suggest one."

There was no response. Finally a big boy, who was busy over his lessons, said without lifting his head, "Call him Joseph."

So Gray-beard entered that name on the school Register.

Joe, as he was called by the boys, grew rapidly, but the helplessness of infancy clung to him. Because he could not fight, he became the butt of every trick a school-boy could devise, and there was no one who would do battle for him. If a big boy looked hard at him he would howl, and if one of his size rushed at him threateningly, he would shrink

134

with fear. He was incapable of creating any mischief, yet he was continually stumbling into scrapes.

One sultry afternoon as I was sitting in the shade of the walnut-tree in front of the school, busy making a sling for Bob out of an old shoe, Joe came up to us, and dropped on his hands and knees. With the greatest interest he watched me cut the leather into a diamond shape; after a while he ventured to ask, "What yer makin'?"

"Wait and see," I answered, and went on working. When I had finished the sling-strap or pocket, I cut from the lappets of my buckskin moccasin two strings, making a noose at the end of one, and then fastened both strings to the sling-strap. Although I did not say anything about it, I had determined to make one for Joe as soon as I had shown Bob how to use the sling. He tried to find out from Bob what I was making; but that little chap would not speak to him.

When the sling was finished, I told Bob to gather some rusty nails and pebbles. He was off with a jump, and returned with a good supply in an amazingly short time. Joe still sat watching, with eyes and mouth wide open. I put a nail in the sling-strap, and, to show Bob how to use the sling, swung it around three or four times, then threw out my arm with force, letting one end of the string slip, and the nail sped on its way through the air, singing. Bob clapped his hands with delight.

A crow was flying lazily over head, croaking as he went. I sent a stone whizzing up to him; it barely missed his head, and he turned a complete somersault in the air, to our great amusement.

"I'm goin' to make one too!" said Joe, suddenly rising and hunting around for materials.

I paid no attention to him, but went on teaching Bob how to throw stones with the sling, little thinking that we were drifting toward an incident which gave Joe much pain temporarily and left an impression on my immature mind unfavorable to the White-chests which lasted many, many years.

"Mine's done!" exclaimed Joe, holding up a sling he had made out of rotten rags.

"Don't use it," I made haste to say, "and I'll make you a good one."

He paid no heed to my words, but went on trying to balance stones in the old piece of rag. The stones dropped before he could swing the sling and throw them. Bob kept me busy throwing stones for him, for he was afraid of hitting the boys who were on the hillside near by playing tag, or of sending a pebble over the fence, where the girls were singing and chatting over some of their games.

"Look now, look!" cried Joe. I turned to see what he was doing. He had succeeded in balancing a clod of earth nearly as large as his head in the rag sling, and was about to swing it.

Just at this moment Gray-beard came out of the carpenter's shop and, shading his eyes with a newspaper, he called loudly to one of the boys who was playing tag, "Ulysses! Ulysses!" He inflated his lungs to call for the third time, and with greater volume of voice. Joe had swung the clod of earth around for the second time, and it was half way up for the third round when the string broke; released from its holdings, the clod flew into the air, revolving, and dropping loose particles as it went. I held my breath as I watched it, for I saw just where it was going to strike.

136

In throwing a stone at some object, I used to imagine that by keeping a steady eye on the stone and bending my body in the direction I desired it to go, I could make the missile reach the place aimed at. In this instance, although I did not throw the clod, I unconsciously bent my body sidewise, keeping my eyes steadily on the lump of earth to draw it away from the spot for which it was making. The two other boys watched with frightened faces.

Gray-beard with head thrown back, lips parted, and chest expanded, called, "Uly—!" when the diminutive planet, which I was trying to guide by my force of will, struck him in the chest, and burst in a thousand bits. For a moment there was coughing and sputtering; then Gray-beard drew out his handkerchief, dusted his beard, and his white shirt front. He looked around to see where the missile that struck him came from. I wished that we three could sink into the earth, or else turn into nothing, as Gray-beard's eyes rested upon us.

"Come here!" he demanded with a vigorous gesture. Like so many guilty curs we walked up to him.

"Which one of you did it?" he cried, grasping me by the collar and shaking me until my teeth chattered.

Joe cringed and cried; it was a confession. I was about to say, "he didn't mean to do it;" when the infuriated man turned, went into the shop, and in a moment came back with a piece of board.

"Hold out your hand!" he said, addressing the shrinking boy.

Joe timidly held out his left hand, keeping his eyes all the while on the uplifted board, which came down with force, but not on the little hand that had been withdrawn

137

to escape the blow. Gray-beard sprang at the boy, caught his hand, and attempted to strike it; but the boy pulled away and the board fell with a vicious thud on the wrist of the man, who now turned white with rage. Catching a firm grip on the hand of the boy, Gray-beard dealt blow after blow on the visibly swelling hand. The man seemed to lose all self-control, gritting his teeth and breathing heavily, while the child writhed with pain, turned blue, and lost his breath.

It was a horrible sight. The scene in the school-room when the naked little boy was first brought there by the old woman rose before me; I heard the words of the grand-mother as she gave the boy to Gray-beard, "I beg that he be kindly treated; that is all I ask!" And she had told the child that the White-chests would be kind to him.

Poor Joe, I did what I never would have done if a boy of his own size had thrashed him, I took him by the hand and tried to comfort him, and cared for his bruises.

As for Gray-beard I did not care in the least about the violent shaking he had given me; but the vengeful way in which he fell upon that innocent boy created in my heart a hatred that was hard to conquer.

The day was spoiled for me; I partly blamed myself for it, though my plans had been to make the two little boys happy, but misery came instead. After supper I slipped away from my companions, and all alone I lay on the grass looking up at the stars, thinking of what had happened that afternoon. I tried to reconcile the act of Gray-beard with the teachings of the Missionaries, but I could not do so from any point of view.

All the boys had come together in the yard, and some one

called out, "Let's play pull." So they divided into two groups, grading each according to the size of the boys. Two of the strongest were selected, one from each side; they held a stout stick between them, then on each side the boys grasped each other around the waist. When all were ready, they began to pull, every boy crying, "Hue! Hue!" as he tugged and strained. In the dusk the contending lines looked like two great dark beasts tearing at each other and lashing their tails from side to side. Bob and Joe were at the very end of one side; Bob had tied a bit of rope around his waist, and Joe had hold of that with his only serviceable hand. The pulling lasted for quite a while; finally one side drew the other over the mark; the game ended, and the boys noisily disbanded.

"Frank! Frank!" I heard; it was Edwin and the rest of the "gang."

"Here I am," I called out, and they gathered around me.

"Joe's hand is awful swelled up," said Bob, as he threw himself down on the grass.

"What's the matter with him?" asked Warren.

"Gray-beard beat Joe's hand like everything; he was so mad I thought he'd kill the boy." Then I recounted the scene, adding, "I can't think of anything else; it was awful!"

"Did he do anything to you?" asked Edwin.

"He shook me right hard when he asked me who did it; but when he saw Joe crying he knew who it was; then he let go of me and whipped him."

Brush had been listening to my story without a word; now he arose and said, "Boys, stay here till I come back."

He went into the house and knocked at the superintendent's door.

"I'm glad to see you Brush," said the superintendent kindly. "Have you finished the book, and do you want another?"

"No, sir; I wish to speak to you about something that happened to-day, which I don't think is quite right, and I thought you ought to know about it." Then he told in a simple straightforward manner the story of Joe's punishment.

When Brush had finished, the superintendent sent for Gray-beard. For a long time the two men talked earnestly together. At length Brush returned, and said, as he took his seat among us:

"Boys, that will not happen again. Gray-beard says he's sorry he did it, and I believe him."

# 16

## The Break

"BRUSH! Brush! Brush!" I ran calling one morning soon after breakfast, down to the barn, to the spring, and back to the house, but I could not find the boy; then I thrust my fingers into my mouth and blew a loud robin call, and the answer came from under a tree up on the hillside. I ran hurriedly to the place; there lay Brush in the shade on the green grass reading.

The occasion of this excited search and call was the announcement by the superintendent that the school would be closed that day, and the children dismissed, so that they might go and see their parents, it being reported by an Indian who had come for his little girl that the people had just returned from the hunt.

"I been everywhere trying to find you," I said to Brush. "My folks have come home. Put that old book away and come go with me to see them. There isn't going to be any school to-day."

"Frank, it's right good of you to ask me, but I don't feel very well; I think I better not go," he replied, in a tone of disappointment. "All my bones ache, and I don't know what's the matter with me; but you go 'long, boy, and have a good time; you can tell me all about your visit when you come back."

"I'm sorry you can't go, Brush; but I'll come back soon and bring you some buffalo meat," I said, starting to go; "you better think about it again and come."

"I think I better stay home and be quiet," he answered, opening his book.

I spent all the forenoon with my parents, and in the afternoon I went in search of some of my village playmates. I found a number of them on the hillside shooting with their bows and arrows. They gave me a noisy welcome in mock English, which made me laugh heartily; then I had to wrestle with one or two of them, and when our peculiar greetings were over, the boys resumed their play, in which they let me join, one of them lending me his bow and arrows.

Our shooting from mark to mark, from one prominent object to another, brought us to a high hill overlooking the ripe fields of corn on the wide bottom below, along the gray Missouri. Here and there among the patches of maize arose little curls of blue smoke, while men and women moved about in their gayly-colored costumes among the broad green leaves of the corn; some, bending under great loads on their backs, were plodding their way laboriously to the fires whence arose the pretty wreaths of smoke.

"They're making sweet corn," exclaimed one of the youngsters whose little naked brown back glinted against

142

the afternoon sun, and he pointed to the workers in the field.

As we stood watching the busy, picturesque scene below us, one little fellow held his bow close to his ear and began strumming on the string, then all the rest played on their bows in the same manner, until one of them suddenly broke into a victory song, in which the others joined.

At the close of the song they gave me a graphic description of the attack on the camp when it was pitched on the Republican River. Although the enemy was repulsed, and the hunting ground secured to our people, the battle cost many lives, several of the enemy's warriors were left on the field, and the Omahas lost some of their bravest men.

While yet the boys were telling of the thrilling incidents of the battle, we arose with a sudden impulse and rushed down the hill with loud war-cries, as though attacking the foe, the tall grass snapping against our moccasined feet as we sped along. We were rapidly approaching a house which stood alone, when one of the older boys who was running ahead suddenly stopped and raised his hand as though to command silence. Immediately our shouts ceased, and, seeing the serious look on the lad's face, "What is it?" we asked in frightened tones as we gathered about him.

Without a word he pointed to a woman who was cutting the tall sunflower stalks that had almost hidden her little dwelling with their golden blossoms. Her long black hair flowed over her shoulders unbraided, a sign of mourning. Now and again she would pause in her work to look up at the humble home and utter sighs and sobs that told a tale of sorrow. Mingled with these outpourings of grief came often the words, "My husband! my little child!" with terms

143

of endearment and tenderness for which I can find no equivalent in English. On a blanket spread over the ground near by sat a tot of a child babbling to itself and making the beheaded sunflowers kiss each other, innocently oblivious of its mother's grief. It was a sad home-coming for the woman; the spirit of her husband had fled to the dark clouds of the west to join the host of warriors who had died on the field of battle, and his bones lay bleaching in the sands of a far-off country.

"It is Gre-don-ste-win weeping for her husband who was killed in the battle last summer," whispered the big boy; "let us go away quietly."

When we had withdrawn to a distance where we were sure our noise would not disturb the mourner, one of the boys called out, "Let's play Oo-hae′ba-shon-shon!" (Tortuous path.) Years after I learned that this game was played by the children of the white people, and that they called it, "Follow my leader."

We graded ourselves according to size, the biggest boy at the head as leader. Each one took hold of the belt of the boy in front of him, and then we started off at a rapid jog-trot, keeping time to this little song which we sang at the top of our voices.

## CHILDREN'S SONG
### "Follow my Leader"

Yo hay    yo ae    ha ra  o  ha

Ya hay  yo   ae     yo ha o ha.

Whatever the leader did, all were bound to do likewise. If he touched a post, we touched it too; if he kicked the side of a tent, all of us kicked it; so on we went, winding around the dwellings, in and out of vacant lodges, through mud puddles and queer, almost inaccessible places, and even entering the village, where we made the place ring with our song.

At last, tired out, the boys broke line and scattered to their homes. It was then that I suddenly realized the lateness of the hour, and remembered my promise to Brush. I ran to the house, took a hurried leave of my parents, picked up the package of buffalo meat my mother had prepared for my school-mate, and fairly flew over the hill between the village and the Mission.

As I came running down the hill to the school I saw Lester, Warren, and Edwin sitting in a row on the fence.

"Hello!" I shouted, "what you sitting on that fence for, like a lot of little crows?"

No answer came, nor did the boys move. I began to wonder if they were displeased with me, although I could not think of anything I had done to give them offence. As I drew near, I noticed that the expression on their faces indicated alarm rather than displeasure, and, becoming anxious in my turn, I hurriedly asked, "What's the matter; what's happened; where's Brush?"

The boys looked at one another, then at me; finally Lester replied, almost with a sob, "Brush is awful sick; he's been raising blood; they sent for the Doctor."

"Where is he? I must go see him," I said, springing over the fence, and starting toward the house.

"He's in that little room next the girls' play-room; but they won't let anybody see him," said Warren.

I went to the room in which Brush lay, and knocked very gently on the door. There was a rustling movement inside, then the door slowly opened and one of the lady teachers stood before me.

"What is it, Frank?" she asked in a low tone.

I tried to look over her shoulder to see the bed, but she was too tall. "I want to see Brush; can't I see him? They say he is sick. I want to see him a moment," I pleaded. "I'm just come back from the village, and brought some buffalo meat I promised him."

"No, Frank, you cannot see him," was the reply. "He is very sick. The superintendent is with him trying to relieve his suffering. Run away now," said the lady, stroking my bare head with her small hand. "Don't make any noise, and tell the rest of the boys to be very quiet."

I went away reproaching myself for not coming back from the village soon, as I told Brush I would. When I rejoined the boys, they looked anxiously into my face, and Edwin asked, "Did you see him?"

"No, they would not let me." After a pause, I asked, "When did he get sick; who was with him?"

"It was under the walnut-tree," said Lester; "he was reading to us about Joseph, out of his little black Bible he always carries. He began to cough hard and choke; he dropped the book all covered with blood, and took hold of my brother's arm. I ran to tell the superintendent. Just as they carried Brush into the house, Edwin came back and we told him about it."

In the evening, after the small boys had gone to bed, the doctor came, a tall gray-haired man. At the gate he was met by the superintendent, and the two walked slowly up the steps, talking earnestly. We four had been watching for the doctor on the porch; as he came along we caught now and then a word, but we did not understand its meaning. We judged by the shaking of the doctor's head that he thought Brush's case was serious.

Days passed; the doctor came and went; yet Brush's door was closed to us, nor had we any hopeful news of him. We missed him sadly; we missed his whittling, his harmless scolding; and our play was only half-hearted.

Indians who came to the school on business missed his ready offer to help. There was no one to take his place; no one who could interpret for them as well as he. Each one, as he went away, left a word of cheer for the lad, with expressions of hope for his recovery.

As school was dismissed one afternoon, the teacher gave special injunctions to the scholars not to make any noise as they passed out, or while moving about the house, so as not to disturb the sick boy. We four strolled toward the spring. Frost had come, and the leaves were beginning to turn red and yellow. Wild geese flew noisily overhead, fleeing from the coming winter to sunnier climes. While we were counting, as we often did, the gray birds, floating through the air like a great V, Warren suddenly exclaimed, "Say, boys, plums!"

We looked at him inquiringly. "Let's go get plums for Brush!" he continued excitedly. Then we remembered that we had pre-empted a small grove of choice plum bushes at the head of the ravine, as against all the boys of the school, and acquired a right in it which even the Big Seven respected.

Edwin ran to the kitchen and borrowed from one of the

cooks a small tin pail. We hurried to our orchard, where we saw no signs of trespass; the bushes were laden with beautiful ripe fruit. We filled the little pail with the choicest, then each one picked for himself. It was nearly supper-time when we appeared at Brush's door. The three boys looked at me; so I tapped very gently, and the teacher who was nursing the sick boy opened the door.

"We've brought some plums for Brush," I said, offering the tin pail.

"That's very nice," said the lady, softly; "I will give them to him." She was about to close the door, when I whispered, "Can we take just a little look at him?"

"Yes," she answered, throwing the door open.

We four leaned forward and looked in. A smile lit up Brush's face as he saw us. "How are you now?" I asked, in a loud whisper.

"I'm all right," he whispered back, although his hollow eyes and cheeks told a tale that stole away all our hopes. We withdrew, and the door was slowly closed.

Next morning as I was coming down from the dormitory I paused at Brush's door to listen. I heard footsteps moving about softly, then the door opened and one of the big girls came out with a white pitcher in her hand. I started to go on downstairs, when she called to me in a whisper, "Frank, go down to the spring and get some fresh water for Brush, will you, that's a good boy?"

I took the pitcher and went quietly downstairs. As soon as I was outside the yard, I ran as hard as I could to the spring, glad at the prospect of a chance to see my friend again. Warren and Lester met me as I was coming up the hill.

"Did you see him?" one of them asked.

"No, but I'm going to," I answered.

"Ask him if we can do anything for him?" said Lester.

Just as I reached the head of the stairs the same big girl appeared. I handed her the pitcher; she took it and was about to enter the room, when I caught her arm. "Just let me take a look at Brush, will you?" I whispered.

"No, Frank, I can't. Superintendent says to let nobody in."

I heard a cough, then a feeble voice say pleadingly, "Maria, let him in, just a minute!"

The girl looked cautiously around, then said to me, "Come, but don't let anybody see you. Don't stay long, be quick!"

I stepped in, and a thin hand was stretched out to receive me. "I can't talk much, I'm so weak," said Brush. Overcome with emotion, I could not speak but stood holding his hot hand. The girl at the door moved uneasily.

"Tell the boys I'm all right," said Brush. "They mustn't worry. Come nearer." I bent over him and he whispered, "To-night, when everybody is asleep, come down and see me. I want to talk to you when I'm alone."

As night came on we four sat under the walnut-tree watching Brush's window. A candle was lit, then the curtain was drawn. Below in the dining-room, the large girls moved quietly to and fro, busy with their evening work. When this was finished, they gathered at the door, and softly sang that beautiful hymn, "Nearer my God to Thee." We joined in the chorus, the wind wafting the words to the broad skies. The singing came to a close; the dining-room lights were put out, and we were called to bed.

149

As we knelt by the side of our beds to repeat the Lord's prayer, I could not keep back the tears that came, thinking of the emaciated little form that I was to see once more that night.

One by one the boys fell asleep, and I alone, among the forty or fifty in that big room, remained awake. The clock down in Gray-beard's room struck eleven; the only sounds that came to my ears were those of the heavy breathing of the boys, the soughing of the wind through the trees, the rushing of the waters in the river, and now and then the calls of the wild geese, migrating in the night.

The clock struck the hour of twelve; I sat up listening. There was a stir and the sound of a voice that startled me. It was only Warren moving and talking in his sleep. I went stealthily to the head of the stairs, then listened again. I could only hear the throbbing of my heart, and the rasping pulsations in my ears. After a pause which seemed interminable, I put one foot down the first step, the board sprang under my weight, and creaked. Again I paused to listen; there was no stir, and I went on. Every little sound in the stillness of the night seemed exaggerated, and I was often startled, but I went on and reached the door of Brush's room. I scratched the panel three times. There was a movement within, and a slight cough. Slowly I turned the knob and opened the door. I entered, closed the door, but left it unlatched.

A candle stood burning in the midst of a number of bottles on a little table near the head of the bed. I knelt by the bedside, and Brush put his arm around my neck. We were silent for a while, finally he whispered in the Omaha tongue:

"I'm glad you came; I've been wanting to talk to you. They tell me I am better; but I know I am dying."

Oppressed with ominous dread, I cried out, interrupting him, "Don't say that! Oh, don't say that!"

But he went on, "You mustn't be troubled; I'm all right; I'm not afraid; I know God will take care of me. I have wanted to stay with you boys, but I can't. You've all been good to me. My strength is going, I must hurry, — tell the boys I want them to learn; I know you will, but the other boys don't care. I want them to learn, and to think. You'll tell them, won't you?"

He slipped his hand under the pillow, brought out his broken-bladed jack-knife, and put it in my hand, then said, "I wish I had something to give to each one of the boys before I go. I have nothing in the world but this knife. I love all of you; but you understand me, so I give it to you. That's all. Let me rest a little, then you must go."

After a moment's stillness the door opened very gently, and the floor near it creaked as though there were footsteps. A breath of wind came and moved the flickering flame of the candle round and round. The boy stared fixedly through the vacant doorway. There was something strange and unnatural in his look as, with one arm still around me, he stretched the other toward the door, and, in a loud whisper, said, "My grandfather! He calls me. I'm coming, I'm coming!"

There was a sound as of a movement around the room; Brush's eyes followed it until they again rested upon the open door, which swung to with a soft click; then he closed his eyes.

I crept closer to the sick boy; I was quivering with fear.

151

Brush opened his eyes again, he had felt me trembling. "Are you cold?" he asked.

Just then I heard footsteps in the girls' play-room; this time they were real; Brush heard them too.

"Superintendent," he said with an effort.

When I crept into my bed the clock below struck one. For a long while I lay awake. I could hear noises downstairs, Gray-beard's door open and close, and the door of Brush's room. I heard a window raised, then everything became still.

We did not know how fondly we were attached to Brush, how truly he had been our leader, until we four, left alone, lingered around his grave in the shadowy darkness of night, each one reluctant to leave.

The Mission bell rang for evening service, and with slow steps we moved toward the school — no longer "The Middle Five."

# Coping in a Troubled Society

**An Environmental Approach to Mental Health**

**Marion R. Just**
Wellesley College

**Carolyn Shaw Bell**
Wellesley College

**Walter Fisher**
Elgin State Hospital

**Stephen L. Schensul**
Illinois State Psychiatric
   Institute

**Lexington Books**
D.C. Heath and Company
Lexington, Massachusetts
Toronto          London

**Library of Congress Cataloging in Publication Data**

Main entry under title:

Coping in a troubled society.

   1. Mental hygiene. 2. Stress (Psychology). 3. Mental health services.
I. Just, Marion. [DNLM: 1. Environment. 2. Mental health. WM100 C783]
RA790.C6818      362.2      74-13719
ISBN 0-669-95851-4

For Hal, Nelson, Irene
and Jean-Jessica

# Contents

# List of Figures

# List of Tables

# Preface

Chapters 2 through 5 of this volume evolved from earlier papers prepared by the authors for a study conference on "The Future of Mental Health," held in January 1974, under the sponsorship of the National Institute for Mental Health and San Francisco State College. While each writer benefited from the critical comments of other participants at that conference, the present chapters represent considerable rethinking and extensive revision along lines worked out by the four collaborators. We owe much, individually and collectively, to those friends who, from their several fields of expertise, have read various drafts and provided many helpful suggestions. We take responsibility, however, for any errors of commission and omission in this effort.

# 1

# An Environmental Approach to Mental Health

**Marion R. Just**

In *Civilization and its Discontents*, Sigmund Freud asks whether "systems of civilization—or epochs of it—possibly even the whole of humanity—have become 'neurotic' under the pressure of civilizing trends."[1] That diagnosis seems particularly apt, here and now. Certainly there is a widespread feeling among Americans that life is becoming more difficult to live. A large segment of society believes "something is deeply wrong" and that, in the face of affluence, the "quality of American life" has deteriorated. People cite inflation, crime, drugs, pollution, taxes, and political scandals as examples of this deterioration. Americans are concerned not only with "making ends meet," but with "making it." A significant percentage of them find the day-to-day pressure of their lives a "real problem."[2] For many, the mechanics of living have long ceased to be simple, and coping with life has become a serious business.

One response to the anxiety of today's living is a nostalgia for a simpler time. In film, literature, and fashion, Americans romanticize hard times and rural life. It is difficult, however, to judge whether or not the stress of contemporary living is greater than in previous periods such as the Great Depression or World War II.

It is also not certain that the tension of life in this country is greater than in less developed countries like India or Chile. Cross-cultural comparisons of mental health are fraught with hazard. National standards and attitudes toward mental illness vary widely; note, for example, the Soviet diagnostic criterion of "deviation from the socialist reality." The mere admission of emotional strain is less culturally acceptable in some societies than in others, and the recognition of anxiety appears to depend on certain kinds of education and knowledge. It would be precarious, therefore, to compare the perceived level of anxiety in the United States, where awareness of psychological stress must be almost universal, to that of, say, Hungary, which has the world's highest suicide rate. Even within American society itself, it is difficult to make interpersonal comparisons of emotional strain. Is the minimum-wage worker who can't properly house and clothe his family more anxious than the harried executive who faces a production deadline? Who is under more strain, the rebellious adolescent or his heartsick parents?

Given the difficulty, therefore, in substantiating cross-cultural, cross-epochal, and even cross-personal comparisons of mental well-being, it would be presumptuous to maintain that our current level of anxiety is greater than in other times

1

and places. The anxiety itself, however, is undeniable; its symptoms can scarcely be overlooked. Consider, for example, the rates of alcoholism, drug abuse, job absenteeism, and heart attacks in the United States. But these do not identify a single cause. Our society may be breeding a particularly anxious lot of individuals; on the other hand, the structuring of our society may make a lot of individuals anxious.

Until some hard evidence turns up in psychogenetics, it will be useful to investigate external causalities. After all, some statistical evidence, such as suicide rates, supports sociological causation. Our hypothesis in this book is that the structure of modern life makes it painful for many people to cope. We further suggest that the forces that strain all of us strain some people to the psychological breaking point, that is, to mental illness.

The American Mental Health Association announced recently that as many as four out of every ten Americans suffer from some form of mental illness. One implication, of course, is that many Americans should be receiving help. But if the figure of 40 percent is staggering in terms of numbers who suffer, it is unthinkable in terms of giving care. It may only be fantasy, but useful fantasy, to compute the percentage of the gross national product required for providing a weekly hour of psychotherapy to those eighty million Americans. How many thousands of psychologists, psychiatrists, psychiatric social workers, ministerial counselors, etc. would have to be employed to give that minimal therapy? How many million people would accept and use that therapy if it were offered to them? Such calculation leads inevitably to a declaration of bankruptcy, on the part of psychotherapy, for public mental health.

But since psychotherapy is the dominant mode of treatment, it is equally inevitable that until now American society has cared only for the most desperate of the mentally ill and for the most wealthy. Therapy for the well-to-do is traditionally supplied in costly one-to-one encounters between middle- or upper-class patients and highly trained professionals. Among the working class and the poor only the direst psychological casualties find their way into publicly supported mental institutions. Those with less acute troubles receive no care—unless or until their problems impinge on society. Treatment for the poor occurs only if their problems translate into behavior that is a nuisance or a menace to others. One might think that as long as only the most acute cases among the poor are being treated, the wider problem would not be apparent. But even acute cases have proliferated. In the late 1950s in the United States, the number of individuals committed to mental hospitals was so great that treatment became impossible for the overwhelming majority of patients. Only the advent of chemotherapy in the treatment of mental disease alleviated the institutionalized population explosion. In Chapter 5, Fisher describes the decline of overburdened mental hospitals in general and the psychoanalytic modality in particular.

Both the costly dyadic therapy and the institutional psychotherapeutic approach are based on the premise that the root causes of maladjustment lie in intrapsychic processes. It is apparent, however, that in many instances the causes of aberrant feelings or behaviors may be external to the individual. It is noteworthy that Freud himself regarded not only the psyche, but the individual's environment and life-tasks, as possible sources of psychosis. Psychotherapy, however, does little to improve an individual's skills or resources for coping with his environment. The onset of therapy is marked by the "patient's" admission of "illness." The process of psychotherapy then tends to establish a dependent relationship between the expert provider of care and the recipient. By defining the problem as endogenous, the patient who accepts his illness also absolves society of responsibility for the condition. In this way, psychotherapy treats the individual's failure to cope, while it excludes society's failure to supply the means for coping.

It should be noted that traditional psychotherapy has devoted scant attention to public mental health. Consequently, the public benefits of psychotherapy have also been modest. An alternative approach, however, has emerged alongside the dominant psychotherapeutic model. "Human service" therapy shifts the emphasis from intrapsychic inquiry to the social milieu. This approach to mental health involves not only mental health professionals but economists, anthropologists, political scientists, and sociologists. This human service approach provides the major thrust of this book.

The human service model focuses on the impact of social institutions, cultural expectations, and cultural behavioral modification patterns on the individual. The theoretical orientations of Lewin (1935) and Skinner (1971) are more relevant to the human service approach than the orientation of Freud and the other intraorganismic theorists. In this mode, deviance and alienation are considered expressions of the pattern of society. The alleged schizophrenics, criminals, or economic failures are, after all, as indigenous to the society as good students, successful businessmen, or policemen. While our society is built around the normal distribution curve, the fallouts from that distribution are extremes of success and extremes of failure. This brings us to the key theme of the book: Where and how society intervenes in aiding those individuals designated as deviant, alienated, and or failures? One perspective views deviance as a disease of the individual that can be eradicated through "treatment" or with a "medicine." The opposite perspective sees the individual's problems purely as a function of society's failures. From this point of view, the individual is relieved of personal responsibility and the solution is sought in political, economic, or social activity.

The human service model relates to both perspectives. It does not ignore the importance of changing the inner person by intraorganismic therapies. However, this approach sensitizes the caregiver to aiding the individual by altering his life space. Human service therapy can be labeled "treatment through institutional change." It is assumed that through this process clients are provided with new "modules of experience" that allow them to grow. The human service worker becomes a problem-solver who involves himself with this process by identifying the appropriate structures for individual development.

The authors of this volume share a common interest in the human service model. They are convinced that the malfunctioning of American society today produces tensions and stress that pose a constant and generalized threat to everyone's mental health.

Innovation in mental health gained momentum about a decade ago, when the federal government began to explore programs to reduce the high cost of institutionalization and to equalize the distribution of mental health services. The Community Mental Health Centers Act of 1962 attempted to develop a new structure for public mental health services. It designed a network of over seven hundred community mental health centers to give access to psychiatric treatment to people of limited means. These centers were to strike at the external causes of mental illness by attacking the negative aspects of the local environment. Psychiatric personnel, working with community residents, would establish programs of preventive care, while the centers provided treatment for those already in need. Hence, the community mental health movement, described in Chapters 4 and 5, committed the federal government to provide resources for the service of poor and marginal groups in the society.

Within a few years (by the late 1960s) the new community health network met with mounting criticism. Few significant changes in mental health institutions had occurred. Little progress was made in developing new treatment modalities. The centers were underutilized, and above all, they were ineffective in changing the social environment. This failure is really not very surprising in view of the essential continuity of personnel between the old and new schemes for mental health. The community mental health movement was a good idea that went wrong in practice. It aimed at narrowing the gap between the troubled poor and the troubled rich by sharing the rich man's psychotherapy with the poor. But in attempting to write "high-quality" care into the program, the legislators had locked community health into the psychotherapeutic model. The training of psychiatrists and psychologists directed them toward treating the "sick" and not toward solving social problems at the community level. It was this latter condition, it is argued in Chapters 4 and 5, which prevented community mental health centers from making any impression on the environment. Furthermore, the stigma of psychiatric service actually discouraged access, particularly for the poor. Finally, community mental health legitimized the underlying assumption of psychotherapy: the sick individual can become well only by conforming to a "healthy" society's pattern.

What was innovative in the community mental health program was its recognition that it is useful to care for people within their own environments. But even this innovation implies that the community is well and healthy and that the individual is sick. This may not be the case. Some people who have problems coping with life could be helped by satisfying work, a private place to live, enough or better food, or perhaps just a vacation from their problems. Chapters 2 through 5 argue that public mental health may be more efficiently achieved by changing social milieus rather than intervening in numerous individual psyches.

In this volume the authors call for a broader approach to mental health, one that includes exogenous as well as endogenous factors and which encompasses the functioning as well as dysfunctioning members of the society. If some critical component of stress can be identified as external, then efforts at palliation must logically include externalia. Treatment cannot consist solely of inducing resignation to one's environment. In helping individuals with their living problems, treatment can better prepare people to cope with, and even to change, their environment. That is to say, treatment should be educational.

The education we are concerned with consists of learning about the external environment, about society, about the political, economic, and social structures of the local and national communities. People can become less anxious through an understanding of the forces that affect their lives. Merely identifying the external factors can relieve people of *self*-doubt, of fear that they themselves are wholly and utterly responsible for their condition. Furthermore, "knowing" individuals can better control the environment in which they function.

There is ample evidence that the more educated strata of the population feel more efficacious in dealing with external problems. College graduates, for example, participate more actively in politics than the less educated. They also participate more confidently and with greater faith in effecting changes. But one need not go to college to feel politically efficacious. People who actually participate in politics tend to feel efficacious, no matter what their level of education. Experience itself is a good teacher. On the other hand "book learning" is probably the least effective way to convey what experience teaches. The success of experiential learning for community action has been demonstrated by the late Saul Alinsky and other community organizers. For many people, however, experience in the world of work, community, or politics tend to mystify rather than to enhance their understanding. The communal experiences that aim at teaching people to cope must be organized to overcome the negative and fearful experiences of the past. Experiential learning must build hierarchically on successful efforts. The need for ordering such experiential educational was demonstrated quite forcefully in national politics a few years ago. The young people who flocked to the McCarthy presidential campaign in 1968 become the apathetic students of 1972. Their frustration at losing politics' highest stakes alienated many students altogether. If these students had had a greater appreciation of American political structures and their dynamics, however, they might have been able to cope with short-term defeat. As for disadvantaged groups in the society, experiential learning may be the crucial second chance for learning to cope with their life circumstances.

Teaching people how to cope with their external environment provides an eminently transferable skill. For example, by learning how to cope with the bureaucracy of the welfare system, people can learn to deal with the bureaucracy of Social Security, educational establishments, the army, or even mental health institutions. Successful coping with external structures can also be transferred inwardly. Competency even for simple tasks tends to enhance optimism, to lighten depression, and to increase activity. In fact, the positive effects of goal attainment are more evident than positive effects of intrapsychic inquiry. Furthermore, learning about one's environment is not at all marked by the cultural stigma of psychotherapy. Experiential learning need not be reserved only to the desperately anxious, but can be made widely available to all those who seek it.

Finally, teaching people to cope with the environment can be considerably more economical than mass psychotherapy. A program of communal experiential learning can be socially efficient in many ways. First of all, it requires only a few highly trained instigators. Larger numbers of teachers and researchers can be generated from within the community itself. The New Mental Health Careers and Community Mental Health programs have demonstrated the relative ease and economy with which such training can take place. (See Chapter 4 for a description of these programs.) In the end, communal learning programs can be entirely self-sufficient in both research and teaching. The benefits from such low-cost programs are considerable: the community gains skilled personnel; the community has increased capacity to deal with new problems as they arise; troubled individuals have increased resources to turn to within the community; and, most important, the community can manipulate the environment so as to remove or alleviate common problems.

The implications for mental health care should be clearly understood. The national debate over health insurance has been underway for some time, and in 1974 was formally engaged in both houses of Congress. It is useful to keep in mind that a national health program has only recently become acceptable as an item on our national agenda. True, Medicare and Medicaid may be thought of as the first steps toward national health insurance. It seems fairly clear, however, that it was their failures which precipitated the call for further action. The enormous cost of these first steps and the resulting increases in the costs of private health care made national health insurance a public concern. Medicare and Medicaid were superimposed on an existing system of medical services with little planning for their impact. The existing methods of producing and distributing medical care were taken for granted; and the new programs were not seen as creating additional (and new) demands. It would be tragic if the debate over a national health program fell into a similar error of miscalculation. The omission, to date, of mental health care from most proposals for a national health scheme is significant.

To write a comprehensive medical care program, including mental health care, for everyone in this country would be to write in water. No program based on the present structure of mental health services and delivery could be carried out. Consciously or unconsciously aware of this, the designers of national health programs have so far omitted mental health from their plans. But if mental health can itself be reexamined, then facilities and programs to provide mental health care may be devised that do not depend on the present structure of services and delivery. (They may also be more effective, as Chapters 4 and 5 in this volume suggest.) Consequently, a comprehensive national health program, including mental health, might be written on a scale at once both larger and smaller. Larger because it would not omit this area of people's well-being, but smaller because the medical sector would be relieved of the sole responsibility for helping people to feel better.

This book grew out of a conference the writers attended, where they discovered the common convictions and concerns sketched above. As social scientists they share a common perception of the relationships between a malfunctioning society and the diminution of mental health. Bell, as an economist, analyzes some of the more disturbing phenomena of our socioeconomic structure. She calls for a better understanding of those structures as a prerequisite to change. Using data on political alienation, Just, a political scientist, tests the hypothesis that society contributes to individual anxiety. These two papers stress that an understanding of social problems can itself be reassuring to people. Because understanding enables people to feel control over their situation, the political scientist and the economist argue for less "expertise" and more "do-it-yourself" action.

Fisher echoes this emphasis in his paper. As a staff psychologist and institutional administrator, he approaches the theme of social change from a conviction that conventional mental institutions have failed. He suggests that the individual who is seriously ill can become healthier by gaining some control over his environment. To the patient in a mental hospital, this may mean reducing the barriers between patient, staff, and support personnel as well as between the institution and society.

Schensul's paper in many ways links the other three to common convictions and concerns. An anthropologist by training, Schensul was the director of a community mental health research program. Like Fisher, he too views control of environment as a significant factor in individual and social development. Schensul studies the impact of social change on those who effect change. His conclusions support the belief, implicit in both Bell's and Just's papers, that the ills of society are remediable and that the public interest includes public efforts and public actions.

Parallels can be drawn between the community of Fisher's state hospital, the urban community served by Schensul's research group, the national political culture described in Just's paper, and the overlapping and sometimes conflicting economic concerns described by Bell. Each of the studies explores an aspect of the concept of knowledge as power.

The authors hope that this volume will broaden the outlook of mental health planners by introducing the perspectives of social science. The authors also hope to introduce the discussion of mental health to those disciplines of social science that have not grappled with this problem. For those engaged in mental health services, this book aims to bring some understanding of how a society itself can be said to be ill. Once we realize that we cannot institutionalize a sick society, perhaps we can change our social institutions to make us well.

**Notes**

1. Sigmund Freud, *Civilization and its Discontents* (New York: W.W. Norton, 1961), p. 91.

2. See the report by Louis Harris to the Subcommittee on Intergovernmental Relations of the Committee on Government Operations of the United States Senate, *Confidence and Concern: Citizens View American Government, A Survey of Public Attitudes* (U.S. Government Printing Office, December 1973), parts 1 and 2.

# 2  A Sane Economy for a Sane People

**Carolyn Shaw Bell**

By nature I am not a builder of utopias and by training I am a marginalist, one who thinks in terms of small, but not unimportant changes. To think about moving from our present economy to one that is utterly sane offends both these predispositions of mine, and I take refuge, therefore, in reversing the approach. On the surface, certain aspects of our present economy, in my opinion, do not appear wholly sane: they may threaten, therefore, the mental health of the population. These observations stem from original research whose methodology does not take long to describe. It consists of merely thinking twice—and noticing that irrationalities crop up when one attempts (as most economists do most of the time) to analyze what is going on in the economy. It takes a modicum of sensitivity—really only putting one's mind to it—to discover what seems to be economic insanities. Let me describe two.

In Hawaii, relief programs have been expanded, yet costs have declined. How? By using welfare clients who have freely volunteered their services. They work as clerical aides, receptionists, child care aides, translators, interpreters, and groundskeepers. "In the past five months," says an administrator, "they have given more than 13,000 hours to public welfare service. If we had to pay for this, it would cost the state more than $32,000 in salaries."[1] What sense does this make? People become eligible for welfare payments when they can't earn incomes. But these welfare "volunteers" are working and provide useful services. Why not pay them wages and get them off welfare?

Another example concerns eighty-five-year-old Isaac Tabor, who voluntarily returned to prison after completing a twelve-year sentence because he couldn't cope with life on the outside. He can't read or write, and during his exile, society grew sufficiently complex to make it impossible for him to survive without such skills. Now he's eager to help those of his fellow prisoners who, like him, are illiterate, and so he's established a program to hire teachers and buy instructional materials. The $7500 he's spent so far came from his Social Security checks. Think of the nonsense implied here. A jail sentence effectively removed this elderly man from the world permanently. Even with retirement pay he couldn't be at home outside. But during the time he spent in jail his Social Security checks accumulated and now provide the resources to enable him to help others, so that they will be able to grapple with a situation defeating him.

These two situations jar the professional framework within which most

9

economists operate, because economists rarely feel comfortable dealing with questions of social values. Many would deny that economics can contribute anything to the larger questions of how society, as opposed to the economy, functions. If I say, therefore, that Isaac Tabor and the Hawaiian welfare setup are symptoms of economic insanity, I state my personal judgment; pure economic analysis does not lead to such a conclusion. Yet more and more economists are becoming concerned with the impact of such problems on society.[2] The aim of this chapter is not only to develop some understanding of the circumstances that give rise to economic anomalies but to suggest changes in those circumstances.

## Economic and Emotional Disequilibrium

Economics can impinge on people's mental welfare at two levels. On the one hand, economic forces shape individual circumstances. On the other, individuals need a working knowledge of "the economic facts of life" to achieve equanimity. Both processes can engender personal strain. People need emotional as well as intellectual strengths to deal with unsolved (or unsolvable) problems in their lives. If economic irrationalities add to these anxieties, then the demands on people's psychic resources may be overwhelming. The individual whose life is directly affected by some species of economic irrationality suffers a multiple threat to his security. Along with the dramatic loss of income or other economic welfare, but perhaps more complex, can be the injury to self-confidence, independence, or even personal identity.

A familiar example is forced retirement at sixty-five, the typical experience in this country. Economists can measure quite precisely the loss of productive potential from people willing to work but forbidden the opportunity. Economists can design programs of Social Security benefits, private pensions, welfare, and other schemes so that income remains available after the ability to earn income has been taken away. But in many cases such people suffer not so much a loss of income as a loss of dignity; the injury is not so much to their financial worth as to their feeling worth while; they have been deprived not of purchasing power but of power to control their personal lives. "Among 65-year-old male pension beneficiaries who were not employed in July-December 1968, the major reason for leaving the last job was mandatory retirement . . . and though two-fifths of all mandatory retirees reported that they wanted to quit working, three-fifths would have liked to continue."[3] Economists know vaguely about these things but have so far allowed analysts from politics and psychology to dwell on their impact. A human services approach to mental health may help to change the attitudes of social scientists. Then, perhaps, people's psychological and emotional reaction to economic programs may have some effect in shaping policy.

Besides its threat to individual security, the surrounding economy troubles people by its apparent mysteries. The amount of emotion aroused by economic controversies frequently seems excessive. It often reflects, however, a fear of the unknown, the threat to inner security that comes from uncertainty. But much of this unknown quality can be removed. Economists themselves have not been very helpful, so far, in demystifying their field; educating the public does not rank high among their concerns. Equally irresponsible, of course, is the economist who claims the experts are also mystified. In fact, the chief economic source of psychological tension in this country exists not because economic problems exist but because people don't understand the simple mechanics of how the economy is put together. Even those who condemn "the system" frequently lack the basic economic understanding to build a new one.

Certain economic phenomena bother people today, to the point of evoking strong inner feelings of personal resentment or rage, feelings of helplessness or deprivation. This chapter attempts to analyze common elements of many stressful economic situations, on the grounds that we can better handle our feelings when we can define our problems, even if we can't solve them. Economic developments have challenged so many basic values and beliefs that our ideas of what is good, what is progress, what is approved of appear irrelevant. Economic circumstances require people to cope with a new view of economic growth and new attitudes toward children, with conflicting prescriptions about work and dismaying reports about education. Nor can these questions of economic growth, of population, of work, and of education be given the attention they need while people are troubled with a deep, nagging anxiety about money, about credit, or about rising prices. Although other economic issues can be cited, each of those listed currently threaten people's stability as human beings. Stability, as a desideratum in economics, isn't much compared to growth and development, and physical and mental health also require growth and development. But focusing on stability and equilibrium makes the impact of economic issues on individuals more apparent. A sane economy may therefore be defined as one in which economic events do not upset people too much.

## Economic Growth: Its Frustration, Our Resentment

The current controversy over economic growth arouses intense emotional reaction in many people. Curiously, none of the no-growth proselytizers has dealt with its emotional impact; but for that matter neither has any advocate of growthsman ship. The controversy disturbs people on two levels, as individuals and as members of a society.

Throughout the economic and political history of this country aggregate growth has been synonymous with progress. From Paul Bunyan to Babbitt, those who boast of America talk of bigger and better and faster and more powerful. Samuel Gompers stated labor's demands, almost a century ago, in one word that still holds true: "More."[4] American parents have always wanted their children to be better off than they have been: a better job, a nicer house, fewer financial straits, a college education—in short, *more*. Now, within a very short space of time, perhaps two or three years, the concept of growth, of more, has changed from good to bad. For two centuries we have turned to growth for solutions, or pseudosolutions, to problems of poverty and income. If they take economic growth away from us, what have we got left?

In the international sphere the push to slow down or stop growth appears to the less developed countries as a hypocritical means of preserving the existing economic disparities among people in different parts of the world. Those in rich countries, who know that economic growth has brought them wealth, has reduced the grinding misery of their poor, and has averted, in some ways, internal strife and dissension, nevertheless urge others to abjure economic growth. Pious urgings from the rich to avoid the environmental destruction inherent in increased production might be more credible if they were accompanied by any concrete offers to share the wealth. Those in poor countries have learned the success story of economic growth as well as their richer neighbors. They have ample reason to resist worldwide cooperation aimed at accommodating nature at their expense.[5] Poorer countries may also resort to blackmail as a weapon to gain some more equitable distribution of existing riches. Countries with crucial reserves of mercury, cobalt, tungsten, and other ingredients essential to the industrialized processes of the wealthy developed countries may learn to stage an even more suspenseful drama than the recent cliffhanger about oil. Ironically, the critics of economic growth, by spotlighting those resources that they see imposing absolute limits to growth within a relatively short period of time, have revealed to the owners of those resources a powerful tool for hastening their own economic growth. It should also be noted that much of the pressure for conservation, preservation of natural shorelines, and the like actually represents a call for increased economic growth. The conservationists wish a rising growth rate in their own sector. The output *they* value—privacy in public parks, land devoted to wilderness, available fishing and swimming in natural waters—these things have not been increasing, while the output of everything else has been going up.[6]

As on the international scene, the arguments for no-growth mean, for individuals, a block to the aspirations of the have-nots and a denigration of the achievements of the haves. Clearly, emotional reactions take place when one's personal goals—moving to an air-conditioned, appliance-laden house, buying a second car, going round the world on retirement—must not only be abandoned but can be blamed for contributing to environmental problems. How do people feel when their personal goals, which used to be universal goals, now come under fire as antisocial? During the fifties more college-educated families began having larger families, and this was generally taken to be progress; it could only result in a "better" population, brighter, more ambitious, and more productive.[7] What is the impact, on a couple with six children, of the message that overpopulation has caused most of our grief and that the ideal number of children is two? How do parents handle their feelings about themselves and their children, when their ideas of progress come in for criticism that hits home? If more is not better and nobody knows what is better, can we find emotional equilibrium by asking, "*Is there a better? Is the concept of progress a delusion?*"

It is possible to conceive of various reactions to the proponents of no-growth, whom Solow has called the "prophets of doom."[8] First is resignation: Yes, the world is coming to an end, and there isn't anything we can do about it. Next, a serious attempt (like Solow's) to analyze the prophecy and put the prophets into a better perspective. Neither of these, however, expresses the bitter resentment that no-growth arouses in people. It is not inappropriate to remember the ancients who slew the messenger bringing bad news: if we can't murder Forrester, the Meadows, and Commoner, some other outlet for rage would be useful.

From this point of view, the unpopularity of environmentalists appearing in the wake of the oil crisis may very well be healthy. The opposition has become more than voluble. The current hostility may be a measure of the resentment that had earlier been suppressed, when pollution was truly a dirty word. Proposals to repeal environmental controls, the failure of environmentalists to defeat or even postpone the Alaskan pipeline, requests to repeal measures that benefited the environment at the expense of higher energy use—every day new examples occur in the trade-off between energy use and environmental protection. And they frequently come with "ecology-be-damned" epithets or ill-concealed glee at having gotten rid of uncalled for interference in the usual way of doing business. At a conference the author attended, she asked a group of assorted businessmen about their experiences with current shortages: they listed plastics, fertilizers, copper, newsprint, cotton textiles, and Mason jars, before mentioning fuel. When asked about the causes of particular supply problems, they blamed the "environmentalists" and the "no-growth guys" for each and every one of these shortages, and more than one executive spoke bitterly about the "shortsighted dreamers" and "dumb birdlovers" who almost wrecked the economy.

It is not clear, however, that merely venting one's rage achieves much in the way of positive comprehension of economic realities. But to put the notion of spaceship earth, with human beings at the helm, above the controversial acrimony of growth/no-growth allows feelings of responsibility and control to replace helpless resentment. It is true that the total resources at our disposal, including the land and its mines, water, soil, and atmosphere, are finite. What is lacking are the linkages between this appreciation of our finite heritage and its implications for any local problem of community or person. Whether it be a vote on building an oil refinery near a beach or a family dispute about recycling soft drink bottles, people need to relate the individual, microcosmic responsibility to what looks like an aggregate, macrocosmic error.

When these issues can be explored, at length and sometimes at leisure, people arrive at a better understanding of the competing demands on the limited resources available. On a local scale, one can argue the merits—and the ecology—of cutting down a tree to improve one's lawn or letting it stand to shade one's own and a neighbor's porch. Within a neighborhood people can cope with the battle between preserving a historic commercial area and building better housing for large families with low incomes. At the community level, conflict over zoning a swampland tract can pit demands for recreational space against the needs of preserving a river basin. Solving such problems requires that people consider their basic values, which is, after all, the only way to solve the ultimate question: How shall we divide up what we've got? By doing this, they may bring about the massive public support needed for concrete actions to change the conditions of economic growth.

## Zero Population Growth: Recrimination and Guilt

One sector of the no-growth lobby, population specialists, has aroused especially strong feelings. ZPG, aiming for not more than two children per family, to say nothing of NON (the newer organization supporting the decision to remain childless), arouses intense opposition on religious or moral grounds for some; that population can also be an economic problem is even more disturbing for others.

Economists have long thought of population as a kind of natural resource, like land or fishing banks or a tourist attraction of sandy beaches or the Grand Canyon. Children constitute "exogenous factors," a term economists prefer to "a little bundle from heaven," but one whose meaning is the same. Natural resources, and by analogy the size of the population, stay relatively unaffected by economic happenings in the short run, so that economics lacks a viable theory about population growth or nongrowth: most economists think that people have children more for noneconomic than economic reasons, and that having children remains a highly personal decision.

Public policy has also reflected a similar outlook: legislators and others who draft social policy measures think in terms of families and make automatic adjustments for the number of children. The federal income tax law and those of several states allow a flat dollar deduction for each dependent, most commonly a child. The deduction is automatically allowed for any number of children. Public housing rules, school lunch programs, the calculation of need for welfare assistance or for college scholarships—they all follow the same procedure of automatically allowing for family size, as if having children were totally beyond the control of parents, as if there were no *choice* involved. But the proponents of ZPG insist that we accept the realities that choice does and must exist. And their insistence also means that the choice is economic.

To consider people's offspring in terms of economic choice offers the alternative of defining children as current consumption or investment for the future. We may agree that most elements of current consumption, the satisfaction or pleasure or entertainment children provide, go to the parents, while the investment return, the productive output and social contributions yielded when young people enter the adult world, accrues to society. For economics has begun to look at children and young people in terms of the investment in human capital represented by schooling, preventive medicine, public health programs, and the like.[9] To speak of "investment" implies that the current cost of these efforts can be calculated in relation to their future payoff in healthier, more productive people. And the logical next step is to calculate how many human beings we should invest in.

From such thinking we come to the inevitable realization that parents do not, in any circumstance, entirely pay for their children. Social costs as well as social benefits cluster around young people; hence, we are gradually, and painfully, coming to regard children as endogenous to the economy. This kind of thinking supports the argument that having children involves economic choice, just like deciding to buy a second car or choosing between natural gas and electricity for household utilities. Nor need we single out the pill or the increase of women in the labor force for particular attention in this matter, although a subsidiary and bothersome choice-problem arises from our awareness that childbearing and childrearing can be separated. But to accept the notion that children need *not* be totally exogenous means to face the conflicts possible between parents' choosing to have children and society's choosing to support them or, if you like, to invest in them.

Not all these conflicts have yet been identified: probably the clearest manifestation so far consists of grumblings or outright rebellion by taxpayers against increased expenditures for local schools. At the state level the conflict accounts for the contrasting financial problems of public and private institutions of higher learning. Despite efforts to raise tuition at state colleges and universities, the differential between attending a local public institution and one that is privately endowed may be anywhere from $1000 to $4000 yearly. As this differential has widened, more families whose children might have applied to private institutions find the public system a thoroughly satisfactory substitute. As a result, private colleges with declining enrollment face imminent or eventual insolvency, while both enrollment and costs rise inexorably at public colleges. Taxpayers asked to expand the system, to provide new residences, parking lots, and other services for the growing student body, find no clear rationale for limiting the number of students nor any rational argument to oppose the dictum that Education Is a Good Thing.

But people do have strong feelings. Some have protested that the taxpayer could help maintain existing private institutions and require them to offer space for additional students, rather than expand the public sector. Their proposal arouses emotional references to state control as a threat to academic freedom or the constitutional separation of church and state. Others charge pampering in state schools and urge that tuition be raised or at least be based on ability to pay. But this prompts an equally emotional invocation of the right to higher education and the American tradition of free public schooling. Neither argument reaches the heart of the controversy, which is whether children should be supported publicly or privately. The supporters of ZPG or NON force people to recognize this unsolved dilemma, which is probably one reason why so many react defensively or with hostility. It is one thing to argue population growth as a kind of abstract question like foreign exchange rates; it is another thing to have the abstraction brought home in terms of one's own children.

The systems of financial aid to education can impose various burdens of guilt on children and their families. For example, when a student applies for financial aid, the family files a confidential form containing data on income, assets and liabilities, family members or claimants, and so on. Each college or university then calculates what is called "need," using the same basic data but not necessarily the same formula. What happens to the young person whose father refuses to file such information? Or whose father, although earning a six-figure income, refuses to pay because he disapproves of his children's life style? Most privately endowed schools treat such students as independent individuals, whose own financial statement provides the data to calculate need. At what point does this acceptance of nonsupport by parents apply to *all* students? At what point do children become independent adults? To state the same thing in a personal way: How much of what your offspring costs will you shift to society and how much will you bear yourself?

People display various emotional responses to the problems involved. More than one financial aid officer has nightmares about families abandoning, *en masse*, their present habit of willingly providing financial information. After all, if right now some students get aid and others don't simply because some families refuse to file returns while others do, does that make economic sense? More to the point, what's to prevent everyone from demanding the same kind of treatment?

Some people distrust the system, like the "needy" parents who see their son's classmate not only receiving financial aid but enjoying a spring cruise. They resent not only the apparent inequity but their own honesty, which they may come to see as gullibility. Yet if they subsequently decide to omit an income increase from their next financial statement ("just to make things even!"), they may confront a load of guilt feelings far more troublesome than their former disgust with others or with the system. And financial problems trouble some students precisely because their families are involved: they worry not only about maintaining or increasing their own contributions but about the added burden to their parents and the limitation on opportunities for younger brothers and sisters. In general, it is probably true that children and their families have difficulties enough in coming to terms with each other without the additional tensions caused by economic conflict.

In order to cope with these feelings, a straightforward explanation of the economics involved will be in order. Under our present system, society bears the costs of education. Public schools in this country are not free, but their services are available at zero prices.[10] The distinction is crucial, for in education, as elsewhere, the basic question is how to divide a limited supply of resources. Because society bears the costs, society has the right to decide, and has decided (although not always consistently) what kind of education to provide and how much of it to whom. Aside from this contribution to raising children, society has assumed other costs: welfare and Medicaid, school lunch programs, youth centers, and so on. What is the same thing, society has shifted more and more resources to this area of caring for young people and their human growth and development. But total resources are limited, and so other demands for their use arise. The taxpayers express this conflict by protesting that taxes are too high; the economist points out that higher taxes are merely the monetary expression of a larger share of scarce resources being diverted from other things people want and need.

In general there are two ways to economize the use of scarce resources or, what is the same thing, to minimize costs. One is cutting back the kinds of services; the other is limiting the numbers of those who receive the service. For example, a local school district may reduce extracurricular activities like music or photography, or it may raise the kindergarten age from four-and-a-half to five. So far, with respect to services for children and young people, the overall movement has been to expand, rather than to cut back, the quantity and diversity of programs offered. The question arises, at what point will this lead to limiting participation in these programs?

It is here that we find the intimate connection between social costs and population control. There may be a point at which it is said: "No more than two children per family, if families get public care for their children." Added to this is the threat of population growth. If society must figure *excess* population as an additional cost over and above what it takes to maintain a given number of people, then society may look for ways to minimize total social costs.

The distinction between private and social costs is well understood in terms of the polluter and the public.[11] The private firm pouring wastes into the river gains by shifting the costs of waste disposal onto those members of the public downstream who lose, by being unable to fish or swim. The economist's solution to this conflict calls for shifting the social costs back to the private polluter. By analogy, the private decision to have a child imposes costs on the public if it is to support that child with school, library, recreation and transportation facilities, supplemented if need be by health and income provisions. In this case, how far does the economist's remedy of shifting social costs back to the private procreator apply? Evidently the emerging controversies about expanding education and other services for young people stems from an unconscious awareness of this question. And the answer, of course, is that children represent both private and social costs and benefits: their existence cannot be solely a matter of public policy, but neither can it any longer be utterly reserved to individual decision.

Working out the demands on society that will follow the birth of a child (including the possibility that society may have to take over entire support) should lead any potential parents to more acceptable decisions. And continuous scrutiny of the boundary between parental and societal responsibility can only be a functional attitude for all. The twin feelings of guilt for one's own actions and/or recrimination for those of others can be squarely faced. Instead of feeling guilt about their own demands on society's scarce resources, parents and children can focus on two technical questions. Using education as an example, the first would establish how much schooling the young person really wants, and what kind. The second technical question then becomes how to achieve this investment at the least cost, both to the individual and to society. The same questions can substitute for the taxpayers' anger and recrimination: that is, how much education (or other services) do people really want to provide to young people, and how can it be supplied at least cost? Solutions to these problems will not, of course, be readily apparent, but the exercise of seeking information and examining basic values should reassure the troubled person that the problems are real, shared, and not beyond solution.


**Segregation and Status**

Recent economic developments have led to an increased consciousness of economic class and rank. Outbreaks of racial, sexual, or ethnic antagonism tend to carry a heavy economic content. Those who have recently "made it" feel both angry at and frightened by the people just below who are struggling to reach their rung on the ladder.

It has long been known that the incidence of mental illness varies inversely with economic and social characteristics: the well-off have fewer psychological or emotional disorders. Later investigations have also shown that economic instability itself is associated with hospitalization for mental illness.[12] And the various movements in contemporary American society to integrate racial, sexual, or ethnic minorities have introduced new elements of instability, as well as changing, for many, the certainty of upper socioeconomic status. The white male college graduate can no longer be as sure of admission to graduate school or a successful managerial career; the white male high-schooler sees prospects for his apprenticeship or acceptance on the police force threatened by affirmative action programs requiring greater numbers of blacks, Chicanos, and women.

Twenty years after *Brown v. Board of Education*, the stresses of bringing about integrated educational systems ought to be familiar, yet new reactions have appeared as northern cities face the issues. The economics involved also have aroused some very troublesome feelings, as it becomes apparent that education benefits those who are already well-off at the expense of the poor. This finding may not yet be generally known, since no popular version has appeared, even in the first-level journals of dissemination to the public like *Harper's, Psychology Today*, or *The New York Times Magazine*. But the analysis that our system of higher education accentuates rather than reduces the inequality of income in this country has been almost completely accepted by most social scientists. In response, they offer widely dissimilar policy recommendations. Some argue for radical change in the educational system to make it more useful to the poor; others point out that low-income people might benefit more from direct income supplements or tax relief than from higher educational opportunities.[13] That public education benefits the rich more than the poor has also, of course, been reported for the lower grades by comparing the per pupil expenditures, appropriations for schools, tax rates, and tax bases in different school districts.[14]

A variety of stressful situations can be observed. If you live in an area with mediocre schools you may be indifferent or you may be working hard to improve them or, of course, you may be consciously resisting any increase in public expenditures. But if you have school-aged children your reactions will be more complex. Parents can agonize over the following dilemma: "I believe in public education, in diversity and heterogeneity of people, and I want my child to learn with companions from families that differ from ours. Therefore, I will send my child to PS 16. But I also believe in the beauty and excitement of continuous learning, and I want my child to cultivate an exploring intelligence and a trained mind. And PS 16 deadens every instinct for learning that a child brings! The school is repressive, its curriculum outdated, the faculty sexist and reactionary, and the children who go there test two grades below the state average in reading. How can I subject my own child to this kind of atmosphere?" No matter what their solution, the parents will have grounds for self-criticism. If they move or send their children to private schools, they may be ashamed of shirking their responsibilities as public-spirited citizens; if they stick it out and attempt to "enrich" the education of their own children, they may feel guilty about their parental responsibilities.

Other dilemmas exist: the ghetto parent fearing for the safety of children bussed to "better" schools in white neighborhoods; the taxpayer believing that Education is a Good Thing who watches vandalism in the schools soar in upper-income neighborhoods; the suburbanite deploring the overcrowded, segregated city schools who feels threatened by proposals for a metropolitan school system; the alumna, donating consistently to scholarship funds, who fears that standards of excellence must drop as "less qualified" students enter; the school dropout returning to class, who finds his work experience and knowledge of human behavior belittled in comparison to academic credentials.

Most people realize, whether they like it or not, that integration in schools will finally be achieved only when residential patterns also become integrated. Employment and therefore the opportunity to earn higher income has also been linked to residence. Many neighborhoods in the United States fall into one of two categories: the ethnic and racial ghettos of the inner city, where people of widely different incomes live together, and the "developments" of the suburbs, where people with similar incomes live in similar homes. Overcoming barriers to housing markets would not produce a homogenized society, but it would lessen the frequency of racial enclaves and make housing more dependent on economic status per se. Overcoming barriers to employment would change the composition of any given work force to make it more homogeneous in terms of people's ability and motivation but less so in terms of their background and outlook. Consciously or unconsciously, most people count the costs of such changes, as of school integration, in terms of what they think may be their personal loss. The economics of discrimination can help them to reckon costs differently.

When discrimination exists, the individual concerned acts as if he were willing to pay a price for satisfying his taste for discrimination. Thus, the consumer objecting to Jewish merchants may lose bargains, the employer refusing to have women in the shop incurs greater labor costs, the landlord denying a vacancy to a black family gives up a higher rent. Society's concern over discrimination reflects the fact that many of these costs have not, in fact, been paid by those with a taste for discrimination but have instead been shifted to minority groups.[15] For example, white families that would pay higher prices to live in segregated communities need not do so if nonmarket methods of exclusion (including harassment) can keep blacks out. The costs have been successfully shifted to ghetto dwellers, in the form of crowded and overpriced living places. The men who would be willing to take a cut in pay rather than risk their camaraderie by welcoming women need not make such a sacrifice if no women apply, excluded by the "old boy network" from the knowledge that jobs exist. But it is also true that not all costs have been thus shifted; the burden remaining for society grows increasingly larger.

Chief among the real costs to us all is the loss of output from potentially productive people who are not properly employed. Educated women and blacks trapped in dead-end jobs or bright young people unable to pursue professional training contribute much less to social welfare than they could. Although the exact amount of involuntary short-time, sporadic employment, part-time work, and underutilized skills cannot be quantified precisely, two facts are clear: it is significantly large, and it is concentrated among minority groups. Much of the poverty among women and blacks stems from such underemployment, and to the extent that taxpayers support the poor, the costs of poverty multiply. Above all, the loss of output (and of the income these people could earn) is irreversible: what is not produced today cannot be made up tomorrow.

Understanding how these social costs impinge on us as taxpayers and citizens may help to deal with the personal problems of adjustment required by new systems of integration at home, at school, and on the job. Many young men in the preferred applicant pool or on their way up the promotion ladder feel considerable anger and fear about their future. Rather than suppress these feelings or try to rationalize the reverse backlash that is now developing, everyone in the society can face them openly, accepting the emotions but developing appropriate modes of behavior to adjust to such situations. These circumstances can be eased when it is clearly understood, from the economic analysis of discrimination, that black gains need not be at the expense of white people and that men will not necessarily be displaced to make room for women. As people realize the potential for increased productivity, they can participate more fully in programs to reduce segregation, thereby achieving greater efficiency as well as equity.

## Work and Welfare

Along with massive changes in occupational structure, in job classification, in wages and hours and conditions of work, society is developing a whole new set of attitudes toward work, to which people react quite differently.

The phenomenon of worker alienation must surely be widely appreciated: its symptoms range from increased absenteeism and faulty production to rebellion against demeaning jobs and demands for more worker control over factory tasks. People disagree, however, about the prevalence of such attitudes, as well as on the appropriate remedies. Economists are not alone in suspecting that a larger paycheck may make the job of a disgruntled worker bearable, that both efficiency and profits might increase if women and minorities could work to their full capacities, and that realistic opportunities can transform the so-called discouraged workers who have dropped out of the labor force. Nevertheless, many of us also suspect that the world contains only a few very good jobs, and we join the tacit conspiracy to keep this fact from the young. Some people would add that the scarcity of enjoyable, exciting, or otherwise attractive openings has been the norm for years and serves to explain the use of the work ethic as a means of keeping the rest of humanity at hard labor.

Clearly, the work ethic, or rather its apparent inapplicability to much of what goes on in today's economy, causes more psychological disturbance than does worker alienation. In order to understand this emotional problem, it is useful to approach the work ethic from the vantage of pure economic analysis. To economists, work, or labor, consists of an input for production. The services of human beings combine with the services of machines and the yield from land and other natural resources into output. In this process human services, like other inputs, can be exchanged or given away in various simple and complex ways. The market system provides a method of exchange where labor, like any other input (or output) carries a price and provides income to the seller. In less weighty terms, people work for wages.

The economist's statement implies no motivational content; it merely observes what exists. For example, two equally valid analyses of labor supply exist. One shows that people will work more if wages are high; the other shows that people will work less. To an economist, the term *waste* implies no value judgment but simply means (as in the previous section) that labor goes unused or produces something nobody wants. An economist talks like this: "Underlying earned income and work-related benefits is, of course, work itself. We have provided evidence that work is the best income-producing mechanism available to the average family or individuals; earned income is highly correlated with not being needy. In saying this, we prescribe no ethical considerations to the concept of work; rather we state an empirical truism: generally, work produces more income than do welfare or transfer programs."[16]

The work ethic, on the other hand, carries a strong burden of both motivation and value, and it does not originate in the field of economics. The work *ethic* means the belief that work is good and idleness bad, that workers should be rewarded and idlers should be penalized. The psychology inherent in this belief can be traced, if one likes, to Freud's statement that work gives us "a secure place in a portion of reality."[17] Our social structure and our economy have developed many ramifications of this statement.[18] Chief among these is the belief that people who are old enough and physically able *ought* to work, and the conviction that earned income is deserved or merited income. Discussing the welfare volunteers described at the beginning of this chapter, an administrator

emphasizes that while the volunteers have in fact saved the state money, the worth of their own efforts for themselves cannot be measured in dollar signs. She has found that the volunteer experience gives the much criticized welfare recipient a "sense of self worth. Many of them have a failure syndrome," she said. "They have never succeeded in anything and are often the victims of community hostility. Then they have this opportunity to help someone else. They see that they can do something of value."[19]

The impact of these notions on people's feelings can be illustrated by two contributions to a symposium on mental health, concerned with a positive definition of its attributes. The first states simply: "A man in sound physical health, for example, is expected to do remunerative work."[20] The second amplifies this remark:

We conceive of the total self-identity of a person as organized into sub-identities, that is clusters of attributes corresponding to the roles into which the person has been socialized. Thus, for example, a man may have a sub-identity as a father, which encompasses specific attributes such as his strictness in disciplining his children, his skill in teaching them, his ability to provide for their material needs, etc. Similarly, a man has an occupational sub-identity as a doctor, teacher, or truckdriver: and associated with the sub-identity is an occupational self-esteem based on the evaluation of this sub-identity.[21]

Both writers, like others in many fields, take for granted that a man's work is a critical reference point. His competence at his job, the ability to perform his tasks, will be rated by others. He will also judge himself in this sphere as well as being sensitive to the opinions of others. Both writers refer to earnings as well as to work, confirming the social ethic that work *should* be the source of income.

But the statement "people ought to work for a living" no longer is a firmly accepted precept for living. We have discovered that it is truly a value judgment. For years it represented the simple fact of life that if you didn't work you didn't eat, but today there are ways around this. Welfare allows people to eat even if they don't have a job. Successful chicanery or criminality allows people to eat very well without doing an honest day's work. As a result, those who hold to the work ethic may experience severe self-doubt, while for the general public new sources of hostility and antagonism have appeared.

One development in particular has tended to erode, for some, the solidity of the work ethic. Both writers quoted above suggest that the link between a man's work and his income has something to do with his providing for a family, i.e., the role of breadwinner. Both evidently recognize that this responsibility, this role, refers to men because of cultural rather than biological destiny, but the masculine terms, nevertheless, pose a newly vexing problem. If the quotations reflect an accepted social *conviction* that the family depends on the husband and father and that a man ought to support his family, they contradict the existing social *circumstances*. In reality, millions of families depend on mothers alone, and in more than half the marriages, both partners work to support the family.

Because the work ethic has always been couched in masculine terms, it causes psychological stress when people learn about the increasing number of women in the labor force. The problem may be epitomized by substituting the word *woman* in the previous quotation:

We conceive of the total self-identity of a person as organized into sub-identities, that is clusters of attributes corresponding to the roles into which the person has been socialized. Thus, for example, a woman may have a sub-identity as a mother, which encompasses specific attributes such as her strictness in disci- plining her children, her skill in teaching them, her ability to provide for their material needs, etc. Similarly, a woman has an occupational sub-identity as a doctor, teacher, or truckdriver: and associated with the sub-identity is an occupational self-esteem based on the evaluation of this sub-identity.

This small exercise will evoke, from many readers, questions like "Don't mothers usually 'take care of' or 'nurture' their children rather than disciplining them? It's okay for women to be teachers and maybe a few can be doctors, but since when is truck-driving a woman's job? Doesn't self-esteem for a woman depend more on her husband and his occupation? Can't she establish her identity by being a good wife and mother?" Most such questions arouse varying degrees of discomfort. The dictum of the work ethic that "people ought to work" causes qualms. Either it must be admitted that women ought to do remunerative work, or it must be claimed that women are not people.

To return to the main argument, the validity of the work ethic has been threatened by swindlers at high- and low-income levels whose existence creates resentment and anger. The reaction to evildoers in high places seems to be cynical resignation: all politicians are crooks; all businessmen are out to get you. Corporate villainy and the existence of fat cats, however, do not threaten the work ethic in the same way that successful welfare chiselers do. Because poor people outnumber the rich, those who "live off the government instead of working" are more visible at low income levels than high. Furthermore, the average wage earner or working family can comprehend the sums paid to welfare recipients much more easily than the amounts involved in dubious government contracts or high level chicanery. The vital challenge to the work ethic is the relatively small income difference between those on welfare and those supporting themselves. Hostility to the poor is also more disturbing. Because welfare recipients are so numerous, it becomes natural to separate them into groups, and this frequently allows prejudices and stereotypes—ethnic, racist, sexist—to come into play. Finally, the gut reactions to welfare seem especially likely to yield arguments *ad hominem* or generalizations from particular, anecdotal evidence.

Again, neutral economic analysis can provide some useful perspective. Welfare differs from other types of government transfer payments, because those who receive welfare must prove need. Transfer payments, that is, income received by someone who does not provide any current service in exchange, go to millionaire owners of government bonds, retired workers with private pensions and Social Security benefits, veterans with disability eligibility, and farmers cutting back their crops. None must file statement of net worth and income or otherwise prove need in order to receive their checks. Transfer income that constitutes welfare payments requires families and individuals to prove they "need" financial assistance, usually because their current income from other sources falls below some minimum sum specified by the particular welfare program. Total transfer benefits of about $100 billion during fiscal 1972 went to about 120 million recipients; the number of *people* involved was smaller; since it is possible to receive more than one type of transfer payment (interest on government bonds and Social Security retirement benefits, for instance). But only about 25 to 30 million people received welfare. Most of these were female, and most lacked the ability to earn "enough" income, because of their age or disability.

Now if, according to the economic theory that labor consists of a productive service, people work for wages, then the welfare system has two effects. It provides income for those people who cannot sell their services, but it also deters people from selling their labor if their total income will be adversely affected as a result. Economists call this the disincentive effect and try to analyze it without adding any moral judgment. But the work ethic does add such a dimension of value, and hence some strong feelings of disapproval for welfare recipients. The pair of epithets used above, "welfare chiselers" and "fat cats," carry contrasting moral overtones. A chiseler is actively destructive, but a fat cat is not.

Economic analysis reveals two things. First, that disincentive effects exist at high-income levels in the form of taxes. Anyone in the 35 percent or over income tax bracket may find it advantageous to bargain with an employer for a longer vacation, higher pension, insurance or college tuition payments for his children, rather than receive a higher salary. Such bargains all go under the heading of avoiding taxes, and no one disapproves as long as it's legal. It can be instructive, therefore, to compare taxes and transfers by thinking of transfer income as a kind of negative tax.

The moderate-income family whose teenager takes on a paper route gains social approval and a minimal rise in total family income; the proceeds usually go to the youngster, illustrating, it is thought, the rewards from work. The low-income family whose teenager takes on a paper route finds its welfare payments reduced; the family suffers a confiscatory "tax" on its total income, and the demonstration effect for the youngster does not enhance the value of work. Another example is the low-income family, going into debt and, as a result, becoming eligible for welfare, contrasted with a similarly poor family that, having saved a few hundred dollars, will be ineligible. In this case, the transfer system provides an incentive to shift savings out of cash balances into durable goods, just as a 50 percent marginal income tax rate provides an incentive to shift savings out of cash balances into real estate or tax-free municipal bonds.

The second finding of economic analysis concerns the extraordinary effort on the part of low-income people to work, to seek and find employment, to stay off welfare, even when coupled with strong monetary incentives working in the opposite direction. Data revealing such attitudes and behavior has nowhere received the attention or emphasis it deserves. For example, a study by the New York City Human Resources Administration finds that one out of three New Yorkers met the criteria for being needy, "a pool of past, present and potential welfare recipients," and that 22 percent of the city's population was immediately eligible for welfare aid. The number of people actually being assisted was far smaller; only six out of ten of those eligible were being helped, and of these, 40 percent were also working to earn income.[22] Another example comes from the Institute for Research on Poverty and its experimentation with cash supplements to low-income families; the general findings show that married men do not alter their work patterns significantly, while married women reduce their employment outside the home slightly.[23]

Women solely responsible for their families may have the most severe problems in coping with both economic and emotional stress. A study of such mothers who received payments from the program of Aid to Families of Dependent Children found that significant numbers worked to supplement their incomes, despite the punishingly high rates of benefit-loss (equivalent to taxation) imposed on their earnings. Working for wages, they incurred both payroll taxes and cutbacks in welfare. For each dollar earned, the majority of these women gained only about 33 cents. Only 5 percent of them could keep as much as 75 cents from each dollar of wages. Yet the percentage of families where income was earned to supplement AFDC benefits ranged from 23 percent of the total in the East to 58 percent in the West and 70 percent in the South.[24]

All these data support the conclusions of Goodwin's social-psychological study of work intentions among the poor:

Evidence from this study unambiguously supports the following conclusion: poor people—males and females, blacks and whites, youths and adults—identify their self-esteem with work as strongly as do the nonpoor. They express as much willingness to take job training if unable to earn a living, and to work even if they were to have an adequate income. They have, moreover, as high life aspirations as do the nonpoor and want the same things, among them a good education and a nice place to live. This study reveals no difference between poor and nonpoor when it comes to life goals and wanting to work.[25]

Despite such evidence, statements in common circulation refer to good-for-nothing welfare clients, those who are so lazy they'd rather go on relief than work, the families with cars and color TVs who cheat by getting six checks for three people, the women who get pregnant so as to increase their welfare benefits. Probably the most prevalent reaction to welfare recipients is resentment rather than sympathy, to low-income people, hostility rather than helpfulness. Welfare recipients themselves respond to these perceived attitudes with resignation and shame in some cases and with outright antagonism in others. A factor analysis of AFDC female clients' attitudes toward work, welfare, and their orientation toward life discerned four types categorized as worker, mother, the hostile client, and the timid client. The worker "believes in . . . honesty and hard work, and getting ahead"; the mother is "a traditionalist vis à vis the role of women in society, needing material and emotional support." The hostile client, "outspoken and openly critical of welfare . . . skeptical about any connection between hard work on her part and success" contrasts with the timid woman, who, "afraid of a job and too discouraged to look for one . . . remains on welfare, but with a certain amount of shame and guilt."[26] In the population surveyed, workers and mothers each accounted for one-quarter of the women, while the hostile and timid clients each comprised 16 percent of the cases; the remainder were unassigned to these categories. Interestingly, both hostile and worker types were better educated than the others; they differed in that workers were older.

On both sides of the interpersonal transactions between those on welfare and those not, the strength of the work ethic persists, whether it generates favorable reactions or disapproval. Some have argued that income maintenance programs must be designed so as to minimize the disincentive effect on work because these conventional attitudes, being so strong, must be accepted.

There are at least two reasons for the concern with the work disincentive effects of income transfers—cost and morality . . . . If a transfer program induces many poor male family heads to reduce work from 50 to 40 hours a week, or causes many wives or children in poor families to work less, we are not likely to be very upset. But because it would constitute a flagrant violation of the work ethic, we would be profoundly disturbed if such a program induced many poor male family heads to permanently quit work.[27]

It should be noted that this argument implies that men should be gainfully employed and that women should stay home to take care of the children. Deriving these details from "morality" concerning the "work ethic" illustrates the conflict about women and work already noted previously.

It can also be argued that the convention of the work ethic itself needs rethinking, as does the notion that only earned income is deserved or merited. Not only have there been, historically, other approved sources of income, like property rents, royalties from inventions, and prizes for scholarly or athletic prowess, but there have been and are, culturally, other rewards for work. Honors and titles may be less common in the United States than elsewhere, but they nevertheless exert considerable influence on some. Furthermore, what is earned from working, the correlation between personal effort and monetary reward or between good intentions and payoff, has always been diluted by the effects of birth, home and community surroundings, and other accidents of health and living conditions. If people come to realize that in many cases the work ethic *seems* inapplicable because it *is* inapplicable, they can face the need to provide income with less emotion, and therefore with greater success in solving the technical questions involved.

## Economic Value and Personal Value

Four economic sources of psychic distress have now been identified: economic growth, population and the social benefit/cost analysis of children, discrimination, and the conflict of work and welfare. Like most topics in economics, these are all interdependent; an analysis of one fairly rapidly encroaches upon another. For example, one reason the work ethic has persisted for so long is that it supported, very usefully, the notion that progress consists of increases in output. One reason people resent welfare mothers is their fear of illegitimate births as an increasing element in the overpopulation threat. But these topics also share another characteristic: they all concern the distribution of income within the country.

The proposal to slow down growth means that our national product must be shared out differently; we can no longer decrease poverty simply by expanding the total pie. Asking public services for young people is to ask those without children to give part of their income to those with children. Efforts to lessen segregation will change the income shares of those with favored racial or ethnic characteristics. To question the validity of the work ethic requires some new ideas of how to divide income among people. Before dealing specifically with income distribution itself, we should recognize that some added complexities have recently been introduced into these issues by inflation.

In our economy, like those of most industrialized nations, a system of interrelated prices serves to allocate the scarce resources available. In the absence of laws or regulations or customs, people will work when they can earn the highest wages, will sell their produce to the highest bidder, will raise their rents if many tenants want more space. Whatever is produced from the resources at hand will also be distributed by an exchange mechanism using prices. It follows that the amount of things one can get, as a buyer, depends on the amount of purchasing power one has, and that in turn depends on the amount of resources one has, as a seller. Within broad limits, people who are born with property have more purchasing power, or income, than those who have only their own labor to sell, but differences in income among people reflect other circumstances as well. What is essential about this system is the interdependence between all markets and prices. If the Arabs raise the price of oil, it affects many types of production, many possible uses for other resources like chemicals, many types of jobs, and, of course, the amount of fuel oil and gasoline many of us can "afford" to buy. It is this commingling of effects that makes inflation such a problem, and this interdependence exists whether the price and market system operates under capitalism, socialism, or some other version of political economy.

Typically, the price structure, the way in which prices are related to each other, is changing all the time, but slowly. The ratio between what we paid, twenty years ago, for a cup of coffee at a lunch counter and a broiler chicken in the market differs markedly from that ratio today: chicken is now cheaper in terms of coffee, or the price of coffee compared to chicken is much higher. The price ratio, in a Latin American country, between a ream of quality typing paper and the charge for laundering a man's shirt does not resemble that ratio in the United States. As prices change slowly over time, people can adjust their spending habits, get used to the differences in "real" income, and manage to stay in control of their economic functioning. A good illustration of the importance of the price *structure* as opposed to the *level* of prices is to consider what difference it would make if all prices, including wages and rents and everything else, doubled overnight. The difficulty in times of inflation, of course, is that rising prices do not all change by the same amount in the same period of time. The price structure shifts drastically, unexpectedly, and with little forewarning about specific dislocations. People make unexpected gains and suffer unexpected losses, and their perceptions of what is going on may be disordered by the total disappearance of familiar prices with which to orient their market behavior.

From this point of view, the technical causes or cures for inflation can reasonably be left to those sufficiently adept at analyzing structural details or the mechanics of operation. The dislocating impacts of inflationary price rises occur whether it is easy credit, overspending, government deficits, corporate borrowing, confiscatory taxes, financial irresponsibility, or something else that precipitated inflation. Worrying about any of these instead of about the real hardships of inflation is simily misplaced anxiety.

When prices go up, two things happen to make people worse off. First, their incomes frequently lag behind their purchases; the prices they receive don't go up at the same time or by the same amount as the prices they pay. But second, their incomes change in relation to those of others; they find themselves in a new place in the distribution of income. This can be disturbing whether one moves up or down, because the change occurs unrelated to any personal effort. People whose incomes automatically vary with changes in prices, like union workers covered by escalator clauses or retired people whose Social Security benefits are similarly adjusted, become better off than those whose incomes depend on administrative review and decision, like municipal government employees or white-collar workers in large firms. As incomes rise, people with large amounts of debt find the burden of payment becoming smaller, while those whose income consists partly of interest become worse off by comparison. People who have managed to accumulate savings, to pay for a college education or a retirement trip, find them insufficient and discover that nonsavers do not look as improvident as they once did.

It appears, then, that inflation itself constitutes still another problem in the distribution of income, that whatever the structure of incomes in this country was, say in 1970, it is not the same now. As a people, we are not accustomed to such rapid change among the haves and the have-nots, nor do we take kindly to capricious and inexplicable change in our relative incomes. Inflation, then, has placed an additional load on the psychological strains created by other economic problems. By injecting an unfamiliar amount of uncertainty and unpredictability into all our lives, inflation has added to the feelings of helplessness in the face of random events.

But the distribution of income is not beyond the control of the people in this country. In small instances, like starting a halfway house or staffing a community day-care center, as well as in larger cases, like voting for a state lottery or lobbying for payroll tax exemptions for low-wage workers, the distributional elements of the issues can be clearly identified. Once isolated and examined, people can push for social change or can work to preserve the status quo. Either way, they can accomplish much more by focusing their energies on the strategic points revealed, once the distributional aspects become clear. Economics, either as a field of study or as a structure of social behavior, does not determine income distribution, nor can it contribute much to solve problems in this field. The basic origin of all these issues, of course, is the inexorable scarcity of available resources. What exists must be divided up. Economists can, however, help people handle their feelings about controversial proposals and plan for more effective action by clarifying the facts of scarcity and the inevitability of hard choices.

First, we can work to abolish the casual use of the term *priority* in delineating the choices to be made. To argue or even agree that improving the nation's housing must take priority over cleaning up the rivers tells us nothing about dividing up the human labor, skills, capital equipment, and know-how available between the two proposals. A simple ranking does not provide any formula for how much each gets.

The recently fashionable term *trade-off* introduces some notions of quantity into the choice problem, but it also adds obscurity by implying that only two alternatives exist. Some would claim that both housing and clean water are less important than increasing the supply of public transport or improving the rehabilitation aspects of our penal system or planning international cooperation in using raw materials. For most distributional questions the notion of opportunity costs contributes more understanding than references to priorities or trade-offs. Opportunity costs apply to large and small decisions: the real cost of what we buy is not the money we spend but the other goods and services we don't buy; the real choice in concentrating medical research on cancer is the decision to reduce other research efforts, give up teaching, or do without the medical services that could be immediately provided. Most of our scarce resources can be used in many different ways, so when we assign them to one task we effectively renounce many different alternatives. And, like all the rest of economics, a given choice-problem and the opportunity costs entailed are inextricably bound up with choices in other areas.

Next, we can encourage more thinking in marginal terms: like it or not, we have an effective system of income distribution existing in the country today. Scarce resources, the goods and services we produce, total income, and consumption are now divided up among all the families and individuals in the country. It will be more constructive to work changes in this system than to attempt to design another system, *de novo*. What this means is, for example, that if we urge income-tax deductions for college tuition, we need worry less about calculating total costs and benefits than about estimating how many *more* will attend college, or how many students will shift from state-supported to private institutions, or what other *changes* will ensue. Only with such facts can taxpayers properly decide whether or not to shift income from those who currently receive it to those with children in college. On a more local level, if there is a plan to run buses "free for senior citizens," we need to know what *extra* costs will be imposed by the new passengers, how many fares now being paid will stop, how much taxi service will increase or decrease, how many new customers there will be in retail stores, movies, and restaurants? Only with such information can local citizens reasonably decide whether or not to share their income to provide transportation services not freely, but at zero prices, to older people.

Another essential for people to comprehend is the relation between income distribution and production. Decisions about allocating scarce resources, about distributing all the goods and services in an economy, obviously determine who gets how much real income within a country. These decisions also affect what gets produced, how much of the different kinds of goods and services that the country *could* have, it does have. What is imperative for people to realize is that these two outcomes, production and distribution, can be separately designed.

If a given set of production elements has been arrived at (say by the market system) it is perfectly possible to change the distribution of income that results from that allocation. Society may choose to reward typists and computer programmers over economists or entertainers, with medals or with higher wages. If this happens, production will be affected as will the distribution of income. People will want to become typists and not economists, while those who employ typists and computer programmers to produce books may find their markets shrinking as their costs and prices go up. But if society chooses to reward blondes or six-footers with freckles or the parents of twins by handing out either medals or higher incomes, production will not immediately be affected, although the distribution of income will change significantly.

It is essential that people recognize how income distribution, in real terms, depends not merely on taxation and transfer payments but on the prices and availability of goods and services. Gasoline shortages offer an illustration. How gasoline supplies get distributed may indeed affect production, for example, by changing the conditions of work. But these aspects should be clearly distinguished from the income effects, that is, the changes in the distribution of that part of real income, consisting of gasoline and other goods and services consumed, brought about by shortages and price rises.

Finally, we must do away with any lingering suspicion that economic worth defines personal worth. The economic value of anything under a market system is given by its price. Whatever we purchase must be worth, to us, at least the amount we give for it, or else we would not buy. In most cases we feel that our purchase yields us more gain than loss, for we would frequently be willing to pay a higher price than we do. By the same token, the value of a day's work, to an employer, must be at least equal to the wage paid the worker. But this says nothing about the value of the human being, that is, what the worker is worth as an individual. The employer buys what the human being does, his or her performance or output, and the wage or price paid defines that service alone, not the person who provides it. If society wants more entertainment than education, then it may pay comedians more than teachers, but this does not make the funny man a better person, or the teacher a less valuable human being.

One of the greatest sources of misunderstanding and emotional hurt lies in the confusion between market prices and personal worth, or the misguided belief that economists put price tags on human beings. To do away with this fallacy requires helping people to understand more about prices and the market system. Prices can change rapidly and violently, as they recently have done, but this behavior reflects no comparable erratic shifts among people. Janitors' wages can be very high in larger cities compared to a pittance in country churches, with no parallel differential in character among city dwellers and rural people. On the other hand, this does not mean that human life is priceless, or that the value of a human being should not be calculated in any fashion. Choices about using scarce resrouces remain, even when they are not couched in terms of dollars spent or dollars saved. There are not enough dialysis machines to go around; providing total safety in the air means nobody flies; only four lifeguards came to work today at the city's eight swimming pools—these dilemmas may pose social and moral judgments, conditions for ethical rather than economic choice, but they do not become easy to solve.

Surely, however, people's self-esteem will be heightened and their regard for others enhanced if they realize that personal worth cannot be measured by prices or wages or any facet of the market system. The economic process of determining value cannot inhibit, unless we let it, the personal process of developing value as human beings.

**Notes**

1. United Press International, © 1974. Reprinted by permission.

2. See, for example, Lester Thurow, "Toward a Definition of Economic Justice," *The Public Interest* 31 (Spring 1973); Kenneth Boulding, "The Dimensions of Economic Justice," in his *Beyond Economics* (Ann Arbor Paperbacks, 1970), and two major collections of research papers, *Studies in Public Welfare* (vols. 1-13) Joint Economic Committee, Congress of the United States (U.S. Government Printing Office, Washington, D.C., 1973) and *The Research Reports* (no. 1-18) for the National Commission on Urban Problems (U.S. Government Printing Office, Washington, D.C., 1969). Compare the program of the AEA meeting in December 1973, to that of similar meetings a decade earlier. The general theme of the 1963 meeting was "the efficiency of economic systems and in particular of important parts of the American economy." The former, more recent program found economists dealing with questions of politics, ethics, and radical philosophy.

3. Robert Taggart, "Labor Market Impacts of the Private Retirement System," *Studies in Public Welfare*, no. 11, Joint Economic Committee, Congress of the United States, Oct. 30, 1973, (U.S. Government Printing Office, 1973), p. 84, citing Virginia Reno, "Why Men Stop Working At or Before Age 65." A letter to the author commenting on Social Security contains the following: "I am a 50-60 year old and I cannot retire to 2 or 3 days a week I have too much energy to give." For the contribution of work to self-esteem, see Abraham Maslow, *Motivation and Personality*, 2nd ed. (New York: Harper and Row, 1970) and the same author's article "Human Needs and Work," in *Eupsychian Management* (Homewood, Ill.: Richard D. Irwin, Inc. and the Dorsey Press, 1965). See also Juanita Kreps, *Lifetime Allocation of Work and Income* (Durham, N.C.: Duke University Press, 1971).

4. This is not to say that Gomper's tradition has died, even with new pressures from labor to control the conditions of work. Describing the sophisticated analysis of bargaining issues by the United Steelworkers Union, which provides computor printouts of ninety-one contracts covering such areas as successor clauses, wage escalators, earnings-maintenance provisions, and supplemental unemployment benefits, Roy Harris contrasts it with the approach of the Aluminum Worker International Union. In an article, "The Me-Too Union," Harris points out that the Aluminum Workers concentrate on their pay-checks. The local unions forward their demands for "more" to the AWIU staff, and provide continuous feedback during negotiations. The elaborate bargaining processes of unions like the steelworkers tend to overshadow, in the public's eye, the frequency of simpler issues of economic well-being. Yet most workers emphasize such goals and have no difficulty in translating non-wage demands, like pensions, medical benefits, early retirement, or longer vacations into income gains. It appears, therefore, that Gomper's simple formula remains paramount, even while "more" is becoming more threatening. *Wall Street Journal*, 183:4 (Jan. 7, 1974) p. 24.

5. See the press coverage in June 1972 of the Stockholm conference and the unplanned conference that arose in opposition. A useful account of the conflict occurs in Norman J. Faramelli's "Toying With the Environment and the Poor: A Report on the Stockholm Environmental Conferences" in *Environmental Affairs* 2:3 (Summer 1972).

6. Leopold Kohr, "Toward A New Measurement of Living Standards," *American Journal of Economics and Sociology* 14:4 (October 1955).

7. It is instructive to compare successive editions of Paul Samuelson's *Economics* (New York: McGraw-Hill Inc.) on this point.

*First edition (1948)*: "As everybody knows, poor people have on the average many more children than wealthy. Harvard and Vassar students are not reproducing themselves. Nor are Michigan State and Oberlin students, nor most city dwellers who have gone only to high school" (p. 29)

*Second edition (1951)*: "Everyone knows that the rich seem to have fewer children than the poor. Before the war, Harvard and Vassar students were not reproducing themselves. Neither were Michigan State and Oberlin students or high-school graduates or urban groups generally" (p. 29) "But finally the expert had to admit that at least temporarily there was an important break in the falling trend of the net reproductive rate. . . . Once it began to be fashionable for a middle-class family to have numerous children, many began to do the same. A glance at any college faculty—young, old, and middle-aged—will show the changing trends in this regard: the assistant professors already have more children than the full professors, and the race isn't over yet" (p. 31).

*Fifth edition (1961)*: "A glance at a college faculty—young, old, and middle-aged—will show the changing trends in this regard: the associate professors already have more children than the full professors, and the race is not over yet" (p. 32).

*Sixth edition (1964)*: "A glance at a college faculty—young, old, and middle-aged—will show the changing trends in this regard: the associate professors have already had more children than the retired professors, and the final score is not in yet. Paradoxically, poorer nations such as Japan and Italy, which used to have high birth rates, now restrict family size more than do the rich nations" (p. 31).

8. Robert Solow, "Is the End of the World at Hand? An Evaluation of the New Doomsday School," *Challenge* 16:1 (March/April 1973); also in *The Economic Growth Controversy* (White Plains, N.Y.: International Arts and Sciences Press, Inc., 1973).

9. An excellent overview of this approach, including an extensive bibliography, appears in T.W. Schultz's article "Human Capital: Policy Issues and Research Opportunities," National Bureau of Economic Research, *Human Resources*, (New York, 1972).

10. See any standard economics text for the definition of price as the ratio of exchange between two commodities and of costs as the scarce resources used, e.g., Paul A. Samuelson, *Economics* (New York: McGraw-Hill, 1973), pp. 18-20, 43-45.

11. Ibid., pp. 474-75.

12. M. Harvey Brenner, *Mental Illness and the Economy* (Cambridge, Mass., Harvard University Press, 1973).

13. Christopher Jencks, et al., *Inequality* (New York: Basic Books, 1972).

14. Two good introductions to the entire literature can be found in *Income Inequality*, volume 409 of the *Annals* of the American Academy of Political and Social Science, September 1973: Robert J. Staaf and Gordon Tullock, in "Education and Equality," review the controversy stemming from Hansen and Weisbrod's cost/benefit analysis of the California system (*Journal of Human Resources*, vols. 4-6, 1969-71) and compare the situation in various countries. Joseph E. Stiglitz, in "Education and Inequality," explores the assumptions and methodology of analyzing the impact of education on the distribution of income.

15. Cf. the author's *Economics of the Ghetto* (a Pegasus book, 1970, distributed by Bobbs-Merrill Inc.), pp. 234-40.

16. Stephen Leeds, *Income Sources of the Welfare-Risk Population*, City of New York Human Resources Administration, Office of Policy Research, Dec. 1, 1973, p. 52.

17. Sigmund Freud, *Civilization and Its Discontents* (New York: W.W. Norton, 1961), p. 27n.

18. Among the exponents of human psychology, Marie Jahoda writes:

I shall begin by turning Freud's statement around: that is, if work is man's strongest tie to reality, then the absence of work should leave him less solidly in touch with reality. This is indeed the case. . . . Work encourages the continuous action necessary to maintain objective knowledge of reality; work permits the pleasurable experience of competence; work adds to the store of conventional experience of competence; work adds to the store of conventional knowledge ("Notes on Work," in *Psychoanalysis: A General Psychology*, ed. Rudolph Lowenstein et al. [New York: International Universities Press, 1966], pp. 623-28).

19. United Press International, © 1974. Reprinted by permission.

20. Leo Srole, "Medical and Sociological Models in Assessing Mental Health, in *The Definition and Measurement of Mental Health*, U.S. Department of Health, Education, and Welfare, Public Health Service (Washington, D.C.: U.S. Government Printing Office), p. 62.

21. John R.P. French, "The Conceptualization and Measurement of Mental Health in Terms of Self-Identity Theory," idem, p. 141.

22. Leeds, op. cit., pp. iii-iv.

23. "How Income Supplements Can Affect Work Behavior," *Studies in Public Welfare*, Paper No. 13, Joint Economic Committee, Congress of the United States (Washington, D.C.: U.S. Government Printing Office, 1974).

24. "How Public Welfare Benefits Are Distributed in Low-Income Areas: Additional Materials," *Studies in Public Welfare*, Paper No. 6, Joint Economic Committee, Congress of the United States (Washington, D.C.: U.S. Government Printing Office, 1973) pp. 105-12.

25. Leonard Goodwin, *Do The Poor Want to Work?* (Washington, D.C.: The Brookings Institution, 1972), p. 112.

26. Ardyce Haring, "Work or Welfare," A Study of ADC Clients for the Human Resources Administration, New York City, July 1973, pp. III-3 to III-7.

27. Irwin, Garfinkel, "Income Transfer Programs and Work Effort: A Review," in *Studies in Public Welfare*, Paper No. 13, Joint Economic Committee, Congress of the United States (Washington, D.C.: U.S. Government Printing Office, 1974), pp. 1-2.

# 3 Coping with Political Alienation

**Marion R. Just**

Political alienation in America is no longer a stigma of intellectuals, but rather a nagging complaint of average citizens. In December 1973, Louis Harris presented a report to the Senate Subcommittee on Intergovernmental Relations, entitled "Confidence and Concern: Citizens View American Government."[1] The principal datum of this report was a post-Watergate scale of political alienation. Harris reported that a significant body of Americans are alienated from their political system. What is more, a greater proportion of American citizens recoil from the politics of Watergate than shrank from the war in Vietnam.[2]

The recognition that politics has an impact on mental well-being is not a new concept in social science. Among the ancients, both Plato and Aristotle were concerned with the role of politics in human development. Probably the most dramatic theory of interaction between social psychology and politics has been advanced with reference to the events in Germany before and during World War II. In the opinion of some scholars of the Nazi period, the German people were the victims of a mass political psychosis, manipulated through the sophisticated use of the media of communication and the use of violence. Clearly the emergence of the technological state has imposed new psychosocial problems on society.

According to Karl Marx, the division of labor required for industrialization is the principal factor in the alienation of work.[3] It is plausible to maintain that the political division of labor in the modern state is a principal cause of political alienation in America. Like its sociological counterpart, political alienation is mired in a controversy of definitions. Political scientists employ a variety of surrogate concepts for alienation: lack of trust in government, political dissatisfaction, disaffection from the political system, nonallegiance, political inefficacy, and public apathy. Neither distrust nor inefficacy, however, allude to the feeling of exclusion, which (by right of Marx) belongs in the concept of alienation. "Political dissatisfaction" is too anemic a term to define political alienation, while the concept of "public apathy" signifies too much that is normal.

This paper attempts a new approach to political alienation, one that builds on the many facets of the concept rather than homogenizing its constituents. First, a structured definition is developed, which embraces the political affect, attitudes, and referents of alienation. This multifaceted definition forms the basis of a typology of political outlooks. In the next section, American political attitudes (as expressed in the Harris survey) are analyzed with respect to various facets of political alienation. The analysis characterizes American political alienation as a form of dissatisfaction coupled with political optimism. The final section presents a discussion of how the political system can cope with political alienation in the American setting.

## Political Alienation: A Structured Definition

Political alienation is a psychological condition of discomfort, anxiety, and even despair. These feelings may be entirely sane—that is to say, in touch with reality. For example, if an individual's political circumstances are actually hopeless, then despair may be a proper response to political reality. At the very least, however, political alienation is a negative attitude towards politics.

### Whose Fault is Alienation?

The literature suggests that the responsibility for political alienation may be assumed either by individuals or by the society.[4] Individual responsibility is central to an existential concept of man as a force in his political destiny. Societal responsibility for alienation, on the other hand, points to some behavioral determinism. In the language of social science, political alienation may be either an individual deviation from the social norm or a symptom of social discontinuity. We will attempt a graceful arabesque around this question. Our thesis is that alienation is a plural phenomenon, and therefore, while some forms can be laid to the door of individuals, other forms may be the burden of the sociopolitical system. It should be emphasized, however, that a democracy in which the great majority of the people are politically alienated is probably not functioning successfully.

### Who is Alienated?

Leaving aside the source of alienation, the fact of alienation is itself open to question: Is an individual politically alienated only if he thinks he is? Or, conversely: Can an individual be politically alienated even if he heartily approves of the political system and of his place in it?[5] This question may be side-stepped in favor of the behavioral consequences that follow. As long as people are oblivious to their own alienation they pose no problem whatever to the political system. Therefore, an analysis of alienated behaviors may rely only on the subjective experience of alienation.

*Referrents of Political Alienation*

Let us turn to referrents of subjective alienation. What are people alienated from in politics?

Three principle referrents can be discerned: the political system as a whole, public officials, and other citizens. While some individuals may feel estranged from politics altogether, recent events suggest that many individuals may be alienated from political leadership without carrying that feeling over to the system as a whole. Contemporary Americans may feel politically alienated from the present administration without feeling that American democracy is alien to them. The sociological literature further suggests that alienation may have an internal dimension.[6] In political terms, a citizen's perception of his own role may become the object of his alienated feeling. Agreement that "politics and government seem so complicated a person can't understand what's going on" points to the guilty side of alienation. To flesh out our first attempt at definition then, political alienation may be defined as an individual's negative and subjective attitude towards: *citizens, public officials,* and the *political system.*

*Criteria of Political Alienation*

With regard to the referrents of alienation, it is useful to distinguish criteria by which negative assessments are made. What characteristics of citizenship, public officials, or the political system alienate individuals from politics? The following qualities are often associated with alienation: lack of trust, lack of understanding, lack of fairness, and lack of power.[7] "Distrust" is the most prominent criterion of political alienation. In fact, Louis Harris used "Public Trust" as the "inside" title of his study "Confidence and Concern." "Lack of public trust" is signified by such phrases as "the credibility gap," "you can't fool all of the people all of the time," and "would you let this man sell you a used car?" While public trust is essential for democratic competition, only a minority of Americans have faith in the political competence of their fellow citizens. In fact, politicians, as a group, exhibit more public trust than average citizens.[8]

While a minority of citizens do not trust their peers, even more do not trust their own political intelligence. The feeling that "politics is too complicated" may (and perhaps should) promote a feeling of political powerlessness. In politics knowledge *is* power. On the other hand, citizens do not find their public officials very understanding either. As many as 55 percent of the Harris sample agreed, "People running the country don't really care what happens to you."[9] The implication may be that the politician who "understands" a problem can not be "trusted" to do anything about it.

"Fairness" is another element that appears to be particularly important for egalitarian politics. In their study of political culture, Almond and Verba define "output alienation" as an expectation of *unfair* treatment.[10] The criterion of justice has a long and illustrious history in the study of politics. While the criteria of "fairness" and "trust" are affective, "understanding" is cognitive. There remains an instrumental mode to complete the Parsonian triad.

An instrumental criterion of alienation may be applied to citizens, politicians, and political institutions. Alienated individuals may consider themselves inefficacious, or find particular leaders to be ineffective, or judge the political system to have no impact on their lives. The categories of social action therefore expand our definition: Political alienation is an individual's negative attitude towards the

(understanding )        (citizens           )
(trustworthiness)    of   (public officials    )
(fairness        )        (political institutions).
(effectiveness    )

*Psychology of Alienation*

This definition may be expanded further by focusing on the source of negative attitudes. C. Wright Mills proposes that alienation is a result of a discrepancy between an individual's personal expectations and his subjective perceptions of politics.[11] Combining the other elements of our definitions with this hypothesized discrepancy yields the following typology: Political alienation is an individual's assessment of a *negative* discrepancy between his expectation for the

(understanding )
(trustworthiness)       (citizenship          )
(fairness        )  of   (public officials      )  vis-à-vis his
(effectiveness    )       (political institutions)

                        (understanding )        (citizenship           )
perception of the      (trustworthiness)    of   (public officials       )
                        (fairness        )        (political institutions).
                        (effectiveness    )

This definition may be elucidated by an example. An individual may perceive a discrepancy between his expectation that politicians behave like Washington and Lincoln and his perception that most of them behave like Boss Tweed. Such an individual may become highly anxious about politicians. The discrepancy hypothesis points to a psychological explanation for this anxiety.

Positive expectations and negative perceptions produce a form of cognitive dissonance.[12] An individual may cope with this dissonance by (1) revising his level of expectation in line with his perceptions (e.g., by not expecting politicians to be honest), or (2) revising his perception in line with his expectation (e.g., by believing that Boss Tweed really *was* honest), or (3) holding fast both to his expectations and his perceptions—producing a state of anxiety.

While the discrepancy hypothesis satisfied the case of the disappointed idealist, how does it treat the convinced pessimist? A political pessimist has no hope for the improvement of the system and supports his belief with compelling evidence. The degree of discrepancy between a pessimist's expectations and his perceptions can be very small. But the valence of a pessimist's discrepancy may be more negative than a disappointed idealist's. To illustrate this point, let us consider an example. Suppose we rate an individual's attitudes on a scale from −5 to +5. Let us assume that the disappointed idealist and the convinced pessimist both rate the system at −2. The optimist *expects* the system to perform at +3, while the pessimist *expects* the system to perform at −3. By combining the idealist's perception and expectations (−2 + 3) we find the idealist's attitude amounts to +1, a weak endorsement of the system. But the convinced pessimist's total (−2 −3) is −5, a very heavy indictment. In this case, the discrepancy between the pessimist's expectations and perceptions is very small, but the outcome has a negative valence. The disappointed idealist, on the other hand, experiences a substantial discrepancy between his expectations and perceptions, but the final outlook has a positive valence. Assigning either a positive or a negative value to both expectations and perceptions, the "discrepancy hypothesis" provides a fourfold typology of political attitudes (Table 3-1).

When positive expectations are matched with positive perceptions, we find the satisfied allegiant. Such a citizen may be either apathetic or active, but underlying his behavior will be positive support for the system. He would encourage change only at the margins of the status quo. At the other end of the main diagonal is the nonallegiant citizen. His negative expectations for the system are matched with negative perceptions of its performance. As an apathetic citizen, the nonallegiant poses no danger to the system, but he remains

**Table 3-1**
**A Typology of Political Outlook**

| | | Perception of Politics | |
|---|---|---|---|
| | | Positive | Negative |
| Expectation for Politics | Positive | Allegiance | Dissatisfied Optimism |
| | Negative | Dissatisfied Pessimism | Nonallegiance |

the potential source of radical behaviors. On the other diagonal of the table, we find the two principle types we have been discussing: the dissatisfied optimist and the dissatisfied pessimist. The optimist is the one whose expectations are not being met by his perceptions. If apathetic, he is disgruntled. If active, he is the source of changes that would bring about a better match between his expectations and perceptions. Reform movements would likely draw their supporters from the ranks of dissatisfied optimists. Pessimists, however, may find the current situation not as disturbing; but their underlying negative expectations provide a shaky foundation for public trust. Any negative turn of the current situation will only confirm their base expectation and mobilize them into the camp of nonallegiance.

While this typology distinguishes among kinds of political dissatisfactions, it is missing an estranging element beyond dissatisfaction. We suggest that the missing link in this equation is power. Individuals who feel powerless in the face of their dissatisfaction with politics are politically alienated. While the apathy of contentment may be functional in a democracy, the apathy of alienation may be quite dangerous indeed. In order to associate behaviors with attitudes of alienation, it is important to couple political efficacy to the typology of political satisfaction. Therefore, a definition of political alienation should include two dimensions: the discrepancy between subjective expectations and perceptions, and the felt inability to correct that discrepancy.[13]

## Political Alienation

Individual (X) assesses the extent to which he $\begin{pmatrix} \text{cannot} \\ \text{can} \end{pmatrix}$ correct

a discrepancy between his $\begin{pmatrix} \text{negative} \\ \text{positive} \end{pmatrix}$ expectations and his

$\begin{pmatrix} \text{negative} \\ \text{positive} \end{pmatrix}$ perceptions of $\begin{pmatrix} \text{himself} \\ \text{public officials} \\ \text{public institutions} \end{pmatrix}$ in terms of

of $\begin{pmatrix} \text{honesty} \\ \text{fairness} \\ \text{understanding} \\ \text{effectiveness} \end{pmatrix}$ $\longrightarrow$ $\begin{matrix} \text{(high)} \\ \vdots \\ \text{(low)} \end{matrix}$ political alienation of

individual (X).

Two examples will clarify the definition.

1. A particular individual believes he can correct any discrepancy between his positive expectation and his negative perceptions concerning the honesty of particular public officials. Such an individual is mildly alienated and belongs in our typology above, in the category of dissatisfied optimist.

2. A particular individual believes he cannot correct the discrepancy between his negative expectations and his negative perceptions concerning the effectiveness of political institutions. Such an individual is highly alienated and would be in the category of convinced pessimists.


**Political Alienation: The American Case**

In order to demonstrate the applicability of this structured hypothesis, we will briefly examine some American attitudes towards politics. Our data are taken from the Louis Harris report "Confidence and Concern." This report is based on a survey of 1596 American adults interviewed in September of 1973.[14] The data show that (1) negative attitudes towards politics are widespread in America today; (2) that there is a sizable discrepancy between what most Americans expect and what they perceive of themselves, of public officials, and of political institutions; (3) that this discrepancy centers on qualities of understanding, trustworthiness, fairness, and effectiveness; and (4) that many Americans feel helpless in the face of this discrepancy.


*Negative Attitudes to Politics*

Based on their responses to several items, it appears that a majority of the sample hold strong negative attitudes toward politics. Of the total sample, 74 percent believe, "special interests get more from the government than the people do"; 60 percent maintain, "most elective officials are in politics for all they can get out of it for themselves"; 55 percent feel "the people running the country don't really care what happens to (them);" and 55 percent are convinced "most people with power try to take advantage of people like (themselves)" (Table 3-2).

The seriousness with which Americans view these situations is evidenced by responses to the questions "How much of a problem are the following for you personally: the lack of response by government to problems facing people such as yourself, the inability of the government to solve problems, corrupt politicians, and the lack of trust and confidence in government." The tables below indicate that about two-thirds of the sample found these to be *real* problems, circumstances they cannot take in stride (Table 3-3).

The dynamic of negative attitudes is also impressive. A majority of the respondents report less confidence in the federal government today than they had five years ago (although this varied by party). The respondents principally blamed their loss of confidence on the corruptness of politicians (Tables 3-4 and 3-5).

**Table 3-2**
**Negative Attitudes toward American Politics**

| | Do Feel Percent | Do Not Feel Percent | Not Sure Percent | Total (N) Percent |
|---|---|---|---|---|
| "The people running the country don't really care what happens to you." | 55 | 41 | 4 | 100 (1613.4) |
| "Most elective officials are in politics for all they can get out of it for themselves." | 60 | 33 | 6 | 100 |
| "Most people with power try to take advantage of people like yourself." | 55 | 40 | 5 | 100 |

Source: Based on responses to question 8: A, C, G in "Confidence and Concern," part 2, pp. 129-34.

**Table 3-3**
**Seriousness with which Americans View Their Negative Attitudes toward Politics**

| | Real Problem Percent | Can Take In Stride Percent | Not a Problem Percent | Not Sure Percent | Total (N) Percent |
|---|---|---|---|---|---|
| The lack of response of government to problems facing people such as yourself | 54 | 22 | 19 | 5 | 100 (1614) |
| Inability of government to solve problems | 61 | 22 | 13 | 4 | 100 (1613.4) |
| Corrupt politicians | 70 | 16 | 10 | 4 | 100 (1616.6) |
| Lack of trust and confidence in government | 67 | 18 | 13 | 2 | 100 (1613.4) |

Source: Based on responses to question 10: E, H. J, M in "Confidence and Concern," part 2, pp. 151-55.

**Table 3-4**
**Increasing Negative Attitudes toward Politics: Confidence in Federal Government, Compared to Five Years Ago**

| | More Confidence Percent | Less Confidence Percent | About the Same Percent | Not Sure Percent | Total (N) Percent |
|---|---|---|---|---|---|
| Total | 11 | 57 | 28 | 4 | 100 (1608.5) |
| Republican | 17 | 45 | 35 | 3 | 100 (352.4) |
| Democrat | 8 | 64 | 24 | 4 | 100 (713.4) |
| Independent | 9 | 61 | 26 | 4 | 100 (431.3) |

Source: "Confidence and Concern," part 1, p. 221.

**Table 3-5**
**The Main Reasons for the Decline in Public Confidence**

|  | Total Percent |
|---|:---:|
| Corruption, use of office, public funds for personal gain | 49 |
| Watergate | 28 |
| Government unresponsive, distant, uncontrollable by people | 19 |
| Government misleading, lying to public, false promises | 19 |
| Government bureaucracy, red tape | 14 |
| Distrust, malaise, moral decline | 11 |
| Feeling that problems aren't being resolved | 11 |
| Increased news media coverage | 10 |
| Inflation, dollar devaluation | 8 |
| Taxes, budget too high | 7 |
| Political parties trying to tear each other apart | 6 |
| Corruption of some officials causes blanket condemnation | 6 |
| Public doesn't understand role of government, issues | 5 |
| Officials unqualified, poorly trained | 4 |
| War-Pentagon Papers | 4 |
| Public apathetic | 4 |
| Too much influence by big corporations on government | 4 |
| Improper campaign funding, expenditures | 3 |
| Rebelliousness, generation gap | 3 |
| Public more sophisticated, aware | 3 |
| Too much influence by minorities | 3 |
| Too much foreign aid, not enough on domestic problems | 2 |
| Russian wheat deal | 2 |
| Courts too lenient | 2 |
| Too much federal control over state, local government | 2 |
| Elected officials support socialism | 1 |
| Watergate committee implies guilt without proof | 1 |
| Too many controls, regulations | 1 |
| Unemployment | 1 |
| Other answers | 15 |
| Don't know | — |

Source: "Confidence and Concern," part 1, p. 223.

*Discrepancies Between Expectations and*
*Perceptions of Public Officials*

Let us turn now to the hypothesized discrepancy between expectations and perceptions in politics. The data are most complete with respect to external objects, particularly elected officials. Respondents chose three or four characteristics that best described the kind of people who *should* work in government and the characteristics of those who *do* work in government. The percentages below are based on the total number of responses (answers therefore total more than 100 percent). The ideal characteristic respondents most commonly cited was "honesty." Other preferable characteristics were "dedicated to hard work" (56 percent), "wants to help people" (51 percent), "intelligent" (41 percent), and "courageous" (35 percent). See Table 3-6 for the full list of responses.

**Table 3-6**
**Age Differences in Political Expectations**

(Question: Which Three of Four of the Following Best Describe Most Elected Officials?)

| | Total | 18-29 | 30-49 | 50 and over |
|---|---|---|---|---|
| Total Answers | 16,069 | 4486 | 5655 | 5908 |
| | Percent | Percent | Percent | Percent |
| Courageous | 12 | 8 | 9 | 18 |
| Bureaucratic | 16 | 21 | 15 | 13 |
| Idealistic | 10 | 12 | 10 | 9 |
| Out for Themselves | 29 | 36 | 29 | 23 |
| Dedicated to Hard Work | 22 | 17 | 23 | 24 |
| Play It Safe | 15 | 18 | 17 | 12 |
| Honest | 13 | 7 | 11 | 20 |
| Just Serving Time | 8 | 8 | 8 | 7 |
| Intelligent, Bright | 27 | 28 | 27 | 27 |
| Make Red Tape | 11 | 14 | 11 | 9 |
| Want to Help People | 25 | 20 | 24 | 30 |
| Corrupt | 17 | 22 | 16 | 14 |
| Care About Freedom | 14 | 12 | 15 | 16 |
| Only Want Power | 22 | 23 | 25 | 19 |
| Public Spirited | 21 | 16 | 22 | 24 |
| Dull | 3 | 2 | 4 | 2 |
| Efficient | 8 | 6 | 8 | 8 |
| Couldn't Care Less | 8 | 9 | 7 | 8 |
| Creative, Imaginative | 2 | 1 | 2 | 3 |
| Do Things by the Book | 7 | 9 | 7 | 5 |
| Tells It Like It Is | 3 | 4 | 3 | 3 |
| Make Promises That Are Never Kept | 42 | 46 | 45 | 36 |
| None (volunteered) | 1 | — | 1 | 1 |
| Not Sure | 6 | 5 | 6 | 6 |

Cross-tabulation of the expected qualities against twelve demographic variables revealed a startling uniformity in the responses. Demographic variables included: region, area, age, religion, occupation, sex, education, income, race, political party, voting, attitudes to levels of government and political participation. Subsamples of the population (by age or race) varied by no more than a few percentage points for each characteristic. The only exception was the characteristic "courage." Surprisingly, only 28 percent of young people compared to 33 percent of middle-aged people and 42 percent of older people expected courageous officials. Respondents also varied by religion on this choice. Forty percent of Protestants chose courageous qualities compared to only 29 percent of Catholics and 28 percent of Jews.

On the whole, the results point to an American consensus on the ideal qualities of leadership. American political culture communicates these norms more uniformly than might be expected from the diversity of the population.

With regard to perceptions, however, responses are more broadly distributed over the range of qualities, and the subtables indicate much less consensus. Subgroups of the population varied by more than 10 percent in eight out of twenty-two qualities. The most consistent deviations occurred by age. Young people were much more likely than older people to perceive officials as "bureaucratic," "out for themselves," "playing it safe," "making red tape," "corrupt," and "making promises that are never kept." Older people are significantly more likely to see officials as being "dedicated to hard work," "honest," "wanting to help people," and "public spirited." Very simply, more young people perceived negative qualities in public officials than older people. The obverse was that young people were less likely to perceive good qualities in officialdom. Since younger and older respondents had similar expectations for politicians, the differences between age groups cannot be attributed to political culture. Rather, some experiential factor seems to be at work to produce this difference.

It is not clear whether younger people will be better impressed by politicians as they get older, or whether, over time, negative perceptions will become more characteristic of the population as a whole. The negative perceptions of today's younger generation will influence expectations of future generations. Even now, the sample as a whole expresses a marked discrepancy between their expecations and perceptions. This discrepancy can be appreciated by comparing the order of expected characteristics with the order of perceived characteristics. A rank order correlation of the two lists (Spearman's rho) equals .21. This statistic indicates a very weak relationship between the order of the public expectation and the order of their perceptions of politicians (Table 3-7).

*Discrepancies Between Expectations and*
*Perceptions of Political Institutions*

Let us turn now to public attitudes towards institutions. Unfortunately, the Harris Poll did not pose a symmetrical set of questions for evaluating expec-

**Table 3-7**
**Discrepancy Between Expectations and Perceptions of Public Officials**

| Quality | Officials Should Be Percent | Officials Are Percent |
|---|---|---|
| Honest | 66 | 13 |
| Dedicated to hard work | 56 | 22 |
| Want to help | 51 | 25 |
| Intelligent | 41 | 27 |
| Courageous | 35 | 12 |
| Care about freedom | 28 | 14 |
| Public-spirited | 27 | 21 |
| Efficient | 24 | 8 |
| Tells it like it is | 23 | 3 |
| Idealistic | 16 | 10 |
| Creative | 12 | 2 |
| Do things by book | 4 | 7 |
| Play it safe | 2 | 15 |
| Dull | 1 | 3 |
| Couldn't care less | 1 | 8 |
| Just serving time | 1 | 8 |
| Make red tape | 1 | 11 |
| Bureaucratic | 1 | 16 |
| Corrupt | 1 | 17 |
| Only want power | 1 | 22 |
| Out for selves | 1 | 29 |
| Make promises that are never kept | 0 | 42 |

Source: Based on responses to question 21A and 21E in "Confidence and Concern," part 2, pp. 353-54, 369-70.

tations and perceptions of political institutions. Several items, however, are revealing. First, the sample positively expects an *active* government. A majority (56 percent) do *not* agree "the best government . . . governs least," and an even larger majority (68 percent) agree that the "federal government has a deep responsibility for seeing that the poor are taken care of, that no one goes hungry, and that every person achieves a minimum standard of living." There are some significant differences between subgroups in regard to this latter question. Poor, black, and Jewish respondents favored welfare measures with huge majorities of 80 to 90 percent compared to rural, Southern, and Republican respondents, whose majorities were in the range of 60 percent. Clearly, New Deal ideology retains a majority of Americans. In the eyes of most respondents, however, the problem of distributive justice is still at issue.[15] Three-quarters of the sample agreed that "the rich get richer and the poor get poorer," that "tax laws are written to help the rich, not the average man," and that "special interests get more from the government than the people do" (Table 3-8).

On the question of bias, there was a dramatic discrepancy between the respondents' view of "possible" and "actual" government performance. Of the sample, 85 percent thought "it is possible to have a federal government in which the good of the country is placed above special interests," yet 63 percent of the same sample feel that "we *do not now have* a federal government in which the good of the country is placed above special interests." In the post New Deal era there may not be a consensus as to how distributive justice may be achieved, but there is a great expectation that fairness should be the goal.

*Powerlessness and Negative Attitudes*
*toward the Political Self*

We have briefly shown that expectations and perceptions concerning politicians and government are discrepant. These data also show that individuals are pessimistic with regard to their own political behavior as well. For example, 73 percent feel that voting is the only way people like themselves can have a say about government, and 86 percent find politics and government so complicated that they do not understand what is going on. On the other hand, while a

**Table 3-8**
**Attitudes Concerning Distributive Justice**

|  | Do Feel Percent | Do Not Feel Percent | Not Sure Percent | Total (N) Percent |
|---|---|---|---|---|
| The rich get richer and the poor get poorer. | 76 | 21 | 3 | 100 (1614.4) |
| The tax laws are written to help the rich, not the average man. | 74 | 21 | 6 | 100 (1615.6) |
| Special interests get more from the government than the people do. | 74 | 13 | 13 | 100 (1613.4) |

Source: Based on responses to question 8: B, H, I in "Confidence and Concern," part 2, pp. 125-29.

**Table 3-9**
**Political Alienation and Political Activity**

| | Total Sample Percent | 1972 Voters Percent | 1972 Nonvoters Percent | Active Citizens Percent |
|---|---|---|---|---|
| Voting is the only way people like myself can have a say about how the government runs things: | | | | |
| Agree | 73 | 75 | 69 | 69 |
| Disagree | 24 | 24 | 25 | 30 |
| Not Sure | 3 | 2 | 6 | 1 |
| Total (N) | 100 (1601.9) | 100 (1171.8) | 100 (429.3) | 100 (585.1) |
| Sometimes politics and government seem so complicated that a person can't really understand what's going on: | | | | |
| Agree | 86 | 84 | 90 | 80 |
| Disagree | 12 | 15 | 8 | 19 |
| Not Sure | 2 | 1 | 3 | 1 |
| Total (N) | 100 (1381.1) | 1009 (94.3) | 100 (386) | 100 (468.6) |

Source: Based on table 078, questions 15: E and F in "Confidence and Concern," part 2, p. 272.

majority do feel that "there is something they can do about an unjust or corrupt public official," the modal response was to turn the offender out of office (23 percent). Only 14 percent considered organizing a group effort against a corrupt official. Sadly, 20 percent of the sample expressed the thought that one individual *cannot do anything* about an unjust public official, and another 18 percent feel powerless to take any action at all.

There is clearly some connection between what individuals feel capable of doing and what, in fact, they do. The causal connection between thinking and doing, however, may go both ways. While studies generally show that active participants feel more efficacious than apathetic individuals, these data demonstrate essentially no difference between the two. For example, a majority of the sample feel that "what they think doesn't count very much anymore." Yet the proportion of the "active citizens" who feel powerless (56 percent) is about the same as the proportion of the whole sample (61 percent). The difference between voters and nonvoters was also not significant. This suggests that common acts of citizenship, such as voting, are not sufficient to dispel feelings of political futility (Table 3-10).

**Table 3-10**
**Voting and Active Citizenship**

| | Voted 1972 | | Active Citizen |
|---|---|---|---|
| | Percent Did | Percent Did Not | Percent |
| What You Think Doesn't Count Very Much Anymore: | | | |
| Do Feel | 60 | 65 | 56 |
| Do Not Feel | 35 | 29 | 39 |
| Not Sure | 5 | 6 | 5 |
| Total | 100 | 100 | 100 |
| (N) | (1177.4) | (432.7) | (591.0) |

Source: Based on table 30, question 8: D in "Confidence and Concern," part 2, p. 132.

*Summary*

We may summarize the shape of political alienation in America as one in which the majority have positive but limited feelings of political efficacy. Americans feel that they can only correct political problems through the use of the ballot. Americans generally hold strong positive expectations for, but negative perceptions of, the honesty of politicians and the fairness of government. By our definition, a preponderance of Americans are alienated optimists. They do not appear to have lost faith in the system or in their political values, but feel a crisis of confidence in political leadership and social justice.

**Strategies for Coping with Alienation**

In conclusion, we would like to speculate on the alleviation of alienation. According to our typology, the dimensions of alienation are efficacy, expectations, and perceptions. Each one of these is a proper focus for healthy change. Let us take these elements in reverse order. Americans will have more positive perceptions of public officials if they can find more honest, trustworthy, and public-spirited politicians to lead them. This may be a long shot. While the image of American politicians ranks next to used-car dealers, it is going to be hard to attract more intelligent and self-respecting individuals into politics. The American image of politicians will need some time to recover from Watergate alone.

In order to bring popular perceptions in line with expectations, American politicians must, of course, avoid dishonesty. They must also, however, avoid the *appearance* of dishonesty. What is at stake here is not only a matter of personal morals, but of public purpose. Effective policy is particularly needed in the area of distributive justice. Americans want a "fairer" deal. Unfortunately, Americans do not agree as to what that deal is. A great challenge to future leaders will be the forging of a consensus on the matter of "fairness": how much income for how much work, how much income for how much need, how much income for one group relative to another.

Let us turn to the dimension of political expectations. It might be easier to narrow the discrepancy between perceptions and expectations, if expectations, in turn, were more realistic. Popular expectations need some revision with regard to the capacity to lead. Opinion polls show that political leaders are more popular after taking any decisive action than when they withhold action. According to Edelman, the reason for this is that most people feel so helpless that they need to believe that at least their leader *can* act.[16] Since the common enemies of modern life are inscrutable corporations and public bureaucracies, individuals need to personalize their heroes. If the president and the leaders of Congress are helpless in the face of inflation, war, poverty, and crime, how much more helpless must the average citizen feel? It must be recognized, however, that some problems may be unresolved no matter how dedicated the national leadership. Leaders are constrained by their limited resources, the complexity of problems, the behavior of other national leaders, and the vagaries of fortune. If Americans can revise their expectations for leadership in view of these constraints, they will not only avoid the Scylla of disappointment but also the Charybdis of demagogy.

The third element of political alienation, efficacy, may also be improved by education. Perhaps the greatest failing of American political culture is its lack of realism with respect to individual participation. The overwhelming majority of Americans believe that the only means for influencing public policy is through the ballot box, yet almost every American appreciates what an infinitesimally small contribution his one vote makes in an electoral outcome. Time and again Americans are chided for their lack of interest in voting. Voting, however, is an indivisible social benefit (like national defense). We all share in the democratic process, but each share is meaningless alone. What political education should teach is the value and legitimacy of other forms of political activity.

Organization can be learned as a means for achieving political ends. Pressure groups are a means for like-minded people to maximize their impact on policies—and more directly than by the ballot. "Pressure politics" may be compared to the advocacy system in law, with which it shares a common Anglo-Saxon origin. Advocacy arrives at truth only if the advocates' capabilities are symmetrical and, therefore, not a factor in the outcome. As long as the lawyer for each client argues his case effectively, the court can decide the case on the merits. But when one advocate is more articulate, better prepared, and has more resources, a spurious factor will weight the scale of justice. Likewise in pressure politics. The American system only arrives at justice if all of the potential groups in an issue are symmetrically mobilized. This means that consumers and corporations, the poor and the rich, the old and the young, the sick and the well must have their pressure advocates. It is not realistic to suppose that all potential groups can be equally mobilized, but the balance could be sharply redressed. The key lies in learning how to organize, learning by experience. Saul Alinsky showed that the meek may not inherit the earth, but at least they can have a better crack at it.

Although widespread political mobilization will not be without disruption, there is no reason to assume that its consequences are any worse than those of widespread political alienation. From the point of view of the individual, mobilization has distinct benefits over alienation. The social values and the competence of political participation can be satisfactorily transferred to other life areas. A society of felt competence would undoubtedly be a more satisfying one than a society of estrangement. Nor should this possibility seem farfetched. The civil-rights movement, for example, has already had important educational effects on a variety of groups, such as women, Indians, Chicanoes, welfare mothers, Italian, Irish, Polish, and other hyphenated Americans. As people begin to perceive their potential membership in groups other than ethnic ones, the resulting cross-cleavages will strengthen the fabric of democratic politics. The message of mobilization is that Americans can overcome their feeling of powerlessness through the exercise of power itself.

## Notes

1. Subcommittee on Intergovernmental Relations of the Committee on Government Operations, United States Senate, *Confidence and Concern: Citizens View American Government*, parts 1 and 2, (Washington, D.C.: U.S. Government Printing Office, December 1973).

2. Ibid., part 1, pp. 29-30, 212.

3. See Karl Marx, *Early Writings*, trans. and ed. T.B. Bottomore, (New York: McGraw-Hill, 1963) pp. 121-134 passim.

4. See the discussion in Richard Schacht, *Alienation* (Garden City, N.Y.: Doubleday and Company, Inc., Anchor Books, 1971), p. 250 and passim.

5. Ibid., p. 253 and passim. Also see the discussion in Joachim Israel, *Alienation from Marx to Modern Sociology: A Macrosociological Analysis* (Boston: Allyn and Bacon, 1971), p. 221 and passim.

6. See Schacht, *Alienation* and also Israel, *Alienation from Marx to Modern Sociology*. Melvin Seeman presents an interesting classification in the use of the term *alienation* in the sociological literature in his article "On the Meaning of Alienation," *American Sociological Review* 24: 6 (1959).

7. Erik Allardt offers a typology somewhat different from Seeman's. See chapter 2, in Allardt and Stein Rokkan, *Mass Politics: Studies in Political Sociology* (New York: The Free Press, 1970).

8. See Herbert McClosky, "Consensus and Ideology in American Politics," *American Political Science Review* vol. 58 (1964).

9. *Confidence and Concern*, p. 30.

10. Gabriel A. Almond and Sidney Verba, *The Civic Culture: Political Attitudes and Democracy in Five Nations* (Boston: Little, Brown and Company, 1965), p. 69.

11. See the discussion of Mills's writings in Israel, pp. 185-204; also C.W. Mills, *White Collar* (New York: Oxford University Press, 1956) and *The Power Elite* (New York: Oxford University Press, 1959).

12. For a diagrammatic presentation of dissonance see Robert E. Lane and David O. Sears, *Public Opinion* (Englewood Cliffs, N.J.: Prentice-Hall, Inc., 1964), p. 45. Full treatment of the subject is found in Leon Festinger, *A Theory of Cognitive Dissonance* (Evanston, Ill.: Row-Peterson, 1957).

13. For a discussion and several examples of mapping sentences, see Louis Guttman, ed., *Readings in Facet Theory* (Jerusalem, Israel, Hebrew University, offset).

14. *Confidence and Concern*, p. 9.

15. See the discussion in Chapter 2, "Economic Value and Personal Value."

16. Murray Edelman, *The Symbolic Uses of Politics* (Urbana, Ill.: University of Illinois Press, 1970), pp. 76-77.

# 4 Toward Community-Oriented Mental Health Services

Stephen L. Schensul

In the late 1950s proponents of community mental health called for a radical change in the treatment of disorders and in the delivery of psychiatric services. The movement sought to shift the emphasis of psychiatric care from narrow considerations of psychodynamic factors in the service of middle-class populations to a socioenvironnmental approach to the treatment of disorder which would be accessible to all populations. The ideological and theoretical underpinnings for these changes had emerged from research developments in several psychiatric and social science fields. One body of research results, epitomized in several large epidemiological projects begun in the 1950s, demonstrated a relationship among sociocultural, environmental, and community factors and individual psychological well-being.[1] Elements such as low income, community disorganization, and migration were identified as causal factors in psychiatric disorders.

Another research line, begun in the early thirties in a collaboration between anthropologists and psychiatrists, has been labeled "cultural and personality" studies. Work in this area caused a rethinking of the concept of the psychic unity of mankind by identifying significant crosscultural differences *in the content* of mental phenomena. Early research showed that such basic features in personality development as the Oedipal complex[2] and the anxiety connected with post-pubescence[3] may not be universal to all cultures. Later research showed important cross-cultural differences in perception[4] and world view.[5] This is not to say that there are not important cross-cultural similarities in psychodynamic processes. Leighton, Edgerton and others have identified similar psychiatric syndromes in a number of diverse cultures and societies.[6] However, the main contribution of the developing field of transcultural psychiatry has been in helping psychiatric practitioners to recognize that culture exerts a dominant influence in determining the content, form, and classification of mental disorders.[7] As a result, attempts at cross-cultural psychotherapy based on Western treatment modalities have frequently been difficult or unsuccessful.[8]

The community mental health movement sought to respond to these challenges to traditional psychiatric ideas and practices by (1) extending mental health services to populations in our society who had previously little or no access to such services; generally, this was synonymous with populations who were poor and culturally different from the mainstream of American society;

(2) directing an important part of program resources and attention to changing the environmental, community and sociocultural factors that play a role in producing mental illness; and (3) designing new treatment modalities to be specific and relevant to the populations to be served.

Thus, community mental health centers were to establish preventative and treatment programs based on the social, cultural, and community factors important in the lives of the populations served. This objective called for a considerable research effort devoted to assessing the social, economic, and psychological situations of these "new" populations from which to build new treatment modalities and prevention programs. However, few community mental health programs bothered to establish such research components. Most of these centers limited their research input to the minimum requirements of evaluation of patient statistics as set forth by the National Institute of Mental Health. While ideological statements proclaimed new and sensitive methods, implementation consisted of standard techniques transformed to new settings.

One program that did have a commitment to understanding the sociocultural and psychological environments of its clients was the community mental health program at the West Side Medical Complex in Chicago. The director of this program hired the author, an anthropologist, to set up a community research unit that would be a major component of the community mental health program.[9] Anthropology was selected as the major social science discipline in the program because of its cross-cultural perspective and its orientation toward the study of communities as functional units of human organization. This community approach fit well with the catchment area concept, in which community mental health centers were designed to provide services to designated geographic locales consisting of one or several communities. The information on structure, major institutions, and sociopolitical dynamics that the anthropologist can provide from this community approach could be crucial for planning preventative programs. The anthropologist's cross-cultural perspectives can help to generate the kind of social and cultural information important to the development of new modes of service delivery and treatment.

Ideally, the anthropologists should collect such cultural and community information and disseminate the results to the administrators and clinicians who can utilize them to plan and implement preventative and clinical programs. This conception of anthropological input represented our starting point in 1969.

Over the past five years, we have had a great deal of experience as applied researchers working with mental health staff in a variety of programs and settings. We have worked with mental health staff drawn from both within and outside the community. They have included highly trained professionals as well as community residents who had little or no training. We have done our work in programs that were controlled by mental health institutions as well as in programs controlled by the community. These experiences have changed our initial conceptions of mental health, of programs designed for the community, of appropriate training and experience for mental health workers, and of the role of applied research in a community-based program.

The first part of this paper describes our experiences in a variety of mental health settings in Chicago. The second part draws on these experiences to generalize about appropriate research, training, and models for programs directed toward the mental health of a community.

### Applied Anthropology and Mental Health in the Chicano Community

The community mental health program was established in 1967 by members of the West Side Medical Center with funds from the National Institute of Mental Health. A segment of the Lower West Side with Mexican, Middle-European and black populations was chosen as the area to be served by the program. Inpatient services at the Medical Center were linked with "outpost" clinics located in each of the communities and staffed with teams consisting of psychiatrists, psychologists, each with several psychiatric social workers, nurses, and community workers.

In the first several months the outpost clinic serving the Chicano community found itself devoting most of its time to serving older Middle-European patients who had long histories of mental illness and hospitalizations. Few Mexican residents sought help at the clinic, and on the whole its existence and services were largely ignored. The difficulties in establishing an effective mental health service in the community were exacerbated by the fact that the clinic was staffed almost exclusively by Anglos who lacked an understanding of Mexican and Chicano culture and the necessary bilingual ability for communicating effectively with Spanish-speaking patients. In addition, the clinic was burdened by a series of bureaucratic and political contingencies in the Medical Center that made it difficult for the various components of the mental health program to effectively coordinate their services.

Another problem faced by the community mental health program was the failure to achieve effective citizen participation. An important part of the community mental health movement was the involvement of citizens and consumers in the direction and formulation of program policies and objectives. Several attempts to form advisory boards for the clinic failed, and the idea was eventually abandoned (although advisory boards have been recently and more effectively revived). Thus, residents neither used the services nor interested themselves in the clinic's operations. The clinic, and in turn the entire community mental health program, stood outside of the mainstream of community life and was only tangentially related to the community's health needs.

I came into the community mental health program a year and a half after it was established, and in succeeding months several other anthropologists and

social researchers joined the community research unit. There were great
expectations on the part of the clinical staff that our research team would
quickly discover the key cultural and community factors to ease their problems.
Since these problems were very real and immediate, the clinical staff felt that the
anthropologists had to provide this information almost immediately. It soon
became apparent to the clinicians that we did not have a ready-made set of
principles or gimmicks that could help them out of the difficulties they faced in
the community. The clinicians also had little understanding of usual anthropological research methods, which generally require time to get to know the
people and the communities on a first-hand basis. When clear-cut results and new
facts were not quickly forthcoming, clinical personnel lost interest in hearing
from us. From our perspective we believed we would prove our utility to the
program once we began to be more involved in the communities.

We began our work among the Chicano populations, who had rapidly become
the largest ethnic group in the area, replacing the established Middle-European
Polish and Czech residents. Early in our research we found that the residents of
the Chicano community have very close ties with Mexico. This seemed to us to
have great implications for the design of mental health services. Nearly 80
percent of the Chicano adult population came to Chicago in the 1960s directly
from Mexico; approximately 15 percent of the adults are from Texas, and only 5
percent are Chicago born.[10] The great majority of the people are Spanish
speaking, young, and have large families. The West Side community has become
a port of entry for Mexican immigrants and the major residential enclave for
Chicanos in Chicago.

Our early research identified clear differences between Chicanos and other
populations concerning perceptions, practices, and beliefs about mental health.
Although many of these factors have been described for Chicano communities in
other areas, we found that the recency of arrival of migrants and the close ties
residents maintain with Mexico created a stronger pattern for practices and
beliefs that were different from those of mainstream America.

1. Unlike Anglo medical beliefs, the traditional Mexican view of disease
causation and symptomatology does not reflect a sharp distinction between the
mental and physical aspects of health; this interrelationship between physical
and mental factors may be one factor in the negative attitude of Chicanos
toward the separation of medical and psychiatric services.

2. Chicano beliefs about disease causation and symptomatology include a
large number of illnesses that are distinct from those of Anglo-Americans. These
disease configurations, or "folk illnesses," include *el ojo malo* (the evil eye),
*empacho* (stomach upset), *bilis* (the product of extreme anger), and *suste*
(resulting from fright or shock).

3. The existence of a complex of indigenous resources including *curanderos*,
or traditional Mexican medical practitioners, is a very important health resource
in the West Side area. From our research we can say with some confidence that

Chicano individuals utilize folk curers more often than they do "standard" psychiatric facilities.[11] The *curanderos*, or folk medical specialists, provide low-cost care with an emphasis on a personalized and "sacred" approach. They use a large herbal inventory in addition to other techniques, such as dietary restrictions, chiropractics, and religio-magical curing.

4. Chicano psychiatric patients show pathology and personality structures different from those reported for other ethnic groups. For example, visions and voices are a widely acceptable part of normal functioning and maintenance of health in the Chicano community. A member of our research team has demonstrated the tendency for Anglo psychiatric staff to misinterpret these visions and voices as psychopathology.[12]

When we disseminated this initial information to the professional clinical staff, we were surprised to find that it produced little interest and no perceptible changes in the program. Our status in the program remained low and our alienation from clinical operations increased. Although we can, in retrospect, see that both sides failed to appreciate the point of view and professional concerns of one another, the effect at that time was our withdrawal from intensive involvement in the clinical and policy aspects of the community mental health program. We began to search in the Chicano community for situations in which our research skills and information could make a useful contribution to social action.

An important breakthrough occurred in our relationship with Chicano community groups in the summer of 1969. We became involved, with the staff of the local settlement house, in the organization of block clubs in the Chicano community. Besides being directly involved in the organizing action, our field workers used minutes at meetings, surveys, and other data-collection operations to facilitate block club organizations. This development, six months after the initiation of our field work in the area, led to intensive involvement with a number of action groups in the Chicano community over the past four years.

From that time, we began to seek out action situations in the community where our research could be helpful to community development goals. In this period we participated actively in community action organizations to the extent that such activity was approved by the membership. We constructed research operations in areas that we thought would have maximum benefit for community action research, and seized opportunities in which community action groups, concerned residents, or agency staff could provide us with entry to data-gathering opportunities in the community. Our activities emphasized rapid feedback of research information to organizations and individuals in the Chicano community.

In the beginning of 1971 a new climate began developing in the community. The increasing strength of the Chicano movement on the national level made people in the community aware of the potential for change on the local scene. A significant portion of the newly developed activist groups began to direct their attention toward health and mental health services in the community. For example, one group, with the help of some volunteer medical personnel, organized a free health clinic in the neighborhood settlement house. Another group, consisting of Chicano ex-addicts, developed a volunteer program in drug abuse. These efforts were organized for the most part by Chicano residents who had special experience, training, and talents for working on these health issues.

Our applied research group was fortunate in this period to have established good working relationships with many of these groups. As they were getting organized we were asked to participate in various aspects of the groups' activities and to contribute research results on specific issues of interest to them.

One of these community-developed programs is the Chicano Mental Health Training Program. The objectives of the training program are to increase the number of Chicano mental health practitioners in the community, provide training for community residents in mental health concepts appropriate for Chicanos in Chicago, and to coordinate mental health services with other organizations and programs working for the betterment of the Chicano community. This program is controlled and directed by community residents.

It was only after some initial conflict that this program became community based. When news of New Careers Funding for mental health was first received by the West Side mental health institutions, a committee was formed to develop a proposal for a program to be based in the Medical Center. Several of the Chicano activists interested in mental health issues decided that the proposal developed by this "establishment" committee did not demonstrate any knowledge of the mental health needs of the community. As a result they developed an alternate proposal. Subsequently the Medical Center committee withdrew its application and supported the community proposal. This application for funds became the first federal grant to be received by the community.

Our anthropological research group had developed close relationships with several of the activists. We were invited to help in the planning of the program and in the criticism of the Medical Center proposal. For the first time we found that much of our research data was useful to the planning and construction of education and service models in mental health. Our involvements included:

1. incorporation of our research data on Chicano health and mental health into the funding proposal;
2. use of our health and mental health data and our experience in the community in the planning of a curriculum for the trainees, and in the consideration of new social psychiatric models appropriate for Chicanos;
3. participation in teaching, seminars, and discussions with interns in which research data and their implications for mental health were discussed;
4. conducting sessions on the nature of research and the utility of research for mental health services; and
5. consultation with the program's research assistant in developing evaluation techniques for assessing the effectiveness of the program.

In the last two years there have been several instances of direct collaboration between staff members and trainees of the Chicano Mental Health Training Program and members of our anthropological group. This experience began to give us a more positive view of collaboration between anthropologists and mental health workers. It emphasized to us the effectiveness of community-based groups in planning their own programs.

By 1971 the administrators of the community mental health program, perhaps in part as a result of our activities, decided that more Chicanos should be on the staff of the outpost clinic. A Chicano who had long experience in providing social services in the community was hired as the director. He made several changes that had great implications for the utilization of mental health services by community residents.[13]

As Anglo staff attrition rates increased, they were replaced by Chicano Spanish-speaking mental health workers. Positions were opened for "paraprofessionals," allowing knowledgeable and experienced Chicano residents to join the staff of the mental health outpost. Linkages were developed with other Chicano community health and social service agencies in the attempt to develop a comprehensive network of services.

The changes promoted at the outpost served several ends. The credibility of the outpost in the community was increased and people became more aware of its services and programs. New and more effective mental health services were developed and linked to other community resources. The changes also served to make mental health an issue in the community and increased the interest of community leaders in developing Chicano input into the mental health field. However, the most dramatic results of the changes in the cultural and community orientation of the mental health center are visible in the changes that have occurred in the ethnic composition of the clients coming to the center.

In June of 1969 only 20 percent of the clients were Latinos, although 75 percent of the community was Latino. By June of 1972, after most of the changes in the outpost were affected, the case load closely matched the ethnic composition of the general community. In addition, the total number of patients in the period between 1969 and 1972 increased by almost 90 percent.

The transformation of staff and their involvement in community issues also had great impact on our relationship to the mental health workers of the outpost. Anthropologists and mental health workers began collaborating on community action projects. Research projects were developed that involved anthropologists and mental health workers jointly collecting data relating to aftercare and psychosomatic symptomatology. Anthropologists also participated in case conferences in which Chicano cultural and community input was needed. We found the staff open to our information, willing to participate directly in research activities designed by themselves or by us, and supportive of our role as a community research facility for Chicano action projects. Thus, a community-based staff had a powerful effect in turning the orientation of the clinic from traditional psychiatry to an innovative program designed for the needs of residents.

### Community-Oriented Mental Health

This section draws on our experiences in the Chicano community in Chicago to construct a set of guidelines for community responsive mental health programs. The creation of an effective mental health program in a community involved the following issues: developing a relevant service delivery model, identifying appropriate program personnel, and assessing community structure and needs.

Providing solutions to these issues involves a close collaboration between the clinician or service provider and those individuals responsible for monitoring the pulse of the community. Toward this end we will also discuss applied research as a mental health tool, and useful applied research methods.

### *Types of Service Delivery Models*

There has been a great deal of criticism of community mental health programs around the country for their failure to achieve many of their stated goals.[14] Although prevention of mental illness was seen as one of the primary goals of these programs, there was great naiveté in operating strategies and ineffectiveness in the implementation of preventive programs. Mental health workers were found to be amateurs in matters of sociopolitical and institutional change. Many of these programs were hampered by the basic conservatism and institution-bound orientation of their sponsoring facilities. Most programs used traditional treatment modalities rather than seeking to develop treatment models specific to the cultures and communities within which they were working. As a result, many critics have sounded the death knell for community mental health and signaled a retreat back to traditional nongeographically based psychotherapeutic services.

I believe it is a mistake to consider the ideology and goals of the community mental health movement as a failure. Rather, I feel it has not been given an adequate test. We have seen in the Chicago situation the creation of effective community mental health service and education programs when their orientation shifted from the institutions to the communities in which they were providing service. It has been community residents both as staff and as developers of their own mental health programs who have been the crucial factors in creating that shift in orientation. The following principles of service delivery are based on the crucial role residents play in the creation of effective services in their community:

1. The provision of mental health services needs to be a part of a general process of community development and the improvement of the quality of life for its residents.

2. Mental health services must be seen as only one element in a broad and comprehensive approach in helping individuals to solve their adaptational

problems, and such services must be linked to other health and social services to create a comprehensive service delivery system.

3. New models sensitive and relevant to cultural, intracultural, and community variations must be developed to achieve an adequate service delivery system, since standard techniques of therapy have been clearly demonstrated to be ineffective among populations outside the middle-class mainstream (and perhaps ineffective among this group as well).

4. Service delivery systems must be controlled by, and responsive to, the priority, perceptions, and demands of consumers of those services. As a result of our experiences in the Chicano community in Chicago, I believe that it is crucial that the direction and actual control of program resources be in the hands of an organized group of community residents rather than controlled by institutional and bureaucratic forces outside the service area. Such a community base promotes a more effective development of a comprehensive service system, a more responsive consumer-oriented program, and facilitates the establishment of new approaches to service delivery.

*Types of Mental Health Workers*

Our experiences in Chicago taught us a great deal about the various kinds of mental health workers and gave us a feeling about those that were more amenable to a community orientation and to social and cultural information about residents. The factors to consider include level of training, ethnicity and place of residence, prior knowledge concerning the language and culture of consumers, past experiences in researcher-clinician relationships, and a perception of the need for innovative rather than standard therapeutic and preventative models.

We found, as a result of our experiences in the community mental health program, that individuals who consider themselves "professionals" below the level of M.D.'s or Ph.D.'s (such as those with Master's Degrees in psychology, social work, or nursing), who live outside the service area, who are of a different ethnic group than the consumers of the services, and who have had little experience in the language and culture of the community, are relatively insensitive to information concerning the culture and community of their patients. These individuals are rarely willing to change their treatment methods to make them more appropriate to patient needs. Our work with such individuals was extremely frustrating. They rarely ventured out of the clinic and into the community, nor did they pay much attention to the information we were supplying about the community. In general, those instances of effective collaboration with professional mental health workers of this type were with individuals who already had an established appreciation of cultural and community factors and their relevance to mental health treatment. Thus, in our experience, rather than changing peoples' attitudes and perceptions, we find that data on culture and community is far more effective in supporting and extending the styles of operation of individuals who already have such an orientation.

Conversely, we have found that individuals who live within the communities in the catchment area, who are of the same ethnic group as the consumers of services, and who have had a high degree of experience in the language and culture of the community are relatively more amenable to community information and psychiatric innovation. This applies to individuals with high levels of professional training (including psychiatrists) as well as those who have had a low level of professional training (including neighborhood or community workers).

These individuals have a stake in extending their information about the community, in relating their work to other community actions and developments, and in converting cultural and community information into more effective programs. We have, however, found that some mental health workers are unresponsive to added community information. These indigenous workers, because they are members of a particular ethnic group, consider themselves experts on every aspect of their group. We have seen these mental health workers present highly conflicting cultural or community statements as "facts" when they are simply opinions or results of personal experience. For example, while many Chicano mental health workers affirmed that *curanderos* are a thriving institution in the community, others, based only on their personal experience, denied their importance or even (in one case) their existence. One mental health worker stressed the element of male dominance in the family structure of Chicanos in Chicago, while another, a member of the community in equally good standing, denied this statement and stressed the degree to which such a concept is an Anglo-created stereotype. Ideas based only on personal knowledge and experience can be seriously misleading in the development of a mental health training or service program. Thus, community research can be most beneficial when individuals have considerable knowledge of the culture and the community, but at the same time appreciate the limitations of their perceptions and the need to collect new information they would not get in the course of their regular activities.[15] Thus, the strategy of drawing staff from the population sectors to be served may be a key factor in creating a responsive and innovative program.

*Useful Community Information*

The ethnographic tradition in anthropology has meant a descriptive approach to the events, institutions, habits, and customs of people in a residential community. Anthropologists talk about such categories of phenomena as religious life, economic and subsistence activities, and political institutions. Frequently, these ethnographies describe the operation of these institutions and aspects of life apart from behavior or individual variations that may be present in the group. These ethnographics provide descriptions of "ideal" or "normative" behavior and are designed to make information available about the group to anthropologists and other social scientists living at some distance from the community.

This approach has come under considerable attack by many social scientists as well as by individuals whose groups have been described in such a fashion. For example, Romano[16] and Vaca[17] have shown that descriptions of Chicano communities that focus on ideal patterns produce cultural stereotypes not unlike those held by the lay public. Anthropological research exhibits such stereotypic views as pessimism, fatalism, female martyrdom, male dominance and machismo. Similar portraits of other ethnic groups and communities are producing an equal amount of criticism. Obviously, this nonbehavioral, normative approach can provide little useful information for mental health workers concerned with treatment of individuals.

Another approach to the description of communities is to go beyond the ideal or the normative, to describe the patterns of variation that exist in all human communities. For a mental health worker, a simple description of the institution of *curanderismo* in a Chicano community may be important as an initial orientation, but the essential questions relate to the variability of its use. What types of individuals utilize the services of *curanderos*? Who is likely to define mental health problems in terms of folk categories of illness? While this information is frequently harder to generate, it involves the applied researcher and the mental health worker in a realistic appraisal of diversity in the community and results in the kind of information that can be useful in planning therapeutic programs and constructing new therapeutic approaches.

The cross-cultural and community orientation of an applied researcher in a mental health program results in several kinds of "informational payoffs" that have significance for education and service delivery. The first kind of information deals with analysis of the sociopolitical process in the community, examination of indigenous leaders and study of important institutions, organizations, agencies and services. Such information can make an important contribution to the development of preventative programs, help in establishing linkages between mental health services and other social services in the community, and develop effective outreach programs in which mental health services are disbursed to key sectors of the community.

A second area of informational output is the investigation of that aspect of community life and behavior related to health and mental health problems, and practices and residents' adaptational strategies. Therapeutic programs and treatment modalities must fit into the expectations, perceptions, practices, and use of resources employed by community residents. This does not mean that, for example, therapists in our community must also become folk curers, but it can be extremely helpful to be aware of how *curanderos* work, the way in which Chicanos define illness to *curanderos*, and perhaps even to refer patients to *curanderos* when appropriate.

A third area of potential information is the investigation of issues concerning patients seen at the clinic. Such information can range from research on sociocultural concomitants of mental illness to anthropological evidence concerning the cultural and community aspects of individual cases. The social researcher, rather than playing the role of expert, brings in a body of information about the community and culture which, in conjunction with clinical information, may provide clues concerning kin supports, treatment modality, or need for hospitalization. The researcher can also be helpful in analyzing clinical data and medical records collected in the course of providing direct treatment. Survey data collected in the community can be matched with clinical information to examine similarities and differences between patients and the general population. The results of this kind of research can have significance not only for the development of appropriate therapeutic programs, but also for the evaluation of the effectiveness of clinic operations in the community.

## The Collaboration of Researchers and Mental Health Workers

Probably most important, in influencing mental health workers to use the researcher's information and approaches, is to reduce the rivalry and hostility that has existed between them. Making cultural and community information relevant to preventative and clinical issues must be done as a partnership in which both groups recognize each other's experience and fund of information; a common area of interest must be established, and each group must share an equivalent responsibility to come up with solutions from its own unique perspective. In our own experience, this partnership has worked best when clinicians, administrators, and other mental health workers have research expertise so they can collaborate with researchers in collecting data and seeking solutions to key issues. This experience suggests that an essential part of the mental health workers' training and education should be enough research methodology so that effective communication with researchers can be achieved and mental health workers can develop their own research and information-gathering projects.

On the other hand, the social scientist has to keep his side of the bargain. He should have some training or experience in looking at clinical or preventative issues. He should show a willingness to include nonresearchers in the formulation of research problems. He needs to be the kind of individual that does not hide the shortcomings of social research behind empty jargon or inflated promises. He should not present himself as an expert in the culture or the community but rather provide help in developing questions and methods and techniques for answering them. Mental health workers need to look for the kind of social researcher who evaluates his research work on the basis of its contribution to the success of a clinical or preventative program rather than simply on its utility for his career aspirations or publishing needs.

## Useful Applied Research Methods
## for Mental Health Workers

The elements of research methodology that should be incorporated into mental health education come from a number of social science fields. Anthropology has contributed some of the more qualitative approaches to the study of human behavior, while sociology and psychology have provided research designs and methods for a more structured and quantitative studies. For the mental health worker, discipline lines are less important than achieving a working knowledge of a variety of behavioral science methods.

Since I am an anthropologist I will single out two techniques that are basic to anthropological research in urban and rural communities. These techniques are described as "participant observation" and "key informant" interviewing and can be particularly helpful to mental health workers. The basic elements of these methods involve an immersion of the anthropologist in the ongoing events and interactions of key sectors of a community. Living in the community and participating in community activities, the anthropologist begins to take on and internalize the way of life as residents themselves perceive and are involved in it. For the anthropologist this internalization of community knowledge and experience is an essential process in his understanding and learning about the community. Essential to this participation and involvement is the development of rapport and trusting relationships with community residents. Although the anthropologist gets to know a large number of people, he depends on a core group of close personal friends to help him to guide his actions, provide him with essential information, and to allow him to get a perspective on events and behaviors in the community that may be confusing to him. Thus, the essence of the anthropological approach involves participation in the group and the development of personal relationships with its members in combination with research methodology developed in a number of social science fields.

The standard approaches to research methodology in the social sciences are designed to produce academically oriented research generally unrelated to action and program considerations. One of the reasons for the hostilities between researchers and clinicians has been that research results using these methods have often failed to pay off in terms of program or action implications. Thus, much of what has been written concerning the need for applied research represents little more than lip service. There are few cases from which a set of sophisticated applied research techniques or methods can be drawn. This gap in information concerning action versus research puts severe limitations on the training of both the mental health worker and the anthropologist. Mental health training programs, at least for several years, will have to depend on the personal communications of anthropologists and other social scientists with applied research experience. Mental health workers will probably have to learn many of the applied research techniques on their own.

Our community research unit has had to develop our own set of procedures for maximizing the utility of research results. Space does not permit a detailed discussion of the strategies we have employed, but I can list some useful procedures which, if used as a guide, can allow a mental health worker to critically assess research techniques and to negotiate a set of realistic expectations with researchers.

1. A mental health worker should never assume that a research specialist is going to come up with useful information if the two have not developed some sort of collaborative relationship. Answers to specific questions come only from research procedures directly aimed at the questions the mental health worker has raised.

2. Most research techniques for gathering data, ranging from developing and administering surveys to participant observation to structured interviews, can easily be learned by mental health workers. If mental health workers are to collaborate effectively with researchers, they must also participate in the construction of data-gathering procedures, administration of the instruments, analysis of results, and assessment of the implications of those results.

3. Research results most frequently assess situations rather than indicating clear solutions. Very frequently they may even make things more complicated by introducing more variables for consideration. Mental health workers have as much responsibility as researchers for working out the implications of a body of research data and in seeing that they have an impact on programs and actions.

4. To be effective, research results must be available at the right time to the right people at the right place. It is standard procedure for many researchers to take an inordinate amount of time between initiation of a research project and writing up the resulting data. Neither the applied researcher nor the mental health worker has time for such a slow pace. If a key decision must be made in a week, information-gathering procedures and analysis must be adjusted to that time frame or the entire procedure may be useless.

5. We have also found that written dissemination of research results is inadequate if impact on action is to be maximized. It is necessary to present lectures, make oral reports, show slides, and provide handouts to get across research findings. Another useful technique for increasing impact, perhaps the most effective, is to sit in on planning sessions and other meetings where there are opportunities to introduce information in the context of actual programmatic decision making.

6. An important element in applied research is the necessity of providing continuous feedback of data to programs rather than promising results at some unspecified time in the future. In other words, research and action must interact so that better research questions may be developed, even if this means continuous alterations and midstream shifts in the design of research. Just as in the timing issue, the impact of high-quality results can be lost if either the researcher or the mental health worker fails to relate to new contingencies that have developed in the action situation.

In this chapter I have presented experiences and guidelines that emphasize the need to put the "community" back into community mental health. Programs designed to provide psychiatric services can be most effective when the control of the program is in the hands of consumers, when the staff is drawn from similar backgrounds and experiences to the people they serve, and when services are geared to the adaptational needs of residents. Such a program can not only serve the mentally ill but can significantly contribute to the mental health of the community by:

1. linking into an indigenous service system geared to meet a broad variety of needs;
2. adding to the total resources controlled by the community;
3. providing a base for identification of community needs and of collective community action; and
4. involving residents in a process of creating their own services for themselves and their neighbors.

Applied community researchers can play an important role in bringing about this community orientation by:

1. focusing attention on the significant cultural, social and community factors that affect the provision of mental health services;
2. helping to transform questions that arise out of the provision of services into methods for getting information to answer those questions;
3. developing information that accurately reflects the behavior, attitudes, and perspectives of community residents;
4. using research results to more effectively plan and implement courses of action in treatment and prevention; and
5. evaluating the relevance, effectiveness and utility of mental health programs from the point of view of consumers.

Research can be a tool that develops in the mental health worker the ability to analyze his actions from the point of view of the consumers and community residents he serves.

Mental health and other social service programs cannot afford to treat residents as the objects of service. Service-providers must be integrated into the community and work in partnership with residents if they are to develop a community-oriented program. Institution-oriented programs have failed to provide effective mental health services in local communities. It is now time to give the people a chance.

### Notes

1. A.B. Hollingshead and F.C. Redlich, *Social Class and Mental Illness* (New York: John Wiley and Sons, 1958); L. Srole, T.S. Langer, S.T. Michael, M.K. Opler, and T.A.C. Rennie, *Mental Health in the Metropolis: The Midtown Manhattan Study* (New York: McGraw-Hill, 1962); B. Malzberg and E.S. Lee, *Migration and Mental Disease: A Study of First Admissions to Hospitals for Mental Disease* (Social Research Council, 1956); and A.H. Leighton, *My Name is Legion: Foundations for a Theory of Man in Relation to Culture* (New York: Basic Books, 1959).

2. Bronislau Malinowski, *Sex and Repression in Savage Society* (Cleveland: World Publishers, 1968).

3. Margaret Mead, *Coming of Age in Samoa* (New York: Morrow, 1939).

4. M.H. Segall, D.T. Campbell, and M.J. Herskovits, *The Influence of Culture on Visual Perceptions* (Indianapolis: Bobbs-Merrill, 1966).

5. H. Conklin, "Hanunoo Color Categories," *Southwest Journal of Anthropology* (Winter 1955), pp. 339-44.

6. A.H. Leighton and J. Murphy, "Gross Cultural Psychiatry" in Leighton and Murphy, *Explorations in Social Psychiatry*, 1965.

7. Ari Kiev, *Transcultural Psychiatry* (New York: The Free Press, 1972).

8. E.F. Torrey, *The Mind Game: Witch Doctors and Psychiatrists* (New York: Emerson Hall, 1972).

9. Dr. Harvey Freed has been very supportive of applied research as it relates to psychiatric services and community development. He discusses the development of the program in his *Holy Grail, Chicago Style: Community Development and Mental Health* (unpublished).

10. S.L. Schensul, "Action Research: The Applied Anthropologist in a Community Mental Health Program," in Alden Redfield ed., *Anthropology Beyond the University* (Athens: University of Georgia Press, 1973).

11. Philip Ayala, "The Chicano Mental Health Training Program: Alternatives to Traditional Psychiatric Training," presented at the American Anthropological Association Meetings, Toronto, Ontario, December 1972; and Emile Schepers, "Voices and Visions in Chicano Culture: Some Implications for Psychiatry and Anthropology," ibid.

12. Emile Schepers, "Voices, Visions and Strange Ideas: Delusions and

Hallucinations in a Mexican-Origin Community," for a Doctor of Philosophy degree in Anthropology, Northwestern University, 1973.

13. Albert Vazquez, "The Effects of Change in the Cultural Orientation of a Community Mental Health Clinic," American Anthropological Association Meetings, Toronto, Canada, December 1972.

14. Ralph Nader, *The Mental Health Complex, Part I* (Washington, D.C.: Community Mental Health for Study of Responsive Law, 1972).

15. Personal communication from Emile Schepers.

16. Octavio I. Romano, "The Anthropology and Sociology of the Mexican-Americans: The Distortion of Mexican-American History," *El Grito* 2 (1968): 13-26.

17. Nicholas C. Vaca, "The Mexican-American in the Social Sciences 1912-1970 Part II: 1936-1970," *El Grito* 4:1 (1970): 17-50.

# 5

## Treatment Through Institutional Change

Walter Fisher

### An Overview of Trends in Mental Health

An examination of current mental health practices in the various parts of the United States reveals a variety of trends: returning mental health responsibilities to the local community, eliminating the public sector and turning over mental illness problems to the private sector, turning away from the medical model towards a human service model, expanding research facilities, increasing somatic therapies, reexamining social institutions and studying their impact on deviance, and dealing with deviance through the corrections and criminal justice system.

It is apparent that these divergent trends are based on a multiplicity of heterogenous assumptions. These differences also illustrate the subjectivity of the field of mental health today. Few current strategies, ideologies, or approaches stem from scientific study or objective evaluation systems.[1] Approaches to deviance tend to be predicated more on political, economic, and value issues than on the science of behavior.

As a result of the weak epistemological state of the field, new trends can result from the preferences held by persons with power. It is not unusual for a new state governor to appoint a new director of mental health who, in turn, changes the direction of the whole department. The new direction will most likely reflect the agendas, political pressures, and varying priorities of the director, the governor or the legislature. For example, in order to meet middle-class demands for holding the line on state taxes, governors, through their human service directors, have packaged human service programs that can be provided with fewer tax dollars. One result of these programs is that services for the disadvantaged and minorities have been reduced. The rationales for these reductions are, of course, unproven and without empirical support. The human service field has become a confused culture with vague boundaries, continuously shifting solutions, and little if any evaluation. The victims of most new trends, as usual, are various minority groups, who exericse little political power.

This study approaches the chaos of mental health programs and therapies from the point of view of human service. First, the important trends and therapeutic models of the past twenty years are examined in some detail. Concentration is on the medical-Freudian model and its decline. Then discussion proceeds to the climate for change in the field of human services, new approaches, and the concept of treatment through institutional change. The focus of this section is on experiences by which people grow. Finally, I will indulge in some speculation on the future of human services.

## Personal Observations on Traditional
## Assumption Systems

In 1954, I began working in a state hospital. Prior to that my education and work in the field were limited to the university, a university clinic, and an elitist university psychiatric center. I was educated and trained in what I can best describe as the Medical-Freudian-Disease-Cure-Hospital-Specialist Model. At the time, university students were primarily educated in the information and skills of that system. The students were not sensitized to the political, sociological, and economic significance of the model.

Freud was unquestionably the seminal thinker in the mental health orientation of the 1940s and 1950s. With his emphasis on the unconscious, he laid the burden of determinism and its implications on caregivers for most of the twentieth century up to the present. In brief, he said that during the first five years of life the child, in interaction with the people in his crucial life space over the issues of socialization, develops an irrational unconscious system. For the remainder of his life, the individual's behavior is in a great part determined by these unconscious vectors. With great volitional effort, for brief periods of time, he might alter the powerful dynamics of these vectors, but his "New Year-type Resolutions" decay rapidly under the potent unconscious forces of anxiety, guilt, depression, etc.

The Freudian position established a number of patterns. Freud set the stage for determinism in the field of mental health. The designation of deviant behavior during the twentieth century was encoded for the most part, in concepts that implied that the individual had little or no volitional control over his behavior. Tics, multiple personalities, schizophrenia, amnesias, fugue states, dissociations, and phobias are examples determined behavioral deviance.

Although Freud did not ignore or deny the impact of the individual's life space (milieu), determinism focused on the inner dynamics of the individual. While inner forces were the result of an epigenetic pattern, after the early years, environmental forces had greatly reduced impact. The unconscious was the greatest source of variance in predicting important human behavior.

With the establishment of the concept of unconscious determinism, mental illness emerged in the context of disease. It was assumed that people who performed in a deviant fashion were unable to interrupt their deviancy of their own volition; mental illness was really no different than a broken leg. Although others had viewed deviant behavior as a disease, it was Freud who legitimized the concept. Several interesting implications are worth noting at this point. Once the disease concept was accepted, it led to an obsession with "cure." The aim was to return patients to an idealized mental state. In order to cure people, however, it was necessary to find the cause of their illness. It was assumed that the cause was intraorganismic in nature: early learning experience, biochemical, or neurological. The assumption followed, therefore, that the treatment of patients would be maximized in the medical configuration.

The process of diagnosis and treatment was considered to be terribly complicated and lengthy. The therapist had to gain access to the individual's unconscious and to his past. A therapeutic and diagnostic technology evolved to communicate with unconscious systems: free association, interpretation of dreams, interpretation of everyday pathology, projective techniques, analysis of detailed case histories, etc. All of these processes were time consuming, required considerable expertise, and were difficult to evaluate. The focus of the treatment was on a search of the past through a transference relationship with the therapist. Unless done expertly, the present could be lost and an outpatient career could evolve into a relationship with the therapist that might endure a lifetime.

It was generally accepted that treatment of the "disease" was to be left in the hands of elite therapists, primarily psychoanalysts. In order to assume this responsibility, psychoanalysts had to be carefully trained. Their training in turn was demanding, lengthy, and expensive. Furthermore, it was assumed that the treatment process was most effective in a dyadic relationship between a single patient and a single therapist.

In the tradition of the disease model, patients were judged in regard to their prognosis. The prognosis was based on their achieving a "normal" behavior pattern by means of analytical techniques. As a result, it became fashionable to brand "untreatable" those who did not respond to the analytical method. In the twentieth century, most therapeutic systems adopted the notion that those who do not respond to therapeutic procedures are grave therapeutic risks. A tendency has developed to expel those unable to respond. It is not so much the therapeutic system that is chastised as the individual who does not respond.

In summary, the implications of the Freudian position assigned deviance to the category of a disease. Its treatment focused on finding the cause of the intraorganismic disease and intervening with some corresponding technique. The therapists were to be highly trained, preferably psychoanalysts, and the primary consumers were the good prognostic risks. Out of this work, it was thought, there might ultimately emerge a "cure" for mental illness.

I came to the state hospital indoctrinated and armed with these ideologies and assumptions. From the beginning, I found myself at odds with the hospital administrators and the psychiatrists who were responsible for treatment planning and over-all philosophy within the hospital. Until recently, I do not think that I really understood why this conflict occurred. At the time I developed many conjectures or hypotheses: most of the treatment staff was conservative in contrast to my liberalness; the medical staff wanted to utilize medical skills in order to maintain their power vis-à-vis nonmedical staff; or the medical staff was not bright or well informed. These conjectures might well have been correct, but the real issue was that the staff acted as if they were dealing with mental health issues when, in fact, the problems were more correctional in nature. I will attempt to clarify this vital issue.

Mental health problems studied by Freud related to a small group of people (those labeled hysterics and anxiety hysterics) who felt they were emotionally disturbed and sought help on a *voluntary basis.* This is the crux of the matter: most therapies are organized around individuals who seek self-actualization on a voluntary basis. This is clear from the educational themes communicated to the students of my time. These were, principally, that the client has to be motivated to change, and therefore the therapist should be nondirective and should allow the client to seek his own solutions. The therapist should not advise the client, should not lead the client, and should respect his volitional system. Therapeutic techniques, therefore, attempt to free the volitional system so that the individual can make decisions on a conscious, factual, and rational basis within the constraints and boundaries of our society.

Restating this theme in modern Freudian terminology: the executive ego, taking into consideration the voices and pressures of the id, the super ego, the synthetic ego, and society, makes an ego-free decision that is most adaptive for all "parties" concerned. Obviously, there is serious disagreement as to how to free up an individual's decision-making apparatus.

From the end of the nineteenth century up to the 1950s, it was generally assumed that the medical-Freudian model held the solution for most deviances. The medical-Freudian model was attractive to most mental health workers and helped to recruit them into its system.

There were two motion pictures, Spellbound and Seventh Veil, vintage late forties and early fifties, that provide the romantic metaphor of traditional mental health systems. In both of these motion pictures, the client has an unconscious obstacle that is interfering with his or her life style of achieving happiness. In each case in partnership with an attractive opposite-sexed therapist, the problem is ferreted out and this, of course, leads to the happy-ever-after illusion.[2]

Staffs in most mental health agencies, including myself, were trapped in this medical-Freudian model. No matter how or why a client came to the door, he was offered the same general model for service. Even clients dragged to the door kicking, screaming, and hollering by several burly policemen were offered traditional psychotherapeutic services. Those many clients who refused the services, particularly in state hospitals, were considered poor prognostic possibilities. Even though clients arrived for a variety of reasons, we behaved as if they were all sick and as if they had voluntarily arrived at the agency seeking help.

For each of these clients, we managed to find a psychiatric-sick-label. In some cases, these labels became their primary identification for life. These labels persist even though most clinicians believe that they convey no significant information. In fact, Hollingshead and Redlich have reported that there are no relationships between psychiatric services and psychiatric labels. Their conclusion is that labels correlate only with socioeconomic status and racial identity.[3]

For three or four years, I played the medical-Freudian game within the context of the state hospital. I frequently commented on how few of the residents seemed to be able to utilize the services I offered, but this did not deter me during these early years. I was appalled, however, by the coercive techniques utilized by the psychiatric staff. At that time, in the name of helping patients, state agencies utilized convulsive therapies on a massive scale, as well as lobotomies, hydrotherapy, packs, sulphur and oil, and chemotherapy.

The state hospital became the "garbage can" for the flotsam and jetsam of society. It became the Devil's Island for those who did not fit into correctional institutions or the other mental health agencies. The residents were the "losers" of society, persons who could not make it in other social institutions.[4]

By the middle fifties, the state hospitals reached their nadir (peak patient load, lowest per diems, greatest deterioration of physical plant, and average resident stay at its longest duration). Except on the intake wards, treatment disappeared from the agency. Both staff and residents gave up hope and settled into a state of apathy and despair. Mental health experts in the universities, private practice, and the clinics pointed fingers of derision towards state hospitals. They withdrew accreditation from the state hospitals and called for their immediate destruction. I believe that the failure of state hospitals reflected the massive failure of the medical-Freudian model and not simply the failure of particular agencies. The other mental health agencies only *appeared* to be functioning because they were able to transfer their problems to state hospitals. The most difficult clients were sent to these "leprosariums." The system itself, however, was no better than its weakest link.

## Factors Contributing to the Decline
## of the Model

One reason for the breakdown of the medical-Freudian model lies in the definition of the target population. In designing a treatment system, Freud was heavily influenced by his clients' and his own style of life. This is true, of course, for all mental health theorists. Most of the mental health theories designed in the nineteenth and twentieth centuries were created and generated by those employed in private mental health centers, universities, and private practices. Typically, their clients were intelligent, high-resource, middle- and upper-class persons with well-developed personal equation factors (energy, appearance, personality, and goal orientation). It was therefore assumed that such clients were the primary target population. Clients who did not fit the pattern and who did not respond to the predominant therapeutic models were a disappointment to the therapist and poor prognostic risks. Therapists considered it bad luck to be employed in an agency that did not have "good" clients; as a result, most professionals did not want to be employed in state hospitals.

It took many years actually to identify the target population. In terms of persons who need help, the primary mental health target is the low-resource, involuntary, "high risk," and disadvantaged person who requires services in order to survive. All human service agencies—mental hospitals, schools, prisons and welfare—now realize that their major target population are the unresponsive, involuntary, and least competent persons. These individuals are struggling with issues of existence and survival. Their homicidal patterns have not been buried under reaction formation and intellectualizing defenses. They distrust, they struggle with feelings of inadequacy and persecution, and they find themselves withdrawing because they cannot manage their rages. Theirs are not problems typically solved by existing mental health services. The medical-Freudian model has failed to serve this target population. It is apparent that alternate services are required.

*Inner Man Theme*

A principal reason for the breakdown of the medical-Freudian model is its focus on intraorganismic processes. The medical-Freudian approach *assumes* that the individual is maladaptive because of events taking place within the individual. It further *assumes* that if mental health workers are to aid (treat) clients, they must become experts in the operations of the inner man. At the very heart of the issue is detecting those inner factors that *cause* maladaptations or deviancy. The inner man theme has resulted in myopic vision for the mental health caregivers. Therapists may spend years examining the inner functioning of one person while literally thousands of others are going without services. At the present time there is no essential evidence to prove that these inner searches are effective.

*Technologists and Therapy*

Another weakness of the medical-Freudian model is its emphasis on finding a special therapy for the client's disease. The recent history of the mental health field is marked by frequent reports of new therapies: Gestalt therapy, confrontation therapy, psychodrama, transactional analysis, vitamin therapy, primal therapy, surgical procedures, and/or a new convulsive therapy.

This emphasis on therapy technology has some value for the high-resource people who have good jobs, families, money, friends, and good educational backgrounds. When their symptoms are removed, these clients have a life style with which they can relink.

Unfortunately, most of the persons seeking mental health services need a great deal more. Most clients not only have specific symptoms and problems, but they have major life style difficulties: poor educations, poor job skills, poor interpersonal skills, few community resources, and poor personal equation assets. Once the symptoms are removed, the task has only begun. The client must be aided in developing those skills, abilities, and attitudes necessary to live in society. The failure to recognize the true therapeutic issues results in high recidivism rates, as indicated in Figure 5-1.

*Elitisms: Supply and Demand*

Still another difficulty with the medical-Freudian model is its emphasis on the development of highly credentialed therapists. This is not only true of the medical personnel but also psychologists, social workers, and nurses. It is assumed that a minimum of six years of university work is required in order to provide therapeutic experiences for the client. To provide leadership for the therapeutic team, it has been assumed that an individual must have approximately fifteen years of education and training. Given this expectation, there appears to be a shortage of mental health workers. As long as this elitist expectation dominates the field, there will not be enough professionals to provide the service. From 1950 to 1966 the number of professionals increased: psychiatrists 350 percent, psychologists 500 percent, social workers 400 percent, and psychiatric nurses 250 percent. Despite these increases, however, there continues to be a shortage of highly credentialed staff.[5] The pattern in the mental health field is to omit services when there are insufficient credentialed persons to provide services. If consumers, attentive publics, and service-givers continue to favor an elitist approach to credentials, there will be an increasing imbalance between service-givers and consumers.

*Goals and Objectives of the Model*

From the beginning this model implied that with sufficient money, training, and proper staff it would be possible to "cure" the world of its deviance. This has been a fool's errand. Mental health workers have been committed to a utopian dream, and the attentive mental health publics have become cynical and disenchanted with the hope. It is this aspect of the medical-Freudian approach that has perhaps been most crucial in setting the stage for the deterioration of the model: the inability to live up to promises.

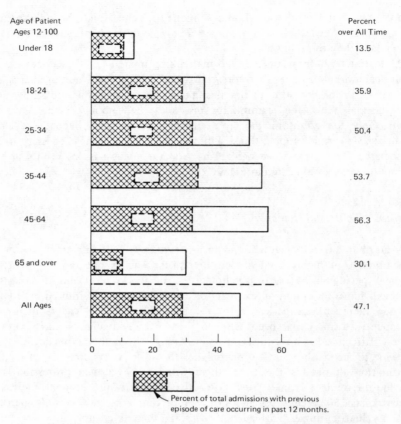

Percent of Admissions with Previous Episodes of Care in Hospitals over All Time and during the Last 12 Months, State and County Mental Hospital Inpatient Services, United States, 1969

**Figure 5-1.** Recidivism in Mental Hospitals. Source: National Institute for Mental Health. *Socioeconomic Characteristics of Admissions to Inpatient Services of State and County Mental Hospitals.* 1969, D.H.E.W. publications no. (HSM) 72-9048. Washington, D.C.: U.S. Government Printing Office, 1971.

As previously indicated, many aspects of the medical-Freudian model contributed to the crisis in the mental health system. Also, other cultural forces—political, sociological and economic—played a role in creating the crisis.

*Rapid Change*

Change factors within a society appear to accelerate with the accumulation of knowledge. It is quite likely that Western society has changed more in the last one hundred years than in the entire previous history of mankind. Certainly most persons over forty can testify to the accelerating changes in values, beliefs, and attitudes within the United States during the post World War II era. The beliefs that appeared so very stable in the twenties, thirties, and forties have become disappearing chichés, stereotypes, and shibboleths in the sixties and seventies. Some of this country's most cherished institutions—the church, the family, and marriage—appear on the edge of obsolescence. There is no longer stability in attitudes towards sex, violence, love, and hate. Most adults, in their thirties, forties, and fifties or more, are probably suffering from cultural shock. The great culture taboos that Freud perceived as the basic themes repressed by mankind—incest, patricide, cannibalism, matricide, and homosexuality—are now on view twenty-four hours a day at the local movie house. Most theories of the twentieth century are being questioned and challenged. It is quite likely that we are not only going through a rapid process of change, but that the process of change is gathering momentum. It is not unfair to say that a rapidly changing society requires new approaches to explain and predict human behavior.

*Process of Change*

Although most persons sense the changes going on around them, they know little about the forces that cause the process of change and govern its course. While historically society has given names to the manifestations of change, the people in the society appear quite helpless to intervene in that process. This is true for those who want to facilitate change as well as those who prefer maintaining the status quo. Even as consumers, attentive publics, and mental health workers view the failure of the mental health model, they cannot predict the major thrust or direction of the mental health system.

The reader can probably best understand this point from a historical perspective. The Freudian model had its origin at the end of the nineteenth century, the Victorian period. It was a period characterized by puritanical and repressive child-rearing patterns. This therapy model focused on reducing inhibitions and returning the repressed to consciousness. This approach created much societal resistance and anger. An examination of the later works of Sigmund Freud and the historical text of Ernest Jones make it clear that social resistance had a major negative impact on Freud.

However, it seems clear in retrospect that Freud was at a growing edge of major societal changes in values, attitudes, and philosophies. The society was changing and traditional child-rearing and human service practices were no longer appropriate for that changing society. I am, of course, suggesting that current mental health delivery models and technologies are both insufficient and inappropriate, and that once again it is time for a change.

*Beginning of Change:*
*Post World War II Era*

After World War II, a variety of new values, beliefs, and attitudes emerged to challenge traditional mental health models. Although the experiences related to the war increased American idealism, the war experience also fostered impatience with traditional human services. As a reaction to the Nazi intolerance, the movement for social justice gained impetus. Racial minorities, women, the mentally ill, and the poor were to receive a greater portion of the "pie." The minority and disadvantaged young men who fought for their country were less willing than their parents to accept traditionally inferior services. They wanted the same kind of services that the middle and upper classes received. Furthermore, many young people who had never received health services became acquainted with the possibilities while they were in the armed forces. It became part of their life. They no longer considered health services to be a privilege, but a right. Suddenly, many more persons sought service than there were services available, a classic situation that demanded change.

*Obsolescence in Technology*

The therapeutic technology that developed in providing services to the middle and upper classes were useless in meeting the needs of the new consumers. The disadvantaged person did not want to spend time investigating his inner self. These new consumers wanted *help* as well as "therapy." If service workers were to aid the disadvantaged person, they would have to alter his environment. It was a time for new service models.

*New Social Movements*

Accompanying these new social demands was a new breed of social scientists. Instead of examining deviance and behavioral disorders in the context of the individual, they focused on social systems. In the fifties and sixties, American society also saw the development of important new social movements: the civil-rights movement, consumer movements, and the women's liberation movement. Each of these developments has brought about changes in society that have benefited members of various scapegoated and disadvantaged groups. They have provided our society with an activist orientation in contrast to the passivity of traditional mental health models. Consumers have demanded more aggressive action and quicker changes. It is quite likely that these new social movements have provided more service to the maladaptive persons than the mental health system.

*Personal Experiences: Vectors of*
*Change in a Particular Agency*

Along with these major societal vectors of change, events in my own work life began to provide some new experiences. In the early 1950s, when the hospital operation was approaching its nadir, the new chemotherapy of tranquilizers was introduced into the treatment system. At the time, it was introduced in the context of a cure for mental illness. In this sense, it had a negative effect. The emergence of the tranquilizers, however, was important as a patient management technique. It changed staff and patient attitudes.

The staff was able to observe dramatic changes in patients. This helped staff feel more optimistic about the care-giving process. Furthermore, the professionals were able to witness dramatic changes *without* long and complicated intervention systems. The staff also began to feel less frightened of the disturbed patient. The emergence of tranqulizers set the stage for closing disturbed wards, reducing the more severe somatic techniques, and opening the door to more flexible discharge procedures. Because the patients were more manageable, the agency did not have to utilize as many employees in purely guarding and protective roles. This, in turn, freed up positions for more therapeutic purposes. It is significant, however, that researchers discovered that some patients reintegrated on *placebos* in place of tranquilizers.[6]

I now think that the recurrent claims of cure for mental illness are themselves important phenomena. I am suggesting that the emergence of the therapeutic modality is not so much the issue as the mobilizations, adrenaline flow, and new configurations that emerge in reaction to projected new cures.

I would like to give an example of the confounding relationship of a specific intraorganismic therapy and the milieu in which it occurred. In the 1930s, insulin shock therapy was introduced into the agency. Because of the need to control diet, a special ward was set aside for patients to receive such treatment. In effect, a staff-patient-community was organized around the therapeutic modality. Typical of pilot projects, the best physical space and best staff was poured into the program. The early reports suggested a 95 percent cure, which probably meant discharge from the hospital. It was assumed that the insulin therapy was the important agent in the recovery. As the years passed, the insulin therapy continued, but the energy put into the community diminished. By the early sixties, the insulin community was gone, and at the time the program was abandoned, the reported cures had reached the zero level.

The psychotropic drugs, partly because they failed to emerge as a cure and because of their value in patient management, probably represented a good starting point for detailing the changing configuration at the facility.

The writings of Mowrer supported some clinical observations I had made at my institution.[7] In the middle fifties, at the request of a psychology intern, I undertook the treatment of a patient who was variously diagnosed schizophrenic reaction, hebephrenic type; and schizophrenic reaction, chronic undifferentiated type. The intern wanted to observe treatment in process, wanted to participate in the process, and, at the same time, didn't want to feel that he would be wasting the patient's time or injure the patient.

We picked out a patient who had been in the institution nine years and now resided on a "back ward." The hospital, at the time, was organized around a system of extruding patients to progressively worse wards as the patient's competency declined. This patient had reached the bottom of the elevator in this system. We picked him as our candidate for several reasons: (1) prior to hospitalization, he had shown certain developed resources, such as being a good musician and attending college for several years; (2) he had certain humorous qualities that appealed to us; and (3) lastly, he came running into the office while the psychology intern and I were discussing the project!

It should be pointed out that initially we had no hope of effectively intervening with this patient. He was a classic example of the alleged process schizophrenic; he had an opening phase of illness that resembled catatonia; this was followed by a regression to paranoid patterns, building his own world, and then a subsequent decline in behavior that was labeled hebephrenic, a kind of anarchy. We would like to have helped him, but we had little hope. This type of patient was considered to have a grave prognosis.

In terms of our feelings about the case, our other obligations, and our reservations about spending time with the patient, we arranged to see him twice a week for one-hour sessions in the office of the senior therapist. Our therapeutic approach was modeled on the various dyadic systems extant at the time: Rogers, Freud, Adler, et al. The therapists were to be primarily listeners; the patient was to recognize his illness and accept responsibility for his illness; the therapists were to achieve communication with the unconscious systems and modify them. Fortunately, the patient did not understand our approach, nor did he choose to participate in our nonsense. The following weeks were much like broncho busting without a saddle.

Before discussing the therapeutic process further, we should take a look at some of the patient's characteristics. He was without inhibition; he constantly and publicly masturbated. He tolerated no tension and passed gas at the slightest provocation. He delighted in his hallucinations, was unconcerned about wearing clothing, and would urinate where he stood. He had a massive greed and devoured everything in sight.

He initially attended the therapy sessions without much coaxing, but once in the session, he refused to participate in the therapeutic contract. His fruit salad associations would have delighted Bleuler; his breakdown in concept formation activities would have made Hanfman and Kasinin ecstatic, and the breakdown in set would have visibly moved Shakow. This was certainly the classic irreversible schizophrenic; without good cause, the two therapists "hung in" when it seemed wise to terminate. Our consumer became tired of his role as client and refused to come to the sessions. The two therapists, disregarding their past training, which indicated that a patient should be well motivated, literally forced the patient to attend the sessions. In the months that followed, the patient attempted to set fires in the therapist's office, he urinated in inappropriate spots, pulling and tugging at any effort to restrain him. Therapy became a structuring and limiting procedure—perhaps it should have been called a fight.

After several effortful months in which therapy was moved out of the office onto the grounds, to the piano, and into various activities, the entire experience reached a climax. The patient, by all considerations, seemed to become totally "crazy," screaming, running, jumping and rolling. When this came to an end through "appropriate" limit setting, the patient appeared to take a total flip-flop. He appeared to capitulate and actually apologized for behaving the way he had for the last nine years. Within a brief period after this, he left the hospital. Unfortunately or fortunately, we never followed up on this patient nor have we ever heard from him again.

Several other psychologists in our agency, taking a cue from our experience, selected long-term regressed patients for treatment. The therapies were organized around encounters, limit setting, tight structures, tenacity, and willingness to invest considerable energy. We might say that in the few instances of employing these strategies, we were successful in getting the patients back to their prehospital level of operation and returning them to the community.

This type of clinical experience began to say some new things to us. First, the patient population was more treatable than we thought. Second, the patient's *volition* and *participation* have considerable importance in this treatment process. Third, treatment need not always focus on inner causes, but rather on external events and experiences.

The change process was given considerable momentum by Menninger. He described a situation of "hopeless" patients, placed in an existential crisis, encumbered with responsibility for themselves, and forced to make a decision, who far exceeded the expectancies of their caregivers.[8]

Szasz in his writings began to question the validity of the concepts of mental illness and Freudian determinism. He dared to ask whether those persons placed in mental institutions are a persecuted minority whose civil rights are being violated and whether the concept of prison is more humane than mental hospitals.

*The 1960s and the Concept of*
*Treatment Through Institutional Change*

In 1961, our agency took the first real step towards change. We started our first patient-government program.[9]

1. The patients would hold meetings twice weekly. They would have their

own officers and conduct the business of the meetings. The ward staff would be present but would function as information-givers, limit-setters, and consultants.

2. Personal problems were not to be discussed at the meetings. The agenda would concern ward community issues. The patients were to develop solutions in the way of proposals to solve their problems.

3. The staff would meet twice weekly to discuss patient proposals. If the local staff could not respond immediately, they would at the following patient meeting. If higher administrative reaction was necessary, the proposals would be properly channeled. There would be eventual feedback at the patient meeting.[10]

The major question in the utilization of this model is raised by Fisher:

Implicit within the milieu therapeutic system is the question whether the psychological systems can be altered with minimum intrapsychic intervention. It is basic to the milieu therapy model that environmental alterations change the role of the patient feedback, and influence the basic behavioral systems. That is, we assume that milieu therapy can reduce symptom pattern, re-establish the premorbid personality and possibly bring about major shifts in the makeup of the individual. If so, at least in part, the milieu therapies reiterate what the specific treatment systems claim to do.[11]

At the time, I was really in no position to evaluate scientifically the effectiveness of the program. I wrote:

The ward meetings have spread throughout the hospital. Instead of one program, there are now twenty, and some of these have gone much farther than the original ward. There is now a Therapeutic Council, the first real middle management group in the hospital, which is made up of chiefs of departments, some ward representatives, and assistant department chiefs. The Council attempts to deal with problems which are beyond the authority of the local wards; it has encouraged the development of ward programs; and has aided in educating the staff. About one-fifth of the patients in the hospital are active in some facet of milieu therapy.[12]

Another major impact of the milieu therapy model was the shift in emphasis in the Freudian theory. Cumming and Cumming brought the role of the executive ego to the fore.[13] The executive ego is the conscious portion of the ego and is that part of the personality that is more responsive to the environment. Basic Freudian theory attempted to bring about changes in the synthetic portion of the ego, which was unconscious. It was assumed that this is where the causal factors lay. Shifting the emphasis towards the executive ego, gives more credence to environmental therapies, role-playing techniques, and sociological therapies.

At our institutions, we became increasingly sensitive to environmental influences. It was becoming clear that our large centralized facility was not adaptive to treatment programs. Rowitz and Levy, in speaking of centralized facilities, state: "This type of hospital does not usually encourage the development of effective treatment programs, although treatment is attempted in acute cases."[14] The centralized hospital is organized according to a pyramidic structure, with the superintendent at the top and patients at the bottom. Staff are linked into the system through departments and speak to the clinical director through the department head, who speaks to the superintendent through the clinical director. As long as the hospital goal is custodial care, the centralized system survives, but if you want to create treatment programs, the system begins to malfunction. It is more of a gate-keeping, inhibiting operation than a facilitating, expediting system.

Typically, in a centralized facility, the staff involved in the treatment cannot directly respond to the patient. They have to wait until requests are channeled through the key administrators. The administrative staff, seldom knowing the patient about whom they are making decisions, are afraid to take risks in planning for the patient. For bureaucratic reasons, patients are moved around in the central facility without specific program delineation. This literally wipes out continuity of treatment. Patients and most staff of the facility do not participate in the decision-making process. As a result, they become alienated and develop major depersonalization and apathy patterns. Furthermore, the system has strong class and caste qualities. Staff has no hope in this system of moving up to the level at which decisions are made. The three or four persons at the top decision-making level resist changes that might reduce their control.

In 1963, our hospital decentralized into a unit system. The large hospital was broken down into ten units: some were specialized units, such as the alcoholic program; others took patients on a random, heterogenous basis. Staff moved out of departments into programs, and the tokens of reward were handed over to program directors instead of department heads. We eventually went out of the department business.

Each program subdivided into ward programs, for the ward appeared the natural unit of operation. The trend was to form a team on each ward and move the clinical decision making to the ward level. The people who were spending their time with the patients now made the crucial decisions. The staff working directly with the patients had more confidence in their decision making; risk taking increased throughout the system. Staff discharged patients that were once considered untreatable. Competition developed between programs in regard to funding, staffing, and reputation. It became easier to establish patterns of responsibility; now there were people responsible for wards and programs.

To meet the needs of such programs, we required a different kind of personnel. The teams that were established were asked to function as generalists; teams were primarily in a nonspecialist orientation (the typical bowling team) rather than a team of specialists (a baseball team). We needed staff who would be willing to participate in all tasks necessary to treat patients. In the past, our staff was polarized into an "upper class," the professionals, and a "lower class," the nonprofessionals. The professionals had many skills and appropriate sensitivities, but only chose to work with the mind. The nonprofessionals appeared willing to do anything, but frequently lacked the sensitivities to deliver services in a therapeutic fashion. As we worked on, it became clear that in a mental health system that is minimally funded, generalists who are willing to do anything are better than specialists who will only do "their thing." The generalist concept also fits well with a career ladder. It becomes possible, theoretically speaking, for any employee to link into a system that will take the person to the "top." This reduces the class and caste systems operating in the hospital. The generalist and the career ladder concepts, furthermore, make it possible for everyone, including patients, to enter the mainstream of the hospital. Again, it becomes theoretically possible for a patient to enter the career ladder and move into the employee system. When you take into account that most patients and many employees are disadvantaged persons who need help in getting back into the mainstream of society, the importance of the career ladder becomes more evident.

I have come to believe that the main ingredient in the role of the mental health caregiver is the personal equation; the energy, appearance, size and interpersonal skills a person brings into the situation is more important than his education. This is not to deny of course that appropriate education and training can add important ingredients to the appropriate persons. Our generalists have been trained primarily in treatment through social experiences. That is, we have come to believe that the primary treatment rests in the everyday experiences that in the past were considered maintenance or custodial situations, but seem, in fact, to have evolved into positive intervention events. Our agency therefore now has a "middle class"—the generalists. No longer a polarized society, we now have a continuum which provides a growth pattern in our service.

In 1968 our agency reorganized into a program labeled the Metrozone. It was later renamed the Chicago Area Zone. In essence, the reorganization introduced the catchment, or geographical, approach to our facility. At the heart of the catchment concept is the nonextrusion theme. That is, all clients coming to the door require a meaningful response. Patients cannot be rejected or expelled because they represent difficult problems. Clients are the catchment area's responsibility from birth to death. It became the responsibility of the catchment programs to assure continuity of treatment. That is to say, treatment occurring in the community had to be related to treatment occurring in the residential facility, which, in turn, had to be related to treatment occurring after discharge.

*Summary*

Institutions falling of their own weight are no longer a novelty in Western society. Our institution declined because we were unable to respond to the various publics and consumers that we served. For several decades, we continued to serve our consumer groups with therapeutic modalities and delivery systems designed for a smaller and different population. I am firmly convinced that organizations must be in a constant process of change to meet the needs and pressures applied by their various consumers and publics. Organizations must remain responsive to these needs or they become stagnant and ineffective.

In the sixties, we began the process of identifying needs and developing reorganizations to meet these needs. We have described the process of these reorganizations, and Figure 5-2 presents the reorganization in summary form. It is this capacity to alter organizations that is at the heart of our approach.

## A New Perspective

When one considers all of the forces involved in creating deviance, it is mind boggling to think that those few mental health outposts called clinics, state

| NEEDS | APPROACHES |
|---|---|
| Improved living conditions | Introduction of Jones and Cumming and Cumming milieu therapy programs in 1961 |
| Greater flexibility, expedite change, and increase innovations | Decentralization of the hospital into Unit System in 1963 |
| To increase patient-staff contacts regarding counseling, problem-solving, and planning | Beginning of the team approach in 1965 with staff being allocated to programs rather than departments |
| Provide wide range of services to maximum number of patients | The development of the generalist philosophy in 1965 and the introduction of the career series. This has only begun to peak in the last year or two |
| Accountability for patient service, attempt to give all patients "some of the action" (no decline option), increase DMH service to community | Development of subzone system in 1968, utilizing catchment/territorial concepts |
| Optimal utilization of personnel, eliminate poor physical plant and equipment, provide increased services to infirmary and geriatric patients, and upgrade and standardize and increase services at admission point | Various reorganizations reflecting a change of the hospital status<br>1. Closing down of redundant services and discontinuing use of obsolete buildings<br>2. Uniting geriatrics and infirmaries<br>3. Establishing a new central admission service<br>4. Construction of new physical plants<br>5. Implementation of increased community services |

**Figure 5-2.** Therapeutic Reorganization

hospitals and day hospitals can prove effective antidotes. In attempting to provide services for individuals considered deviant, we should examine and utilize the embedded therapeutic potential extant in society's social systems and social institutions: aiding the individual to develop an appropriate social role, proper linking to a market economy, and preparing the individual for survival in our society.

The problem of deviancy relates to the entire community and should not be left solely to the professional mental health workers. Chu and Trotter, in their report for the Nader group, find that the major failure of the community mental health movement has been the inability of the community to become influential. There has been little transfer of power from the professional groups to the community groups. In effect, the community mental health movement has simply expanded the power of mental health workers out of their agencies and offices into greater sectors of the community. As the seeds of deviancy have been traced into the various societal systems—political, economic, and sociological—there has been some tendency for mental health workers to want to place the medical-Freudian imprint on these systems. There has not been sufficient effort made to utilize the existing therapeutic potential in most individuals' life space.

The task of the mental health worker is to identify and authenticate those experiences by which we grow. That is, the mental health worker should not only directly deliver services to the client but should also become aware of the growth opportunities available in a society and link the client to such possibilities. Further, whenever possible, it becomes the task of the mental health worker to design new social institutions and social systems that will provide growth experiences. Most of our traditional growth experiences are available in the early years in such social institutions as the family, the school, and peer groups. In concrete terms, additional growth experiences are needed for the early years and an increased number of social institutions are needed for adults who have missed their first opportunities.

If we are to stay with our primary assumption that help in the mental health systems requires the client's volitional cooperation, then we must provide options in addition to the traditional mental health model, the medical-Freudian model. It should seem clear to most mental health workers that many persons classified as deviant will not voluntarily enter into traditional mental health systems in order to find help. In fact, it is not unlikely that many of the recent social movements—the civil-rights movement, women's lib, radical therapists, gay liberation, etc.—have provided growth experiences for many more individuals than the traditional mental health movement. That is, the embedded growth experiences are alternative developmental experiences to the traditional mental health approach.

Without additional options that may be attractive to the client, we tend to end up with continued escalations between staff and the involuntary client. It starts with staff setting limits within their model. If the client refuses to participate in this system, the staff generates consequences for the client. This can lead to increasing encounters, "warfare," brinksmanship, possibly the client capitulating or the staff ultimately writing the client off as a bad prognostic risk. The escalating model is built into most institutions (mental hospitals, prisons, and families), and problem children brought to therapists have typically been through escalation and brinksmanship patterns with their parents. In state hospitals where clients have been least responsive to the medical-Freudian model there have been the most intense efforts to control the volitional system. It has been in this setting that the convulsive therapies, lobotomies, packs, bromides, and psychotropic drugs have been utilized to get the residents into line.

As part of any new attempt to understand mental illness, it should be clear that defining deviancy is a difficult if not impossible task.[15] The work of Hollingshead and Redlich (1964) demonstrated the lack of relationship between diagnosis and services offered and received. Ultimately deviancy has been defined as behavior different and unacceptable to a geographical unit's majority. In many cases it has been tyranny over the minority. Historically, in the field of mental health this has resulted in persons being locked up for hallucinations, suicide attempts, homicidal behavior, incompetency, unusual sexual behavior, delusions, being a pest, being hostile, inappropriate dress, and addiction patterns. We have utilized the classification of mental illness to exile people we didn't want around. Currently most states utilize three criteria for locking persons up in mental hospitals: individuals too incompetent to care for themselves and persons who may potentially commit homicide or suicide as a result of an inner mental illness process. On the surface, in terms of the societal values, this does not sound too inappropriate. However, this model fails because mental health experts are not able to make such predictions with any expertise. This leaves an enormous ambiguous area in which individuals are locked up on the basis of inaccurate predictions. I feel that only Szasz (1961) has arrived at any possible solution to the problem of definition. Mental health agencies, offices, and hospitals should only be utilized for persons seeking help. It should remain a *voluntary system.*

Anyone who is to be locked up involuntarily must be tried through a criminal justice system. That is, the individual must be tried for the violation of existing laws and be tried by the court. Many persons will say that it is inhuman to place mentally ill persons in prisons. I would say, "What's in a name?" Mental hospitals have historically been prisons. Many persons have spent lifetimes there because the length of stay has been indeterminate. As far as treatment is concerned, penal systems have not developed procedures any more barbaric than lobotomies and convulsive therapies. Certainly no one in his right mind will consider mental hospitals a worthwhile growth experience. Basically, at this time in history there are no individuals whom we can trust, on the basis of their professional competency, to take away the rights of other individuals. Deviancy must be defined by the individual identifying it in himself or through a criminal justice system.

It is my feeling that once an act of deviancy has been identified either by the individual or by others, there are no good solutions available. It's really a plague on both of their houses—mental hospitals and corrections systems. Our society has tended to deal with deviance in a first-aid fashion. If a person commits a crime, typically he is locked up (punished), but he is not provided with much opportunity to reconstitute himself. If an individual is not economically viable, we put him on welfare, but we seldom provide the individual with the opportunity to reconstitute himself economically. If an individual demonstrates behavior that we identify as a form of mental illness, we attempt to identify what is wrong with him, but we provide him with few possibilities of altering his life space—his network of friends, his social role, and his occupation.

I am, of course, saying that our failure to reduce deviance directly relates to our failure to design opportunities for growth. We continue to sell the theme that deviance is the inner failure of the person and that if the individual is provided with the correct "medicine" he will be "cured." The ultimate absurdity is a therapist attempting to provide a fifty-year-old state hospital patient with insight, even though his client has none of the characteristics, skills, and abilities necessary to survive in society. It seems a basic premise of any therapeutic process that the individual achievements through the therapeutic process should be reflected in gains in his ability to cope more adequately with the society around him.

I do not think that the issues of deviance are as esoteric or mystical as most professionals have suggested. This is not to deny that on occasions incomprehensible biochemical, neurological, and metabolic processes may not contribute to an individual's deviant behavior. I am suggesting that we have gone out too far on an intraorganismic limb rather than face up to some of the brutal triage decisions implicit within all societies.

*Prevention*

Three principle triage conditions can be discerned: prevention, crisis, and chronic deviance. We can define the task of prevention as making sure that everyone has multiple opportunities to meet his basic attachments. These are, according to Hansel, the need for taking in supplies, maintaining an intimate relationship, being part of a peer group, a sense of identity, a social role, and a linkage to the economy.[16] Theoretically, on any given day, we want all of the citizens to be able to meet their needs and thus avoid crisis situations. In theory, most members of our society would agree with this notion, but it is unlikely that the majority is willing to make the kind of decisions that might result in this Camelot-like situation. For example, in the United States, even in the best of times, we tend to have an unemployment rate of 3 to 5 percent. This appears to be an invariant factor within our economic system. It seems quite probable that this unemployment rate leads to a number of persons not meeting their needs, such as the need to earn income by working. In practical terms, in the light of our priority systems, it is unlikely that we would be willing to alter our economic system to eliminate the unemployment and probably related deviance. My point is that every culture on the basis of its priorities makes triage decisions that result in some persons not meeting their needs and thus every culture has patterns that produce crisis and deviance. It has been customary for mental health workers to ignore macrosocial factors leading to deviance.

It appears clear, however, that prevention goes well beyond the boundaries of mental health. Once we get into the question of preventing deviance, we must relate to almost all of society's social systems: political, economic, legal, penal, sociological, etc. The workers in the field of prevention are ultimately problem-solvers who attempt to design new possibilities when existing systems do not meet individual needs. New possibilities have to be produced when existing social institutions such as career planning, families, church, welfare, mental hospitals, penal systems, and schools begin to malfunction. Examples of such new institutions are Synanon, Daytop, Peer Groups, Alcohol Anonymous, communes, universities without walls, prisons without walls, new professions, the concept of the indigenous worker, and guaranteed annual income. We must provide the individual with a variety of opportunities for solving his problems. Not everyone wants to or can solve his problems through a long introspective search for cause and subsequent insight.

## Crisis Conditions

When prevention is unsuccessful and the individual's needs are not being met, he tends to take on certain crisis characteristics: lack of concentration, diffuse identity, disturbed social role, distractibility, great anxiety, and an increased capacity for learning. In terms of the model being presented, it is suggested that the crisis can best be resolved if we can identify which attachment or attachments have been severed and relink the individual to other systems or objects that can realistically substitute the previous attachment and meet the essential needs of the individual. Appropriate resolution of crisis is considered crucial in the prevention of a chronic deviance pattern. Next to prevention, it is the key to reducing deviance within our society.

Therefore, crisis services have to be available twenty-four hours a day, seven days a week (e.g., hot lines and crisis teams). These services will have to be provided on a "massed time" basis, rather than being distributed over a long period of time. Usually, it will be necessary to work with a rather extensive network of persons in the client's life. It is important to understand, however, that through crisis the client has an increased capacity to learn. The client's capacity to resolve the crisis is, of course, significantly improved if the process leads to realistic gains in his life. For example, if he has been cut off from his income, it is crucial that he foresee a financial solution related to the crisis resolution. In the solving of crisis, it is also important that the individual's decision-making apparatus play a significant role. As much as possible, the situation should be managed so that the client becomes a voluntary and active participant.

Erikson (1950) has postulated that all significant growth in the individual results from the resolution of crisis. In order to move to the next stage of development, the individual passes through a crisis in which he organizationally gives up the previous stage patterns and assumes the organization of the new stage. Each of these stages has certain themes that must be mastered: trust, autonomy, intimacy, etc. These are major learning experiences. The society has created major roles and social institutions to resolve these crises: mothers, fathers, families, schools, wives, marriage, sports, and religion. If we utilize this developmental analog, we can say the adult in crisis must have the same opportunity to move ahead. Unfortunately, as a society, we are not nearly as generous in the opportunities that we make available to the person in the crisis. There are typically no built-in rewards for developmental growth. In order to aid persons to resolve their crises, we have to design new social roles, relinking opportunities, second chances, new credentialing procedures, and new career possibilities.

If the person does not resolve his crisis adequately, he moves out on a trajectory of deviance. As the individual moves along this new trajectory, he becomes increasingly alienated and takes on a chronic pattern of disability and deviance. He begins to meet his needs in patterns that are not socially acceptable. It is these individuals who most frequently become unacceptable to their communities and are exiled to institutions. Once institutionalized, they make their attachments to the institution and, of course, this is how their needs are met. In rather brief periods of time, probably less than a year, the client's community network of resources is no longer available to him. The task of rehabilitation is now doubled. The client has to be helped with the problems that led to his chronic disability, and in addition, he has to be aided in regard to the institutionalizing processes.

It appears crucial, therefore, that we should do everything in our power to prevent a chronic deviance from occurring. Prevention programs and crisis intervention programs should gradually erode the level of chronic deviance in our society. There are no good solutions for these persons who have made deviance a way of life.

For the chronically deviant currently present in the society there appear to be four major possibilities:

1. Those who cannot change and at the same time cannot live in the

mainstream of society have to be provided with decent living conditions. This should be reserved only for individuals who *select* this form of life or are placed there by the criminal justice system.

2. Those persons who intermittently or episodically engage in deviant behavior should be provided with first aid. This would include brief counseling, psychotropic drugs, employment agencies, sheltered care facilities, partial hospitalization, workshop facilities, and ombudsman/expeditors. The recidivism pattern would constitute another style of life.

3. A third system should exist for those persons who attempt to escape recidivism or who the criminal justice system proposes as good candidates for escaping recidivism. Service would include changes in behavior but not necessarily a total "overhaul" (help for an alcoholic who wants to stop drinking). The client would have the following systems available: all the systems in item 2, behavior modification, occupational training, sexual education, survival training, career series, peer groups, Alcoholics Anonymous, Synanon-like groups, communes, universities without walls, job counseling, and counseling sessions with persons who can help in redesigning life patterns.

4. This last system would be available for persons who want to and are able to "overhaul" their entire system. This should be available for voluntary clients and for individuals referred from the criminal justice systems. The client would have the following systems available: all the systems in items 2 and 3, psychoanalysis, services in reconsidering all phases of his life, legal advice and help in redesigning his life at a significant level.

The aim is to provide the individual with the appropriate social institutions, meaningful opportunities, and an appropriate network of persons to make it worth the client's time to begin to grow. It has obviously not been a high-priority item within our society. The triage decision we have made up to now has been to invest our money in those persons who are going to make it.

## Modules of Experience, Treatment Through Institutional Changes, and Vectors of the Future

Every society provides or makes available to its population "modules of experience," social institutions, events, opportunities that have potential maturational force for its citizenry. An example of this theme is the school system, which is the primary elevator to the top. A child enters the school system usually at five and, contingent upon his motivation and skills, can utilize this module of experience as a developmental option to emerge at a higher socioeconomic level.

It is important to remember that not all modules of experience represent growth experiences for all members of the society. We know that traditional schools are utilized much more effectively by white middle-class children than by black lower-class children. In fact, schools probably play a major role in manufacturing and maintaining the status quo of a society.[17] The majorities design school systems in their image, and so the schools can act as a barrier to the minorities. For example, if a person goes through an exclusive private school system and then graduates from Harvard, he or she is considered to have the credentials for a "high station" in life. Yet a person probably cannot pursue this educational pattern without considerable funds and certain early developed attitudes.

In all countries, the primary modules of experience reflect the mainstream patterns of the culture. The American society has provided multiple chances for growth, but these opportunities are primarily accessible to persons who have those resources that link them to the mainstream. We have not traditionally provided many options for minorities, deviants, for lower socioeconomic groups, for women, for retarded persons, and for eccentrics. It is from these persecuted and alienated persons that we have filled our public-aid rolls, prisons, mental hospitals, addiction agencies, and alcoholic programs. Most agencies who serve these individuals have maximized security models and minimized developmental services. These relationships have been dehumanizing, further alienating and destructive to the human spirit.

In order to clarify and concretize the theme of this section, I would like to examine the "plus" and "minus" persons in a society. The plus persons, or "winners," in our culture are the bright, competitive, and "best" persons who have everything going for them: mainstream family, good resources, proper "up-beat" motivation, excellent physical characteristics, and a likable temperament. An individual such as this grooves into our system and obtains high payoffs for efforts. The culture is organized to support this person. If things do happen to go wrong for the plus person and stresses become unmanageable, the first-aid, or therapeutic intervention, techniques are designed so that this type of client can maximize their use. The medical-Freudian model was designed for these people, and they will typically turn to this module of experience when they experience an anxiety overload.

In contrast, if we accept a societal minus person, or "loser," an individual from the ghetto, with few resources, lack of mainstream motivation, unschooled, apathetic, unattractive, and moody—we find the community is organized to punish. He or she does poorly in school, which becomes a nightmare for the unsuccessful student. If he obtains a job, it is typically uninteresting, poor-paying, and demanding. If the stresses become overtaxing, the minus person does not have the resources or skills to utilize the medical-Freudian model. Nor would he voluntarily seek this solution to his problems. When he demonstrates deviancy, he is most likely to be extruded to an institution that is organized around security themes rather than growth forces. Even though he is outside the mainstream, he is expected to live within the moral systems, values, and ethics that have been forged to maintain the status quo of that society.

Recapitulating, we can say that a community molds the behavior of its citizens through its built-in reward and punishment patterns. Through this process each culture differentiates a distribution of citizens, with highly plus persons at one end and highly minus persons at the other end. The potential growth modules in a society are designed to benefit the plus individuals and at the same time support the status quo. The needs of the plus people are reflected in the therapy models, and generally, minus people are said to have a poor prognosis for treatment. In our society few minus people are rescued by traditional mental health systems. In fact, it would seem impossible to rescue the alienated person by therapy models designed for the mainstream citizens.

As stated earlier, the task is not to eliminate existing traditional mental health models. It is more a question of expanding the field and creating new opportunities. Without plan, communities produce counter-mainstream modules of experience.

For example, the labor movement in the thirties became a growth experience for many alienated persons. Many workers were able to utilize the labor movement as a career series that provided them with a reentry link into the mainstream. The civil-rights movement did much for many minority persons. It not only helped in supporting the civil rights, but it began a process for many persons that helped them move up the socioeconomic ladder.

I am obviously recommending that caregivers must involve themselves in the task of creating, supporting, and increasing the number of experience modules available to their consumers. I feel that this is particularly true in regard to their consumers who are labeled as "high risk" or disadvantaged. In this task, I do not expect caregivers to emulate Gandhi, Martin Luther King, or Jesus Christ, but I feel that within their sphere of influence or within the limitations of their power they can bring about changes that will result in treatment through institutional change.

The concept of "treatment through institutional change" has been with us for at least ten years. One result has been an increased effort to focus on persons in crisis. Hospital populations have been reduced because of an increased effectiveness in coping with persons in crisis. Mental health workers have become sensitized to the importance of resolving crisis.

There have been several attempts to link disadvantaged deviant persons into the market economy. On a small scale, state hospitals have begun to tie profit-making occupations into therapeutic programs. At our agency, we have opened a service station run by hospital residents. It serves as a means of preparing persons to live outside the agency and as an employment agency for other service stations. It is a major goal of the agency to tie patients into such projects.

The creation of new professions to serve the mental health clients can become another resource for disadvantaged persons. Indigenous work patterns organize the natural talents and skills of the disadvantaged person into a profession. The movement away from specialists and the development of paraprofessionals has provided a stepladder for persons at the bottom to move towards the top.

Within the last decade, the catchment models in mental health have increased continuity of treatment and reduced the exile of deviants from our community. Szasz's questions concerning the nature of mental health and the rights of the client have, of course, revolutionized mental health workers' perspectives towards their clients.

In education there have been a number of interesting developments. There has been an expansion of adult education and extension programs. There has been a new focus on crediting life experiences and a movement away from credentials-based education towards competency-based education. It has become increasingly possible for adults and disadvantaged groups to link back into the educational system. The seeds for institutional change are prevalent throughout the system.

It seems to me that if we are to pursue concepts like "treatment through institutional change" and "modules of experience," we must begin to catalog experiences by which people grow, identify where such experiences are available, and move away from the custodial pattern.

In this chapter I have attempted to identify vital issues in the mental health field. But the implications of the entire volume are that we need a thorough examination of these crucial issues: "treatment through institutional change," competency based education, "modules of experience," and identification of necessary life experiences. As I see the mental health field today and in the near future, it can only gain from the perspectives of social science. The environmental approach will not produce many objective answers or universal solutions. A mental health worker must still remain primarily a problem-solver. If I had to wish one quality for mental health workers, it would be that they have the capacity to be innovative problem-solvers.

## Notes

1. About a year ago several colleagues and I (Fisher, Mehr and Truckenbrod), put together a text called *Power, Greed and Stupidity in the Mental Health Racket.* While the title sounds like pure muckraker, the purpose was to convey the paucity of scientific data in the field of mental health.

2. Walter Fisher, J. Mehr, and P. Truckenbrod, *Power, Greed, and Stupidity in the Mental Health Racket* (Philadelphia: Westminster Press, 1973).

3. A.B. Hollinghead and F.C. Redlich, "Social Stratification and Psychiatric Disorders" in Milton Ohmer, ed. *Behavior Disorders: Perspectives and Trends* (New York: J.B. Lippincott, 1965).

4. The characteristics of the client population and the institutions have been described in a number of articles and books. See, for example, E. Goffman, *Asylum* (Garden City, N.Y.: Doubleday and Co., 1961); J.K. Wing, "Institutionalism in Mental Hospitals," *British Journal of Social and Clinical Psychology* 1

(1962): 38-51; R. Barton, *Institutional Neurosis* (Bristol, England: John Wright and Sons, 1969).

5. Arnhoff, Rubenstein, and Speisman indicate that the shortage of professional workers has continued to increase and that many professional positions go unfilled. See their article "The Mental Health Fields: An Overview of Manpower, Growth and Development," in their book *Manpower for Mental Health* (Chicago: Aldine, 1969).

6. See Jerome B. Frank, Earl H. Nash, Anthony R. Stone, and Stanley D. Imber, "Immediate and Longterm Symptomatic Course of Psychiatric Outpatients," in *American Journal of Psychiatry* 120:5 (May 1963).

7. In simple form, Mowrer stated that good mental health could only be achieved by bringing the functions of the ego into line with the requirements of the superego. He holds the position that the neurosis or psychosis develops when the individual violates (through deceit) this honest ego-superego relationship. Mowrer contends that the violation of this relationship is often a function of conscious forces, acts of volition. He further states that the deviance can frequently be undone by other acts of volition (e.g. confession and reparation). Mowrer points out that the great emphasis on determinism has allowed patients to abdicate their responsibility. I feel that although many caregivers do not accept Mowrer's basic theme regarding the relationship of the ego and superego, his attack on *determinism* has played a major role in revolutionizing mental health treatment. See his works: "Integrity Therapy: A Self-Help Approach," *Psychotherapy* 3:3 (August 1966); "The Basis of Psychopathology: Malconditioning or Misbehavior?" *Journal of the National Association of Women Deans and Counselors* 29:2 (Winter 1966); "Guilt in the Social Sciences, or the Conflicting Doctrines of Determinism and Personal Accountability," in Helmut Schoek and J.W. Wiggins (eds.) *Psychiatry and Responsibility* (New York: D. Van Nostrand Company, Inc., 1962).

8. Karl Menninger, "The Course of Illness," *Menninger Clinic Bulletin* 25:5 (September 1961). The article described the fate of a French mental hospital during World War II. The hospital was located in the path of the German Army, which had circled the Maginot Line. Most of the patients had been sent home to their relatives, but 153 patients, who were considered too ill to return to their relatives were to be escorted to safety by the hospital staff. As was typical with the time, the Germans moved faster than the French anticipated and the patients were left to their own recognizance. That ended the story until the completion of World War II, when a commission was set up to determine the fate of the patients. Most of the patients were traced, and of these, 37 percent had been found to make appropriate community adjustments.

9. The program was described in a paper by Fisher, "Social Change as a Therapeutic Tool in a Closed Institution," *Psychotherapy* 2:3 (October 1965).

10. The reader can probably better understand the operation of the group by reading J. Cumming and E. Cumming, *Ego and Milieu: The Theory and Practice of Environmental Therapy* (New York: Atherton Press, 1962).

11. Fisher, 1965.

12. Ibid.

13. Cumming and Cumming, 1962.

14. L. Rowitz and L. Levy, "The State Mental Hospital in Transition: An Approach to the Study of Mental Hospital Decentralization," *Mental Hygiene* 55:1 (January 1971).

15. In a recent volume on major mental illness Scheff (1966) points out that upwards of 5000 research studies in schizophrenia have been reported in the past five decades. He cites a number of experts who agree in their essential conclusion that very little headway has been made towards understanding or treating this profound disorder. Somewhat more limited in scope is the review by Kety (1967) of biochemical research in schizophrenia, which, however, also suggests that no single confirmed causative agent, or combination of agents, has yet been successfully identified. Scheff argues that these pessimistic generalizations are appropriate not only for schizophrenia but for the broad field of "functional mental disorder." He is not alone in this view (Braginsky, et al., 1969).

Quoted from M. Zax and E.L. Cowen, *Abnormal Psychology: Changing Conceptions* (New York: Holt, Rinehart and Winston, 1972).

16. N. Hansell et al., "Decision Counseling Method: Expanding Coping at Crisis-in-Transit," *Archives of General Psychiatry* (Spring 1970).

17. See Chapter 2.

# 6

## Reorienting Mental Health Policy

**Marion R. Just**

### Coping

The thesis of each of the preceding chapters is that people can better cope with their problems of living when they are in control of their immediate environment. In order to achieve some control, people need both experience and understanding of the processes that affect their lives.

The foregoing studies not only converge in an emphasis on control of the environment as a condition for mental well-being; each study also focuses on the experience of learning by participation. Chapter 2 argues that individuals can manage their own affairs better when they understand the economics of their options. Chapter 3 suggests that mobilization in the political process counteracts the despair of political alienation, while Chapter 4 shows that group organization in an urban setting does effect concrete changes in the environment. A further example is offered in Chapter 5, with respect to the environment of a public mental hospital. There patients who collectively cope with life in their ward not only succeed, but also become able to cope with their individual emotional problems as well.

Recent research by Geer, Davison, and Gatchel supports our thesis with experimental data. Their experiment was designed to simulate a group of "copers" and a group of "noncopers." Both groups were administered mild electric shocks that lasted exactly three seconds. While the copers were told that they could reduce the shock by rapidly pulling a switch, the noncopers were only asked to endure the shocks. Even though the duration of shock was precisely the same for both groups, subjects who believed that they had some control over their situation were considerably calmer (as measured by galvanic skin response) than those who did not. The copers reported less pain and were observed to tolerate higher levels of shock than the noncopers.

Throughout this book, we have made this point: trying to cope with problems in the environment is better than not trying to cope, even if the problems themselves turn out to be intractable. At the very least, by trying to cope with their environment, individuals gain specific skills that may be otherwise undeveloped. The process of coping provides people with a positive emotional outlook and so promotes mental well-being. This is true both for people who appear to be mentally disturbed as well as for those who do not. The

101

process of coping with the environment should not be merely symbolic or delusionary as it was in the experiment by Geer et al. Coping is not simply "making do" or accepting things as they are. Rather, coping means effecting concrete changes in the human environment. Furthermore, in the process of coping, people can learn to tell the difference between what they can and cannot change in their external world. It is not enough, for example, for an individual to learn resignation to his unemployment or poor housing or unhappy family. In helping people to cope, a human service agency will help in finding employment, improving housing, or restructuring the family. The aim of such service is to help people to manipulate their own environments, and so to reduce emotional stress. This kind of help is appropriate not only for the emotionally handicapped but also for people who are "well." It is true that some people are quite unable to handle even minor stress and strain. For such people, the environment must be shaped in the most gentle way, in sheltered care facilities, for example. But a great many other people could function more successfully if they were helped to look outside themselves and helped to find alternative arrangements in their lives. What is needed is an agency for creative intervention in the human environment.

The need for and the success of environmental intervention can be cited in many life areas, such as employment training, educational extension, and legal aid. Consider, for example, the role of the Bureau of Legal Assistance (of the Office of Economic Opportunity). The BLA's legal assistance in civil as well as criminal actions provided tangible solutions to problems that troubled countless less affluent Americans. On a smaller scale, the Community Legal Clinic of Toronto's York-Finch Hospital offers legal advice to psychiatric patients. Many of the patients it serves were severely depressed following domestic quarrels, tenant-landlord disputes, sudden unemployment, or problems with the police. Most of the patients had little knowledge or experience in finding legal assistance for their problems. According to Dr. Jerry Cooper, the psychiatrist who initiated the program, many depressed patients improved markedly after receiving legal advice.

Both the OEO Bureau of Legal Services and the York-Finch Community Legal Clinic provide the same kind of services. The settings, however, differ. In the case of OEO, the aim is to provide the poor with legal assistance. In the case of York-Finch, the aim is to provide legal assistance for the mentally ill. The two services highlight the theme of this book: most of us need help in solving problems of living, and the mentally ill need much the same kind of help.

Because of the unequal distribution of resources in society, help is generally more available to some people than others. On the one hand are those who have more income, better educations, and higher status in the community. They can afford to pay, know how to find, and have more free access to helping services in the community. What is more, those who have more resources find the caregivers to be people very much like themselves. Therefore, they can better relate to caregivers, and presumably respond more fully and quickly to the service. On the other hand, fewer options are open to people who have little income or who receive public welfare assistance, who have little formal education, and, (by virtue of their employment, or ethnicity, or sex) have lower status in the community. They cannot afford to pay for services, they are ill-equipped to find service-providers in the community, and rarely have personal contacts who can help them gain access. Moreover, lower-status individuals find caregivers to be people very different from themselves. In articulating their problems, they find that they do not share experiences, cultural values, or even a common language with service agencies. In sum, less advantaged people are less comfortable in the helping situation.

## Human Service Centers and Environmental Opportunities

In reorienting mental health policy, the aim must be to expand environmental opportunities for solving problems for everyone—the rich and the poor, the sick and the well. In reaching this goal, the direction should be towards decentralized multiservice agencies. Decentralization, founded on communal self-help agencies, can broaden access to services. The multifaceted aspect of such agencies can also reduce the stigma that attaches to help for mental illness. The system of medical triage (first-line diagnosis) for mental illness currently falls short on both counts. Medical triage aims at separating out patients who are basically sick from those who are basically well. In this case, the "well" are often given short shrift. In the institutional phase of triage, the sick are separated out from the severely sick. In the case of this decision, the poor are at a disadvantage. They are more likely to be diagnosed "severely sick"—and hence, less treatable.

While special protective treatment must be offered to patients who cannot function at all, a human service facility should do more than that. Where the patient arrives voluntarily, it is more useful to focus triage on the patient's problem rather than his illness. The problem orientation has several useful consequences. First, it emphasizes the individual's own participation in solving his endogenous and exogenous difficulties. In distinguishing among problems, the service agency is less likely to elaborate a caste system among the clients. Second, a problem-oriented facility makes more effective use of indigenous, nonelite personnel within the individual's home environment. In a specific localized conflict, members of the community may deal more capably and more rapidly with a problem than even a highly trained outsider. The employment of indigenous personnel is also efficient. The client need not explain so much of his situation to another individual who experiences it firsthand. A community multiservice center is also considerably more likely to identify environmental stresses than a medically oriented facility.[1] Finally, a problem-oriented human service center can extend assistance to many people who would otherwise not be reached because they are not "sick," and because their problems are not "mental."

## Social Science and Mental Health

It is important to reiterate here that this approach is not new. It builds on trends in mental health that have gained momentum in the last decade. The community mental health movement, in particular, was an agent for bringing the social environment into therapeutic consideration. The location of mental health centers in high-risk communities simplified access and strengthened the patients' ties with the community. The New Mental Health Careers program established opportunities in the field of mental health for community personnel and provided a culturally homogeneous atmosphere for therapy.

It will not be easy to reinvigorate the community mental health movement with the dynamic of social action. The era of street-level organization is waning as we pass from the decade of "mobilized action" to the decade of "detachment." If the mood of universities is any guide, American society is shifting emphasis from doing to thinking. This book suggests that this new mood can be a positive factor in reorienting mental health policy. Increasing social science interest in mental health (of which this volume is an example) may provide the necessary force for directing mental health outwards from the psyche. On the whole, social scientists can help orient mental health policy to exogenous as well as endogenous factors in human development. The work of Hollingshead and Redlich, Szasz, and others illustrates the usefulness of coupling social science methodology to research in mental health.

## Social Planning for Mental Health

We hope the environmental approach to mental health will function not only critically and therapeutically, but also preventatively. This will occur only if concern for mental health is an ingredient in all areas of social planning. The emotional responses of individuals should be a consideration in policies ranging from unemployment to school busing, and from the devaluation of the dollar to community child care. The responsibility for reorienting social policy, however, must rest on all of us: social scientists, mental health workers, bureaucrats and politicians, and citizens concerned with their emotional environment.

## Note

1. Such a problem-oriented center was organized with union and management cooperation in the New York City garment industry during the late sixties: its

goals were to help patients solve crises so that they could maintain employment. Many of the findings of this research-demonstration project support the argument of this book. See Hyman J. Weiner, Sheila Akabas and John J. Sommer, *Mental Health Care in the World of Work* (New York: Association Press, 1973).

# Bibliography

# Bibliography

Aberbach, Joel. "Alienation and Political Behavior." *American Political Science Review* 63 (March 1969).

Adler, A. *The Practice and Theory of Individual Psychology.* New York: Harcourt, Brace, 1924.

Allardt, Erik and Stein Rokkan. *Mass Politics: Studies in Political Sociology.* New York: The Free Press, 1970.

Almond, Gabriel A. and Sidney Verba. *The Civic Culture: Political Attitudes and Democracy in Five Nations.* Boston: Little, Brown and Co., 1964.

Arnhoff, F.W., E.A. Rubenstein, B. Shriner, and D.R. Jones. *Manpower for Mental Health.* Chicago: Aldine, 1969.

Arrow, Kenneth. *The Limits of Organization.* New York: W.W. Norton, 1974.

Ayala, Philip. "Folk Practices, Folk Medicine and Curanderismo on the Lower West Side of Chicago." Presented at the Society of Applied Anthropology Meetings, Miami, Florida, April 1971.

_____. "The Chicano Mental Health Training Program: Alternatives to Traditional Psychiatric Training." Presented at the American Anthropological Association Meetings, Toronto, Ontario, December 1972.

Bachrach, Peter. *The Theory of Democratic Elitism: A Critique.* Boston: Little, Brown and Co., 1964.

Barton, R. *Institutional Neurosis.* Bristol, England: John Wright and Sons, 1969.

Becker, Gary S. *The Economics of Discrimination.* Chicago: University of Chicago Press, 1957.

Bleuler, E. *Dementia praecox oder Gruppe der Schizophrenien.* Leipzig: Franz Deuticke, 1911.

Boulding, Kenneth. *The Economy of Love and Fear.* Belmont, Calif.: Wadsworth Publishing Co., 1973.

Braginsky, B.M. and D.D. Braginsky. "Stimulus/Response: Mental Hospitals as Resorts." *Psychology Today* 6:10 (March 1973).

Campbell, Angus et al. *The American Voter.* New York: John Wiley and Sons, 1964.

Chu, F. and S. Trotter. *The Mental Health Complex*, Part I. Washington, D.C.: Community Mental Health Center for the Study of Responsive Law, 1972.

Conklin, H. "Hanunoo Color Categories." *Southwest Journal of Anthropology*, Winter 1955, pp. 339-44.

Cumming, J. and E. Cumming. *Ego and Milieu, the Theory and Practice of Environmental Therapy.* New York: Atherton Press, 1962.

Durkheim, Emile. *Suicide: A Study in Sociology.* Eds. John A. Spaulding and George Simpson, Glencoe, Ill.: The Free Press, 1951.

Edelman, Murray. *The Symbolic Uses of Politics.* Urbana, Ill.: University of Illinois Press, 1970.

Edgerton, R. "Concepts of Psychosis in Four East African Societies." *American Anthropologist* 68 (1966): 408-25.

Eriksen, E.H. *Childhood and Society.* New York: W.W. Norton, 1950.

Festinger, Leon. *A Theory of Cognitive Dissonance.* Evanston, Ill.: Row-Peterson, 1957.

Finifter, Ada W., ed. *Alienation and the Social System.* New York: John Wiley and Sons, Inc., 1972.

Fisher, W. "Social Change as a Therapeutic Tool in a Closed Institution." *Psychotherapy* 2:3 (October 1965).

_____ , J. Mehr, and P. Truckenrod. "Critical Mass # 1: Treatment Through Institutional Change." *Catalog of Selected Documents in Psychology* 3 (Spring 1973).

_____ , J. Mehr, and P. Truckenrod. "Critical Mass # 2: Assumptions, Implications and Problem Solving in Treatment Through Institutional Change." *Catalog of Selected Documents in Psychology* 3 (Summer 1973).

_____ , J. Mehr, and P. Truckenrod. *Power, Greed, and Stupidity in the Mental Health Racket.* Philadelphia: Westminster Press, 1973.

Freed, Harvey. *Holy Grail, Chicago Style: Community Development and Mental Health.* (Unpublished.)

Freud, Sigmund. *Collected Papers.* London: Hogarth Press, 1950.

Friedman, Milton. *Capitalism and Freedom.* Chicago: University of Chicago Press, 1957.

Fromm, Erich. *The Sane Society.* New York: Holt, Rinehart and Winston, 1955.

Goffman, E. *Asylums.* Garden City, N.Y.: Doubleday and Co., 1961.

Guttman, Louis, ed. *Readings in Facet Therapy.* Jerusalem: Hebrew University. (Photo offset.)

Hansell, N. et al. "Decision Counseling Method: Expanding Coping at Crisis-in-Transit." *Archives of General Psychiatry.* Spring 1970.

Hollingshead, A.B. and F.C. Redlich. *Social Class and Mental Illness.* New York: John Wiley and Sons, 1958.

_____ . "Social Stratification and Psychiatric Disorders." Ohmer Milton (ed.). *Behavior Disorders, Perspectives, and Trends.* New York: J.P. Lippincott, 1965.

Israel, Joachim. *Alienation from Marx to Modern Sociology: A Macro-Sociological Analysis.* Boston: Allyn and Bacon, 1971.

Jones, Ernest. *The Life and Work of Sigmund Freud.* New York: Basic Books, 1957.

Kasanin, J.S. (ed.). *Language and Thought in Schizophrenia.* Berkeley and Los Angeles: University of California Press, 1944.

Kiev, Ari. *Transcultural Psychiatry.* New York: The Free Press, 1972.

Lane, Robert E. *Political Ideology.* New York: The Free Press, 1962.

_____ and David O. Sears. *Public Opinion.* Englewood Cliffs, N.J.: Prentice-Hall, Inc., 1964.

Leighton, A.H. *My Name is Legion: Foundations for a Theory of Man in Relation to Culture.* New York: Basic Books, 1959.

_____ and J. Murphy. "Cross Cultural Psychiatry." Murphy and Leighton (eds). *Explorations in Social Psychiatry*, 1965.

Levin, Murry B. *The Alienated Voter: Politics in Boston.* New York: Holt, Rinehart and Winston, 1960.

Lewin, K., *Dynamic Theory of Personality.* New York: McGraw-Hill, 1935.

Lystad, Mary H. *Social Aspects of Alienation: An Annotated Bibliography.* Washington, D.C.: National Institute of Mental Health, 1969.

Malinowski, Bronislau. *Sex and Repression in Savage Society.* Cleveland: World Publishers, 1968.

Malzberg, B. and E.S. Lee. *Migration and Mental Disease: A Study of First Admissions to Hospitals for Mental Disease, New York, 1939-41.* Social Science Research Council, 1956.

Martin, D.V. "Institutionalization." *Lancet* 2 (December 1955).

Marx, Karl. *Early Writings.* T.B. Bottomore (ed.). New York: McGraw-Hill, 1963.

McClosky, Herbert. "Consensus and Ideology in American Politics." *American Political Science Review* 58 (1964).

Mead, Margaret. *Coming of Age in Samoa.* New York: Morrow, 1939.

Menninger, Karl. "The Course of Illness." Menninger Clinic Bulletin 25:5 (September 1961).

Miller, Harmon P. *Rich Man, Poor Man.* New York: Thomas Crowell, 1971.

Mills, C. Wright. *White Collar.* New York: Oxford University Press, 1956.

_____. *The Power Elite.* New York: Oxford University Press, 1956.

Mowrer, O.H. "Guilt in the Social Sciences or the Conflicting Doctrines of Determinism and Personal Accountability." Helmut Schoek and J.W. Wiggins (eds.). *Psychiatry and Responsibility* New York: D. Van Nostrand Company, Inc., 1962.

_____. "Integrity Therapy: A Self-Help Approach." *Psychotherapy* 3:3 (August 1966).

_____. "The Basis of Psychopathology: Malconditioning or Misbehavior?" *Journal of the National Association of Women Deans and Counselors* 29:2 (Winter 1966).

Mundell, Robert A. *Man and Economics.* New York: McGraw-Hill, 1968.

Myrdal, Gunnar. *Objectivity in Social Research.* New York: Pantheon Books, 1969.

Nader, Ralph. *The Mental Health Complex, Part I.* Washington, D.C.: Community Mental Health for Study of Responsive Law, 1972.

National Institute for Mental Health. *Socioeconomic Characteristics of Admissions to Inpatient Services of State and County Mental Hospitals.* 1969, D.H.E.W. publications no. (HSM) 72-9048. Washington, D.C.: U.S. Government Printing Office, 1971.

North, Douglass C. and Roger LeRoy Miller. *The Economics of Public Issues.* New York: Harper and Row, 1973.

Rogers, C.R. *Client-Centered Therapy*. Boston: Houghton Mifflin, 1942.

Romano, Octavio, I. "The Anthropology and Sociology of the Mexican-Americans: The Distortion of Mexican-American History." *El Grito* 2 (1968): 13-26.

Rowitz, L. and L. Levy. "The State Mental Hospital in Transition: An Approach to the Study of Mental Hospital Decentralization." *Mental Hygiene* 55:1 (January 1971).

Schachter, Gustav and Edwin L. Dale, Jr. *The Economist Looks at Society*. Lexington, Massachusetts: Xerox Publishing Company, 1973.

Scheff, T.J. *Being Mentally Ill: A Sociological Theory*. Chicago: Aldine, 1966.

Schensul, S.L. "Action Research: The Applied Anthropologist in a Community Mental Health Program." Alden Redfield, ed. *Anthropology Beyond the University*. Proceedings No. 7, Southern Anthropological Society. Athens, Ga.: University of Georgia Press, 1973.

_____ and M. Bakszysz. "The Role of Applied Research in the Development of Health Services in a Chicano Community in Chicago." *Topias and Utopias*. The Hague: Mouton Press, 1974.

Schepers, Emile. "Comparison of Folk and Professional Diagnoses Using the Hypothetical Case Study Method." Society of Applied Anthropology Meetings, Miami, Florida, April 1971.

_____ . "Voices, Visions and Strange Ideas: Delusions and Hallucinations in a Mexican-Origin Community." For a degree of Doctor of Philosophy in Anthropology, Northwestern University, 1973.

_____ . "Voices and Visions in Chicano Culture: Some Implications for Psychiatry and Anthropology." American Anthropological Association Meetings, Toronto, Ontario, December 1972.

_____ . "Institutional Approaches and Community Approaches to Urban Mental Health Care." In *Processes in Urbanism*. The Hague: Mouton Press, 1974.

Seeman, Melvin. "On the Meaning of Alienation." *American Sociological Review* 24:6 (1959).

Segall, M.H., D.T. Campbell and M.J. Herskovits. *The Influence of Culture on Visual Perceptions* Indianapolis: Bobbs-Merrill, 1966.

Sevilla-Casa, Elias. "A Model for Anthropological Research in a Psychiatric Setting." American Anthropological Association Meetings, Toronto, Ontario, December 1972.

Shakow, D. "The Nature of Deterioration in Schizophrenic Conditions." New York: Nervous and Mental Disease Publications, 1947.

Skinner, B.F. *The Behavior of Organisms*. New York: Appleton-Century-Crofts, 1938.

Srole, L., T.S. Langer, S.T. Michael, M.K. Opler, and T.A.C. Rennie. *Mental Health in the Metropolis: The Midtown Manhattan Study*. New York: McGraw-Hill, 1962.

Szasz, T.S. *The Myth of Mental Illness.* New York: Hoeber-Harper, 1961.

_____ . "From the Slaughterhouse to the Mad House." *Psychotherapy* 8:1 (Spring 1971).

Torrey, E.F. *The Mind Game: Witch Doctors and Psychiatrists.* New York: Emerson Hall, 1972.

Tucker, W.T. *The Social Context of Economic Behavior.* New York: Holt, Rinehart and Winston, Inc., 1964.

United States Senate, Subcommittee on Intergovernmental Relations of the Committee on Governmental Operations. *Confidence and Concern: Citizens View American Government.* Parts 1 and 2. Washington, D.C.: U.S. Government Printing Office, 1973.

Vaca, Nicholas C. "The Mexican-American in the Social Sciences 1912-1970, Part II: 1936-1970." *El Grito* 4:1 (1970), pp. 17-50.

Vazquez, Albert. "The Effects of Change in the Cultural Orientation of a Community Mental Health Clinic." American Anthropological Association Meetings, Toronto, Ontario, December 1972.

Weiner, Hyman J. Sheila H. Akabas and John H. Sommer. *Mental Health Care in the World of Work.* New York: Association Press, 1973.

Wing, J.K. "Institutionalism in Mental Hospitals." *British Journal of Social and Clinical Psychology* 1 (1962): 38-51.

Zax, M. and E.L. Cowen. *Abnormal Psychology: Changing Conceptions.* New York: Holt, Rinehart and Winston, Inc., 1972.

# About the Authors

**Marion R. Just** received the Ph.D. in political science from Columbia University in 1969. She is an assistant professor at Wellesley College and a research associate at the Center for International Studies of the Massachusetts Institute of Technology. Her research has focused on the rational and irrational components of voting behavior in the United States and in Great Britain. Ms. Just has contributed articles to *Current History* and to the *Journal of Political Studies* (U.K.).

**Carolyn Shaw Bell**, an economist specializing in family income and consumption, received the Ph.D. from London University. Her findings on women's earnings, social security, and the distribution of income have been presented to Congressional committees, and on radio and television. Ms. Bell has written syndicated columns and has contributed to *Challenge, Transaction*, and *The Public Interest*. She is the author of *Consumer Choice in the American Economy* and *The Economics of the Ghetto*.

**Walter Fisher** is an Assistant Superintendent of Elgin State Hospital, a Clinical Lecturer at Northwestern, Roosevelt and Northern Illinois Universities and maintains a private practice at the Center for Human Potential in Illinois. His research in mental health has been supported by a number of federal and state grants and has resulted in video tape productions, articles and books, including *Power, Greed and Stupidity in the Mental Health Racket* and *Human Services: The Third Revolution in Mental Health*.

**Stephen L. Schensul** received the Ph.D. from the University of Minnesota in 1969. He has conducted anthropological fieldwork in Northern Minnesota, Southwestern Uganda and a Chicano community in Chicago and he is currently the Director of Community Research of the Community Mental Health Program in Chicago. Mr. Schensul will shortly become Director of Community Mental Health Services at Jackson Memorial Hospital, Miami, Florida and associate professor in the Department of Psychiatry, University of Miami School of Medicine. The results of his research have appeared in *Human Organization* and in the recent book, *Topics and Utopias in Health*.